Christianity and Other Religions

by

E. O. JAMES

D.Litt., D.D., F.S.A.

Professor Emeritus of the History of Religion
in the University of London

Fellow of University College and
King's College, London

Chaplain of All Souls College, Oxford

D1457946

J. B. LIPPINCOTT COMPANY
Philadelphia and New York

EDITOR'S PREFACE

To judge by the unending flow of religious literature from the various publishing houses there is an increasingly large demand on the part of ordinary intelligent people to know more about what Christianity has to say. This series is designed to help to meet this need and to cater for just this kind of people.

It assumes that there is a growing body of readers, both inside and outside the Church, who are prepared to give serious attention to the nature and claims of the Christian faith, and who expect to be given by theologians authoritative and up-to-date answers to the kind of questions thinking people want to ask.

More and more it becomes clear that we are unlikely to get any answers that will satisfy the deepest needs of the human spirit from any other quarter. Present-day science and philosophy give us little help on the ultimate questions of human destiny. Social, political and educational panaceas leave most of us unpersuaded. If we are not to end our quest for the truth about ourselves and the world we live in in cynicism and disillusionment where else can we turn but to religion?

Too often in the past two thousand years the worst advertisement for Christianity has been its supporters and advocates. Yet alone of all the great religions it has shown that a faith which was oriental in origin could be transplanted into the western world and from there strike root again in the east. The present identification of Christianity in the minds of Asians and Africans with European culture and western capitalism is a passing phase. To say that no other religion has the same potentialities as a world-wide faith for everyman is neither to denigrate the God-given truth in Buddhism, Islam and the rest, nor to say that at this stage Christianity as generally practised and understood in the west presents much more than a caricature of its purpose.

Perhaps the best corrective to hasty judgment is to measure these two thousand years against the untold millions of years of man's development. Organized Christianity is still in its infancy, as in the mind of man as he seeks to grapple with truths that could only come to him by revelation. The half has not yet been told and the full implications for human thought and action of the coming of God in Christ have as yet been only dimly grasped by most of us.

It is as a contribution to a deeper understanding of the mystery that surrounds us that this series is offered. The early volumes deal, as is only right, with fundamental issues—the historical impact of Christianity upon mankind based on its Jewish origins and establishing itself in the wider world; the essence of the Christian faith and the character of Christian behaviour. Later volumes in the series will deal with various aspects of Christian thought and practice in relation to human life in all its variety and with its perennial problems.

The intention is to build up over the years a library which under the general title of "Knowing Christianity" will provide for thinking laymen a solid but non-technical presentation of what the Christian religion is and what it has to say in this atomic age.

The writers invited to contribute to this series are not only experts in their own fields but are all men who are deeply concerned that the gulf should be bridged between the specialized studies of the theologian and the untheologically minded average reader who nevertheless wants to know what theology has to say. I am sure that I speak in the name of all my colleagues in this venture when I express the hope that this series will do much to bridge the gap.

WILLIAM NEIL

The University,
Nottingham

AUTHOR'S PREFACE

In a series designed to help intelligent people to know more about the nature and claims of Christianity as the faith which for the last two thousand years has occupied a unique position among the religions of the world, it is of crucial importance to determine historically and comparatively its place, function, validity and potentialities in this setting. Hence the present volume. The higher living faiths and systems fall into two groups, the one Western originating in the ancient Near East, largely Semitic, giving rise to Judaism, Christianity and Islam; the other Oriental based on India where Hinduism and Buddhism arose, the latter having important offshoots in China, Japan and Southeast Asia. In China the indigenous disciplines, Confucianism and Taoism, were primarily ways of life rather than religions, inculcating respectively filial piety as the supreme virtue, and living in accordance with Tao as the moral law and the will of Heaven. In ancient Iran, midway between the occident and the orient, Zoroastrianism emerged from its Indo-Iranian cradleland as an ethical monotheistic prophetic faith which became the national religion of Persia from the third to the seventh century A.D. Having exercised a powerful influence on Judaism and Christianity at the turn of the era, it has now dwindled into obscurity as the highly respected Parsee community centred in Bombay.

As Christianity in the first instance arose in the Middle East as a Jewish sect before it became the dominant dynamic in the far-flung Roman Empire, eventually itself developing into a missionary movement to the ends of the earth, so Islam before it became a world-wide civilization maintained that it was the fulfilment of the Judaeo-Christian revelation. In this welter of religions Christianity, with its oriental ramifications, occupies a unique position historically, geographically and theologically. Indeed, so deeply embedded in the history of religion are its roots that they go back to prehistoric times, and in divers manner they are a recurrent phenomenon in the subsequent divine self-disclosure to mankind in varying cultural conditions. An objective investigation of this course of events, however, is not all that is required in this particular Series, its purpose being to determine wherein lies the uniqueness of the Christian faith in the satisfaction

7

of the deepest needs of the human spirit, without "denigrating the God-given truth in other religions". I have endeavoured, therefore, to show how this has been attained while readily acknowledging the common ground and aims it shares with other traditions and systems; God having not left himself without witness at any time or place throughout the ages. In so doing I have tried to make the inquiry intelligible to readers who do not profess to have a special knowledge of the subject in its historical and theological setting. The glossary devoted especially to the current terms employed in the oriental religions and unavoidable in a serious account of their beliefs and practices, but likely to be unfamiliar to some readers, will, I hope, help to this end. For the guidance of those anxious to go more deeply into the investigation at a scholarly level I have given references in the texts and to the more authoritative literature in the notes, together with selected bibliographies for further reading and consultation.

E. O. JAMES

All Souls College,
    Oxford

CONTENTS

9

GLOSSARY

Advaita The philosophy of non-duality in Hinduism as taught by Sankara.

Amidism The worship of Amitabha Buddha as a saviour god to obtain salvation by grace in and through his merits.

An-atta The Buddhist doctrine of the denial of a human self or soul.

Atman The eternal self within man and in all things (Brahman) in the Upanishads.

Avatar The "descent" of the supreme being to earth in some bodily form in response to human needs.

Avidya Ignorance as to the cause of human misery and evil.

Bhagavad-Gita, or the "Song of the Lord", the most popular Hindu scripture in which all the ways of salvation are brought together in the love of God for man.

Bhakti The Hindu way of devotion to a personal deity.

Bodhisattva A Buddha-being who has delayed his attainment of Nirvana out of compassion for struggling humanity.

Brahman The basic concept in Hinduism concerning the eternal ground of all existence; and the name applied to the priestly caste controlling its operations.

Brahmana Elaborate explanations of the manner in which the sacrificial ritual in Hinduism must be performed.

Communio Mystical union, fellowship and spiritual intercourse often established by sacramental sacrifice.

Dharma The traditional way of life of the Hindu and Buddhist based on an eternally fixed sacred law and principle of existence.

Dukka The Buddhist conception of sorrow and suffering caused by attachment to present existence *(Samsara),* and the will to live.

Isvara The generic name for the Lord, the Creator and divine personality in action, and the personal aspect of Brahman.

11

Karma The effects of the actions performed in successive states of life on earth and the determining cause of rebirth.

Mahayana The "Great Vehicle" of northern Buddhism in which the Buddha is revered as an eternal being ever ready to aid mankind in the attainment of Buddhahood.

Mantic Pertaining to the practice of divination as a systematized art and technique.

Maya The conviction that the phenomenal world is illusory appearance.

Moksa The Hindu doctrine of seeking freedom and liberation from the delusion of phenomenal existence.

Monogram of Christ The first two letters of the name of Christ in Greek used for many purposes as a cipher.

Nirvana (Pali: *Nibbana*) The state of passionless peace beyond rebirth and all temporal and carnal cravings, and desire.

Omophagia The eating of sacred raw flesh for ritual purposes in the Dionysiac.

Omphalos A sacred conical stone regarded as the centre of the earth.

Parousia The expectation of the "second advent" or return of Christ in glory to judge the living and the dead, and to bring the present world order to an end with a final general judgment.

Piaculum A sacrificial expiation of sin or evil as an act of atonement.

Rig-Veda The earliest collection of Vedic hymns in the books dealing with the creative efforts of many of the gods.

Sankhya (or enumeration), a dualistic and atheist division of reality into matter and soul.

Samsara The round of birth and rebirth.

Soteriology The doctrine of salvation, including the redemption of human nature and the final destiny of man.

Tetragrammaton The four letters YHWH of the Hebrew word vocalized as Yahweh as the name of God.

Theophany A divine appearance or manifestation at a particular place, or on a specific occasion.

Theravada named by Mahayana Buddhism *Hinayana*, or the "Little Vehicle", in which it is claimed that the original teaching of the Buddha, especially about Nirvana, is retained and practised by its monks; denying divine grace or divinity in the process of self-salvation.

Torah   The divine revelation claimed to have been revealed through the Hebrew priests, prophets and sages in oral teaching or written records, on which the faith of Judaism rests.

Ugaritic texts   written in an early Canaanite cuneiform script, recently discovered at Ras Shamra, the site of the ancient Ugarit, on the northern coast of Syria.

Upanishads   The most important school of Hindu mystical philosophy centred in the unity of all existence in the Brahman as the Absolute.

Veda   The eternal truth, wisdom and knowledge of Hinduism recorded in the scriptures.

Vedanta   The school of Hindu thought systematizing the mystical teaching of the Upanishads.

Yoga   The Hindu system of ascetic discipline, abstract meditation and concentration to produce with the aid of the prescribed techniques union with Brahman.

Zen Buddhism   A Japanese sect, which in recent years has become widespread in the West, maintaining a rigid mental discipline and technique for the realization of a mystic state of enlightenment and insight called *satori*.

Chapter One

INTRODUCTION

The Comparative Study of Religion

THE place of Christianity among other religions, both ancient and modern, has been the subject of discussion increasingly in recent years from very different points of view. This debate has arisen very largely as a result of the enormous amount of information that has become available from numerous sources during the last few centuries concerning the religious beliefs and practices of people in varying states of culture all over the world. But although the systematic comparative and historical study of religion as a scientific discipline did not come into being until the beginning of the last century, very frequently sporadic attempts had been made for a long time to compare one faith or cult with another, either favourably or adversely for the purposes of proselytism. Thus, in the Roman Empire at the turn of the present era the Early Church engaged in a prolonged controversy with pagans and Jews alike to vindicate the Christian revelation as the unique and final self-disclosure of God to man in the incarnation, ministry, death and resurrection of Christ. Once, however, Christianity became the established faith in the Roman Empire and the rest of Christendom little interest was taken in the subject in its wider aspects, as everything outside the Jewish-Christian tradition was regarded as valueless, and often as a diabolical invention. Throughout the Middle Ages wars were waged in defence of the faith against Islam in Spain, Palestine, Syria, Asia Minor, Byzantium and the eastern Mediterranean. The Renaissance revived interest in the glories of Ancient Greece and the splendours of Pagan Rome, their art, literature, mythology and classical culture. This, however, was soon followed in northern Europe by the Reformation with its return to a circumscribed theological outlook.

Nevertheless, a fresh impetus was then given to biblical studies, and a knowledge of Hebrew created a fresh interest in Jewish faith and practice. But emphasis on the inherent depravity of unredeemed humanity reacted against a sympathetic understanding of non-Christian religions. It was only in isolated individuals here and there that a more enlightened and intelligent approach was made to them. Thus, for example, Joseph Scaliger in 1583 treated the Old Testament as an integral part of ancient history. Similarly, in 1672 John Selden published his *De Dis Syris Syntagmata* in Leipzig showing some critical understanding of Semitic mythology, while in 1678 Cudworth in his *True Intellectual System of the Universe* maintained that Plato's "trinity" was a Hebraism derived from Jewish sources. Dr. John Spencer, the Master of Corpus Christi College, Cambridge, published a book in Latin at the end of the nineteenth century on the Hebrew ritual laws which Robertson Smith regarded as laying the foundations of the science of comparative religion. In France a Jesuit, Lescalopier, and a Benedictine, Calmet, were working on similar lines about this time.

Meanwhile the voyages of the early explorers had been bringing to light new continents, and in an age of discovery knowledge of the religious beliefs and systems current in different parts of the world rapidly increased and called for some interpretation. In the seventeenth and eighteenth centuries the Deists restricted belief in God to the existence of a single Creator, or first cause, who having brought all things into being and set them in motion in the natural order, had no further interest in the world. Revelation, therefore, was impossible. All that could be known about him came by the unaided observation of the physical universe. But this so-called "natural religion" of the "age of reason" at the beginning of the nineteenth century gave place to an emotional imagination in nature which found expression in the landscape art of Turner, Constable, the Norwich school and the pre-Raphaelite brotherhood, and the poetry of Wordsworth and Shelley. This new understanding and appreciation of nature and its kinship with man produced a sense of the mysterious both in the human and natural orders. In Coleridge such awe and amazement, now known as the "numinous", were combined in revolt against the assumption that the relation of the Creator to the universe was that of a mason to his work. Thus, the Deistic doctrine of an "absent God" now underwent a fundamental change in the direction of divine immanentism pervading the universe, in which the relation between God and nature tended towards pantheism in the form of Romanticism.

Collectively the Romantic movement gave a fresh impetus to the study of the nature, origin and development of religion in terms of immanentism, nature-worship and nature-mythology and poetry. Thus, in the middle of the Century Max Müller and his school concentrated attention on the analysis of the names of the gods in the Hindu Veda, the Iranian Avesta, the Hellenic Homeric literature and the Icelandic Edda for the purpose of discovering the origin and nature of religion, and the common elements in these classic texts. Working along these lines they arrived at the conclusion that the personification of natural phenomena, notably the sun, the sky and its constellations, was a "disease of language"; a pathological condition of the human mind arising from an inability to express abstract ideas except in metaphor. But the production of the accumulating evidence of the customs and beliefs of preliterate peoples in a primitive state of culture showed the inadequacy of the foundations on which this philological hypothesis was based.

The Evolutionary Hypothesis

It only then remained for the biologists to bring the entire order of organic life under the reign of natural law to complete the transformation, in spite of the efforts of Paley and the authors of the Bridgewater Treatises at the beginning of the nineteenth century to interpret the cosmic processes as evidence of design on the part of an intelligent personal, beneficent Creator. During the previous century although the doctrine of "special creation" and the "fixity of species", so graphically portrayed by Milton, was firmly established and had the support of the foremost botanist Linnaeus (1707–1778) and the French comparative anatomist Cuvier (1769–1832) the idea of evolution implicit in the Copernican astronomy was beginning to find expression as the key to world-history in the philosophy of Kant (1724–1804), Schelling (1775–1854) and Hegel (1770–1831). But it reached its climax in the positivism of Saint Simon and Auguste Comte (1798–1857), where it was maintained that a theological "age of fiction" in the infancy of mankind passed through that of metaphysical speculation to the final scientific or "positive" stage.

In the biological sphere Georges Leclerc, Comte de Buffon (1707–1788), had detected vestigial organs of little or no use in the bodies of animals inexplicable on the theory of the fixity of species. Erasmus Darwin (1731–1802) and Lamarck (1744–1829), affirmed that in the development of more complex organisms from pre-existent simpler forms, modification, growth or atrophy in the use or disuse of organs was due mainly to physical conditions such as cross-breeding and the stress of necessity. When the changes affected in these ways were transmitted to the offspring they became permanent features. In 1827 von Baer showed the remarkable resemblance between the early embryos of the vertebrates. Schleiden and Swann reduced all plants and animals to a complex cell organization, and in 1844 Barry showed that frequently protozoa are unicellular organisms, thereby opening

17

the way for the derivation of all organic evolution from a single cell. In his *Principles of Geology* Charles Lyell in 1830 disposed of Cuvier's theory of cataclysmic changes in the earth's surface and established a genetic connexion between the fossils brought to light by palaeontological investigation and excavation, and their continuity with modern forms of life. It was, however, the accidental reading of Malthus's *Essay on Population,* published in 1839, that gave Charles Darwin his fresh inspiration which led to the formulation of his theory of evolution based on natural selection. It was this contention in his epoch-making book on *The Origin of Species* in 1859 that changed completely the outlook on the organic universe and its processes, supported by A. R. Wallace who arrived simultaneously at the same results in parallel inquiries. This was destined to have far-reaching effects on the development of human culture, religion and ethics.

As a trained naturalist Darwin realized that a struggle for existence always occurred among animals and plants. This he explained in terms of natural selection as the cause of variation and survival in organic evolution. Species, he maintained, that had developed the best natural equipment to engage in the conflict with their environment were able not only to survive but also to leave behind more descendants to inherit the useful novelties they had acquired. Those that lacked these safeguards and advantages tended to become extinct in course of time since they had less offspring and were more readily eliminated.

This revolutionary hypothesis which brought under the reign of natural law the development and elimination of species in relation to variation, heredity, isolation and the struggle for existence, clearly had a very much wider application, covering almost every aspect of natural and human life. That it produced widespread critical examination, opposition and controversy is hardly surprising, especially as the opposition was led in the first instance by the principal anatomist of the day, Richard Owen (1804-1892), the Hunterian Professor in the Royal College of Surgeons and the founder of the Natural History Museum in South Kensington. With more bitterness and personal prejudice than understanding, wisdom and justice, he dismissed the theory as "nothing more than guesswork and speculation". Adam Sedgwick, the Woodwardian Professor of geology at Cambridge, was even more scathing in his review of *The Origin of Species* in *The Spectator*. Indeed Darwin himself admitted that "all the most eminent palaeontologists, and all the greatest geologists, have unanimously, often vehemently, maintained the immutability of species."[1] And there can be little doubt that the unfortunate ill-informed intervention of Samuel Wilberforce, the Bishop of Oxford, at the meeting of the British Association in his cathedral city in 1860, was engineered by Owen, who used the bishop as his own mouthpiece.

Wilberforce should not have played Owen's role, lacking both technical biological knowledge and the philosophical insight required to pass judgment on the hypothesis. It must be conceded, however, that the evidence in 1860 was very incomplete, and while Darwin pointed out that it was not incompatible with "belief in God as a philosophic doctrine", that with which it did collide and with which it seemed to be absolutely inconsistent, was the theological conception of creation based on the opening chapters of the book of Genesis. The evolutionary process, it appeared, was merely a mechanism operating according to certain fixed laws which pursued their course in complete independence of divine guidance, though admitting the existence of a transcendental deity as a remote first cause on Deistic lines. It is, therefore, the more remarkable that the first zoologist to accept the Darwinian contention was Canon Tristram, followed on general grounds by Charles Kingsley. Indeed, even so jaundiced an anti-clerical as T. H. Huxley (1825–1895) was surprised at the lack of opposition from the "white cravats". In fact, as the century proceeded, in spite of the initial rejection of the theory, not only was the evolutionary process widely accepted in principle, but development in an orderly sequence became of universal application in the Victorian era.

Nowhere was this more apparent than in the anthropological interpretation of the origin and development of religion, and of the organization of society and the family. Comte and Hegel had maintained, as we have seen, that everything was marching in an orderly manner to its goal by virtue of an inner ceaseless urge towards higher and more complex forms in accord with "the laws of phenomena", be it from an age of fiction to an age of science; from the worship of ancestors and heroes to that of gods; or from promiscuity through polygamy to monogamy. Similarly, Hegelian humanity was one progressive and perfectible being or organism which advanced by becoming more complete and reasonable. Thus, Pfleiderer maintained that "as history was dialectic expressed in time so the religious relation is a process within the mind, developing itself from lower to higher stages and forms according to immanent laws, laws which are essentially the same in the macrocosm of humanity as in the microcosm of the individual". Therefore, Herbert Spencer's dictum "from the simple to the complex, and from the homogenous to the heterogeneous", seemed to be an established principle applicable alike in the cosmic, organic, human and religious orders.

It was in this intellectual milieu that the comparative study of religion became a scientific discipline within the domain of the newly created science of anthropology in the second half of the last century, with "evolution" and "progressive development" as the key words. Like the biologists and sociologists the scientific students of religion invented a system to explain comparatively the similarities and distinguishing features of the available data in terms of origin and development. This was based on the doctrine of the invariability of universal laws operative in nature and in human society. The first systematic attempt to apply this method to beliefs and institutions was that of Sir Edward Tylor (1832–1917), who was the leading anthropologist of the period. Following Comte he affirmed that "the history of culture began with the appearance on earth of a semi-civilized race of men, and from that state culture has proceeded in two ways, backward to produce savages, and forward to produce civilized men".[2] Because everywhere and at all times the human mind was alleged to function according to fixed laws of thought and action it continually reproduces recurrent practices, institutions and ideas attributed to "the like working of men's minds under like conditions". The modern savage was regarded as the contemporary representative of early man at corresponding levels of evolutionary advance and decline, the Australian aborigines having similar myths because, as Andrew Lang maintained, "the ancestors of the Greeks passed through the savage intellectual condition in which we find the Australians".[3]

This evolutionary anthropological approach by comparison with the philological theory of Max Müller at least was an empirical attempt to investigate the problem comparatively and critically in the light of the available evidence. Where it failed was in its explanation of similar beliefs and practices as the product of mental processes working according to fixed laws of progress regardless of their history and environment. On the assumption that everywhere in ancient and modern states of culture the same specific laws of thought and action always have been and are operative, Tylor traced the progressive development and decline in beliefs and customs with little or no reference to their purpose and function in the religious and social structure in which they occur.

Following his lead, in the first edition of *The Golden Bough* in 1890, J. G. Frazer acknowledged in the preface his profound debt to his friend Edward Tylor, who, he said, "opened up a mental vista undreamed of by me before". And it was Frazer more than anyone else at the turn of the century who developed and perpetuated the comparative method in the study of religion, myth, ritual, folklore, and human ideas and institutions. From the mass of material he collected the one general conclusion he thought that emerged was "the essential similarity in the workings of the less developed human mind in all races, which corresponds to the essential similarity in their bodily frame revealed by comparative anatomy". But while this general mental similarity may be taken as established, he recognized that "we must always be on our guard against tracing to it a multitude of particular resemblances which may be and often are due to simple diffusion, since nothing is more certain than that the various races of men have borrowed from each other many of their arts and crafts, their ideas, customs and institutions".[4]

Nevertheless, this did not prevent his trying to reconstruct, like Comte, the origin and development of society and its cultural and religious traits in stratified stages of evolution; or of mental ages through which he supposed different peoples have passed in their advance from savagery to civilization. Thus, he postulated a three-fold scheme of transition from an initial "age of magic" through an "age of religion" to an "age of science", determined by the operation of immutable laws working dialectically in Hegelian fashion, priority of type being confused with priority in time based on internal resemblances. Following Tylor he assumed a multiplicity of spiritual beings animating "every nook and hill, every tree and flower, every brook and river, every breeze that blew and every cloud that flecked with silvery white the blue expanse of heaven". From these innumerable spirits a polytheistic system of departmental gods emerged. "Instead of a separate spirit for every individual tree they came to conceive of a god of the woods in general, a Silvanus or what not; instead of personifying all the winds as gods, each with his distinct character and features, they imagined a single god of the winds, an Aeolus, for example, who kept them shut up in bags and could let them out at pleasure to lash the sea to fury". By a further generalization and abstraction, "the instinctive craving of the mind after simplification and unification of its ideas" led to the transformation of the many localized and departmentalized gods into one Supreme Creator and controller of all things. Thus, as polytheism evolved out of animism, polytheism in its turn passed into monotheism.[5]

Similarly, the magical control of nature by "the sheer force of spells and enchantments" was abandoned when this method failed to produce the desired results. Then the magician gave place to the priest who sought instead to "mollify a coy, capricious or irascible deity by the soft insinuation of prayer and sacrifice".[6] Finally, both magic and religion were displaced by science; "the keener minds pressing forward to a deeper solution of the mysteries of the universe, after groping about in the dark for countless ages, hit upon a clue to the labyrinth, a golden key that opens many locks in the treasury of nature".[7] These neat and tidy sequences, however, have in fact never existed at any known stage, or succession of stages, in cultural development. So far from religion having arisen out of the failure of the magician to exercise his functions successfully, in every known community, ancient and modern, the two disciplines occur side by side and are inextricably interwoven; and, indeed are recurrent phenomena in predominantly scientific civilizations, with varying degrees of emphasis. In preliterate states of culture supreme beings, animistic spirits and animatistic conceptions of the sacred and numinous coincide with magical devices, divination and soothsaying. It is impossible therefore, to maintain evolutionary sequences along the lines adopted by Tylor, Frazer and their contemporaries.

Again, as Dr Marett recognized, the interpretation of man and nature as a dualism of body and soul animistically, was a product of conceptual thinking involving a realization of personality foreign to the primitive mind. Therefore, he contended that a far less narrowly intellectualistic definition of religion in terms of spiritual beings as framed by Tylor is required. As conceived by Marett, religion was something "danced out and developed under conditions, psychological and sociological, which favoured emotional or motor processes, whereas ideation remained relatively in abeyance". Belief in spiritual beings and separable souls, he argued, can only arise when the individual is conscious of himself as a human being. So he postulated a pre-animistic, or animatistic, phase at the threshold of religion covering "residual phenomena which a strictly animistic interpretation of rudimentary religion would be likely to ignore, or at all events to misrepresent".[8]

He was careful to point out, however, that this pre-animistic stage was not to be interpreted chronologically though it lay in the background of speculations about dreams and visions and separable souls, heroes, ancestors and departmental gods. It was this concept of sacredness in the sense of supernatural power and non-moral holiness that Otto called the Numinous, and regarded it as a category of value like beauty, truth and goodness, not reducible to any ordinary intellectual or rational knowledge.[9] This, however, is to over-emphasize "the wholly otherness" of religion as a thing apart, eliminating the psychological conditions that called it into being and reducing it to an "unnamed Something". But it is not an "unnamed Something"

22

that stimulates the numinous reaction to the mysterious. It is anything that is awe-inspiring and beyond human control. Moreover, to produce religious behaviour and evaluation the numinous must be not only experienced; it must be accessible. If the "presence" beyond human consciousness experienced in what he calls the *mysterium tremendum* was as completely transcendent as Otto suggests, it would not be within reach of man at all. Therefore, attempts to establish efficacious relations with it, which always have constituted the religious quest, would be of no avail. It must be articulate and intelligible, not wholly transcendent and non-rational. In short, religion is more than a special kind of experience aroused by stress and awe; or, as Freud contended, a psychological projection and illusion.

The Sociological Interpretation of Religion

In opposition to these interpretations, Durkheim, and those associated with him in France in the journal *L'Année Sociologique*, maintained that religion is essentially a social phenomenon which can only be evaluated accurately in relation to the social facts in the structure, organization and sanctions in the society in which it emerges. Indeed, the present generation of social anthropologists and sociologists, particularly in England, are inclined to exclude altogether numinous emotion and its related psychological factors from religious conceptions and practices, together with attempts to explain how and when they have arisen and been formulated. But here, again, caution is needed. Unquestionably it is true that the institutions of religion function within the structure of society, and under specific social conditions, largely for the purpose of maintaining and regulating human relationships and adjustments, stabilizing economic, political, social and spiritual institutions. Thus, at every level of cultural development religion has exercised its functions primarily in a social milieu, enabling human beings to live together in an orderly arrangement of social relations. But the sociological and historical aspects of the discipline should be complementary. As Mr. Christopher Dawson has pointed out, the social way of life influences the approach to religion and the religious attitude influences the way of life.[10] The study of beliefs and customs in this context in recent years has thrown a great deal of light on the understanding of religion in its anthropological phenomenological and theological aspects, as well as on the consolidation and development of culture in general. The history of religion, in fact, has centred to a considerable extent in the interaction of all these elements in the maintenance of a stable way of life.

Nevertheless, so far from society having "all that is necessary to arouse the sensation of the Divine in men's minds by the power it has over them, so that to its members it is what a god is to his worshippers", as Durkheim contended,[11] it has always been to the sacred order transcending natural and human categories that religion has made its appeal. The Divine has been the ultimate object of religious experience and evaluation, interpreted in terms of super-causation rather than a "mirage of social facts". To confine the discipline to its social manifestations is a legacy of Comte's severance of man from nature and his equation of religion with a "subjective synthesis" of humanity as a self-contained and self-created order of existence related to the attributes of deity. The human mind, on the contrary, has looked beyond the social and physical environment to a transcendental extra-mundane "otherness" deeply-rooted in the past, and believed to be a continuous influence in the world and on mankind by virtue of its sacred significance. Thus, the established religious traditions, their institutions, myth and ritual, being regarded as a direct expression of primeval realities, provide supernatural sanctions for faith and conduct, enhancing and codifying belief and practice. Therefore, they fulfil an indispensable religious and social function by justifying the existing order, its institutions and scale of values in terms of a continuous tradition, deriving their efficacy from the initial events in which they claim to take their origin. They are, in short, the means whereby sacred power and divine grace are made accessible through the re-enactment of the reality believed to have once occurred and to have ever since influenced the world and mankind in a representative rite, as, for example, in the case of the Christian eucharistic oblation. The sacred tradition lives on in its worship and in the theology underlying it, constituting the unifying centre of a closely knit religious, cultural and social organization.

The Tradition of Islam

Thus, Islam has welded together a great variety of peoples in a consolidated civilization in a common "submission" to Allah and his Prophet. Embracing more than three hundred and fifty million adherents, this mighty movement based on a relatively simple but fervently held creed, and an equally simple cultus punctiliously observed by Muslims of many races and nationalities, has remained united as a single religious and cultural community by the whole-hearted acceptance of its faith. As a world-wide civilization it has spread from its Arabian cradleland through Persia and India to the

Far East in China; westwards through Egypt and North Africa to Spain; southwards to Malaya and Indonesia; and leaving an indelible impression in the Balkans and on European history and culture. So bound up has it become with every aspect of human life that it has transcended all other allegiances, and over this vast region it has produced a homogeneous society. Scholars in Alexandria, caravan attendants in Morocco, tradesmen in Syria, farmers in Java, and judges and statesmen in Pakistan, regulate their lives and behaviour in accordance with the religious, social, ethical and political norm provided by the Holy Qur'an, and the traditions derived from these sacred scriptures. Inspired and consolidated by this spiritual dynamic one of the greatest world empires, and the numerous Muslim states, have arisen transcending the barriers of race, language and locality, and exercising a profound influence in the coherence of this widespread civilization.

Confucianism

Here, then, is an outstanding instance of a common faith stabilizing and sustaining a remarkable culture, transmitting from one generation to another the beliefs, cultus and sentiments on which its constitution depends, grounded in the conviction of a final revelation having been vouchsafed to its founder as "the Seal of the Prophets". Again, in China it was as a consolidating dynamic that Confucius (551–478 B.C.) insisted upon the traditional ceremonies, customs and music being preserved and maintained, though, unlike Muhammad, he did not commit himself to the acceptance of specific doctrines about the gods. The Chinese people, in fact, have never been a particularly religious people. With theism as such Confucius was not concerned, and he deprecated speculation about spirits and divinities. Nevertheless, he urged conformity to the customary rites because they gave stability to the established order and the moral life. Ceremonies are described in *The Book of Rites* as "the bond that holds the multitudes together, and if the bond be removed these multitudes fall into confusion". And in *The Analects,* which contain the collection of sayings attributed to Confucius, these rites are said to be those enacted by the ancient divine monarchs of the legendary past, Yao and Shun, Wen, Wu, and by Tao, the founder of the Ducal House in his own state of Lu. When these were correctly observed they were the means whereby good government (i.e. the right ordering of society) was preserved and harmonized with the operations of nature. "Through the sacrifices the unity of the people is strengthened," filial piety is maintained and peace preserved. By music and dancing rain is said to be produced, virtues are promoted and laws established. Indeed, if a king could carry out in all its fullness the royal ritual for a single day the whole country, it was affirmed, would "surrender to his goodness" *(Analects* II.3). As for Confucius the nearest approach to a concept of Deity was that of Tien (Heaven), an impersonal pantheistic cosmic principle. It was in conformity with "Heaven" as the unvarying moral order, that the apex of good living in a well-ordered society was attained. The Taoists, on the other hand, endeavoured to re-integrate themselves into the equally impersonal conception of Tao, the "way", embracing all the forces active in the universe as an inner necessity producing the harmony in nature. This was the world-denying facet of Chinese religion in opposition to the positive world-affirming attitude of Confucianism. It did, however, look back to a Golden Age in which the individual was harmoniously merged in the community in a *participation mystique,* comparable to the Hindu conception of Brahman in the mystical treatises known as the *Upanishads* (see chap. IV, pp. 72 ff)

Asian Mysticism

In Hindu India, despite the absence of a unified theology or philosophy, this metaphysical merging of the self in the pantheistic All — the beginning and goal of all existence – was the supreme quest. Unlike China, in Hinduism, however, almost every variety and aspect of belief and practice was adopted by a religiously-minded people with very different temperaments and traditions, ranging from a crude polytheistic fertility cultus going back to prehistoric times in the Harappa Indus valley civilization, to a highly abstract pantheistic and monistic mysticism and metaphysical theism, and loving devotion to virtually a saviour-god in the Bhagavad-Gita (see chap. IV, pp. 75 f). Hinduism, in fact, has been primarily a way of life rather than a consistent form of thought and dogmatic theology. Provided that certain distinctive basic principles are maintained and customs observed, such as the caste system, the sacredness of the cow, the concept of Brahman as Ultimate Reality, and the law of Karma, according to which the actions done in this life are the determining cause of rebirth, very diverse modes of belief and practice have been adopted. Unity in diversity, in fact, always has been the characteristic feature of the indigenous faith of the sub-continent, the Brahmins having preserved intact all that is vital in the Vedic texts and in the Vedanta, a term used to describe the later texts.

While Buddhism had a short life in India, when it emerged from

Hinduism in the sixth century B.C. as a reaction against its metaphysical mysticism and the caste system, it readily became a missionary movement adapting its *dharma,* or sacred law and principle of existence and order of the universe, to the requirements of the countries in which it became established. Thus, in Mongolia, Tibet, China, Japan and in South-east Asia, with their very diverse traditions, it has been an effective discipline and a predominant force in faith and culture. The Vedic ritual order has been replaced by moral asceticism; the priestly caste by the monastic contemplative life and the ideal of self perfection; and the *via negativa* by a way of salvation in the quest of the passionless peace of nirvana. In the Mahayana, or great northern school of Buddhism, the Buddha himself, like Krishna in the Hindu Bhagavad-Gita, has assumed the role virtually of a saviour-god. To fulfil its functions in the social structure Buddhism has had to encourage compassion *(mettakarma),* the ethic of universal love and of social service, as integral in the attainment of Buddhahood, to meet the religious and social needs of mankind, as in the case of Bhakti Hinduism. (See chap. IV.) By these modifications and adaptations both Hinduism and Buddhism have cultivated a cultural vitality with outstanding personalities, who have included not only mystics and ascetics, but statesmen, scholars, artists and poets adorning the histories of the Asian people from 500 B.C. onwards to the present day. In Hindu India among them are Ramakrishna, Mahatma Gandhi and Sarvapillai Radhakrishnan, and with the rise of oriental nationalisms these great Eastern living religions have now become a very powerful influence by no means confined to their original homes.

Christianity and Other Religions

It is, therefore, regrettable that in the West much of the knowledge of them is out of date, and the interest in them often is amateurish, centred in theosophy and the fascination for certain types of mind of reincarnation and popular mysticisms such as Zen Buddhism. Not infrequently this reaction has been aroused as an escape from Christian faith and morals, based on a very imperfect understanding of any of the relevant religions. It is true that a deep gulf lies between the oriental faiths and systems and Christianity, the one being primarily concerned with the cessation of phenomenal existence, the other with a living God directing the course of the world and its history and processes, with whom redeemed humanity stands in a vital relationship. As Dr. Ramsey has recently emphasized, Christianity is intensely other-worldly and at the same time thoroughly down to earth, requiring a dual allegiance to the sacred and the secular. It exercises its mission essentially in this world but it is ever ready and, indeed, anxious to renounce the world for the sake of heavenly citizenship in the eternal order.[12] Thereby it combines the two functions of religion in its transcendental and immanental, its social and supramundane aspects.

That the gulf between the Occidental and the Oriental religions can be nevertheless bridged, notwithstanding its depth, will be considered in due course in this volume. Suffice it to say at this introductory stage in the inquiry that in the study of religion the climate of opinion has now changed and a new approach to the problem of their mutual relations one with the other is becoming more apparent through the combined influences of the historical and comparative investigation of their contents and purposes in an empirical and phenomenological manner, and in the genial climate of the ecumenical movement. Hitherto the non-Christian religions too often have been regarded with suspicion, disdain, repudiation, and more recently, under Barthian influence, even with repugnance, on the assumption that fallen humanity has been so under the dominion of sin that all "natural religion", independent of the Christian revelation, has been radically perverted. Even cultural achievements are said to be rooted in evil. On the empirical side the situation has not been made easier, as Professor Evans-Pritchard has pointed out, by the fact that the Victorian anthropologists and their successors at the turn of the century were nearly all agnostics, and many of them positivists following in the wake of Bentham, Comte and Saint-Simon, with their Deistic background. Consequently, they looked upon religion as an illusion, all of them "children of fancy" composed of discarded survivals from a distant past when such outworn superstitions and irrationalities predominated.[13] Approaching the subject with this sceptical bias and undiscerning detachment from its values, realities and purposes as a way of life, they were in much the same position towards the discipline as a whole as have been the Barthians and fundamentalists towards faiths other than their own.

It is now becoming more widely recognized, however, that religion at all the stages of its emergence and development is a living reality expressing and adapting itself to the prevailing conditions of culture and knowledge. Therefore, it must be studied and evaluated seriously, sympathetically, ethically and comparatively at its respective horizons and within its spheres of influence, neither paleontologically as fossils and obsolescent survivals and relics, nor as irreconcilable rivals in conflict with each other in diametrical opposition. As the Early

Church adapted its faith and practice to the requirements of its Graeco-Roman environment, so today in India, China, Japan and the Islamic world a similar approach is needed to make Christianity intelligible and acceptable to these nations; in India, in the case of Hinduism, having antecedents considerably older than those of either Christianity or Judaism, with roots going back to the second and third millennia B.C. Moreover, in Asian mysticism depths are reached of spiritual experience comparable to those attained in Western Christendom by St. John of the Cross and St. Teresa of Avila, notwithstanding their very different theological setting.[14] Here common ground is to be found, each learning from the other as co-partners in the ascent to the "castle of the soul".

Thus, while there are divergences in the Christian and Oriental religions which must be given their full weight, there is much also to be learnt by Christianity from the Eastern faiths as well as much for it to give them. This, indeed, applies in varying degrees to all the higher living religions, and in some measure to their preliterate and proto-literate background in which in many instances their foundations are deeply laid. Christ came not to destroy but to fulfil the strivings of mankind everywhere throughout the ages from the threshold of religion onwards. Being "the light that lighteth every man that cometh into the world" he has not left himself without witness in any nation or state of culture. It is the purpose of the historical and comparative study of the religions of the world to determine how this has been accomplished, and how it can be made more effective today.

FURTHER READING

Bouquet, A. C., *Comparative Religion,* 1942
Bouquet, A. C., *Christian Faith and Non-Christian Religions,* 1958
Dewick, E. C., *The Christian Attitude to Other Religions,* 1953
Durkheim, E., *Elementary Forms of the Religious Life,* E. T. 1915
Eliade, M. and Kitagawa, *The History of Religions* (Chicago Press) 1959
Evans-Pritchard, E. E., *Social Anthropology,* 1951
Gundry, D. W., *Religions,* 1958
James, E. O., *Comparative Religion,* 1961
James, E. O., *History of Religions,* 1964
Kraemer, H., *World Cultures and World Religions,* 1960
Kraemer, H., *The Christian Message in a Non-Christian World,* 1938
Lewis, H. D. and Slater, R. L., *World Religions,* 1966
Neill, S., *Christian Faith and Other Faiths,* 1961

Parrinder, E. G., *Comparative Religion*, 1962
Penniman, T. K., *A Hundred Years of Anthropology*, 1935
Toynbee, A., *Christianity among Other Religions*, 1958
Wach, J., *The Comparative Study of Religions*, 1958
Zaehner, R. C., *At Sundry Times*, 1958
Zaehner, R. C., *The Catholic Church and World Religions*, 1964

Chapter Two

THE PREHISTORIC AND PRELITERATE BACKGROUND

THE evolutionary approach to the study of the origin and development of the human race, its culture and religion, as we have seen, had revolutionary effects upon the theological situation in the middle and latter part of the last century. This in no small measure was due to the conflict it produced concerning the generally accepted biblical presentation and interpretation of the course of events as they are recorded in the opening chapters of the book of Genesis. This outworn controversy has now spent its force, and except perhaps in some fundamentalist circles, no one today is troubled very much about it. Nevertheless, it cannot be denied that the impact of the scientific evidence has had very far-reaching effects upon the Judaeo-Christian conception of creation and its doctrinal implications.

The Hebrew Creation Stories

It has now become generally recognized that behind the Hebrew stories lies a long and complicated mythology which in the Genesis version was derived from the Mesopotamian and Palestinian myths after having undergone a considerable amount of significant revision and editing in Israel when the prophetic ethical monotheism had become paramount before and after the exile in the sixth century B.C. In addition to these narratives several other very ancient traditions occur elsewhere in the Old Testament in which a primordial cosmic struggle between the opposed forces of good and evil was a prominent feature (Ps. 104; Job 38 cf. Ps. 74. 12–17; Job 26. 10–13; 9. 13). Taken together in the form in which they acquired their final shape, Yahweh was represented as the Creator of the entire universe, though before the exile other national deities were recognized, and the hostile forces were personified in Leviathan, Rahab and the crocodile dwelling in the primeval waters of the deep *(Tĕhom)*, who played much the same role as Tiamat in the Babylonian creation drama.

The Semitic conception of the three-storied geocentric universe was retained with the sky as the dome-shaped "firmament" resting on the circle of the earth, stretched out like a tent above it. Beneath was the watery chaos *(Têhom* or *Apsu)* out of which the earth was fashioned. In place of the combat between the rival gods, the Jewish priestly redactors when they compiled their creation story (Gen. 1. 2. 3), substituted the creation of vegetation and of the sun, moon and stars after the upper firmament had been erected and the dry land had been separated from the sea. This was followed by the creation of the birds, fishes, beasts, reptiles and finally man, on their respective days, leading up to the Sabbatical rest of the Creator on the seventh day of the momentous week.

In both the Babylonian epic and the Priestly Hebrew narrative virtually the same order of events recurs, whereas in the pre-exilic combination of two versions of what took place, current in the southern kingdom of Judah and the northern kingdom of Israel (distinguished by two names for God, Yahweh and Elohim, in the respective narratives commonly known as J and E) quite a different account is given from that in the Priestly story. According to the Yahwist, originally only an arid uninhabited waste existed until Yahweh-Elohim "planted a garden to the east" and caused a mist to descend upon it; or moisture to spring up as a foundation from beneath, to render it fertile and ready for human habitation (Gen. 2. 4. ff.) This suggests a Palestinian setting where, unlike Mesopotamia, the country depended upon the rainfall for its crops. From its moist soil *(adamah)* the Creator moulded man, as in ancient Egypt the god Khnum formed mankind on his potter's wheel, or in Greece Prometheus fashioned him out of clay in Phocia. Having breathed into his nostrils "the breath of Life" in order to make him a living soul, he consigned to him the care of the garden without toil and the hazards of husbandry. In the centre stood the mysterious Tree of Knowledge while next to it was the Tree of Life, which after the fatal encounter of the first parents of the human race with the serpent, later identified with the devil, was carefully guarded by cherubim with a flaming whirling sword to prevent their partaking of its life-giving fruit after their expulsion from Eden (Gen. 3. 19, 22–4).

This version of the creation and fall of man whereby primal innocence, happiness and immortality on earth were lost, is in striking contrast to its post-exilic counterpart. Clearly the two accounts are independent and are as mutually irreconcilable with each other as they are with the scientific evidence. Thus, all attempts to harmonize these diametrically opposed records, and to bring them into line with the historical situation have completely failed. Moreover, the critical investigation of the Hebrew narratives in the light of our knowledge of the parallel mythology in the ancient Near East has revealed the much earlier traditions from which they were derived and formulated by the later redactors, chiefly from their Babylonian sources. Then, as has been pointed out, it was the Semitic conception of the world and its chronology, contents and processes that formed the background of the stories, and it cannot be regarded as in any sense a revelation of the physical and historical facts and events. Indeed, there is reason to think from the didactic construction of the opening chapter of Genesis and its repeated refrain that it was composed originally for liturgical purposes; perhaps to be sung in the temple at Jerusalem at the annual festival when the enthronement of Yahweh as Creator was celebrated. His victory was re-enacted annually at the new year as a primeval event to give renewed hope and confidence in his continual beneficence, and of his loving kindness to his chosen people. The value and significance of the stories lie in their theological reinterpretation concerning the monotheistic conception of God and his relation to man as a divine creation, as later expressed and developed in the Judaeo-Christian revelation, first by the Hebrew prophets and then by the Christian Church.

Now it is true that throughout the ages the generally accepted Christian belief about an original Fall as a result of a primeval act of disobedience on the part of Adam and Eve in the garden of Eden rested on the traditional story, regarded as a record of an historical event at the threshold of human history (Rom. 5. 12 ff.; 16. 20; I Cor. 15. 22) with varying degrees of emphasis on human depravity and involvement in the initial catastrophe. It is the rejection of this interpretation of the situation as a result of the accumulation of the biological, geological, palaeontological, archaeological and anthropological evidence since the middle of the last century that has tended to throw serious doubts upon the theological deductions. Various efforts have been made to restate the doctrine in evolutionary terms, but the problem of evil, its nature, purpose and remedy, remains the most intractable and obscure of all human experiences however it is approached, especially in a monotheistic context.

Whether or not it is insoluble, at least a comparative study of the conditions in which it has arisen throws some light on its obscurities and the human reaction to them in varying states of culture. But before an investigation from this standpoint can be undertaken with hope of success, the historical course of events as they actually occurred in prehistoric times must be determined, so far as the available evidence admits of such an inquiry. As religion in its varied aspects in all probability is as old as humanity itself, inevitably it comes within the do main of the ancient origin-stories, sagas and epics, and all that lies behind them in the historical situation. Moreover, as so many of the beliefs and practices in the higher religions, both ancient and modern, are rooted in their prehistoric prototypes, going back to the Old Stone Age, the initial phase of the discipline requires elucidation. The empirical evidence, however, is confined for the most part to the archaeological material consisting of objects, sites and their equipment which have escaped the ravages of time and other destructive forces. This in its turn requires interpretation, often with the aid of similar cult objects, sacred places and their beliefs and practices still current among peoples in a preliterate state of culture, who in other respects have survived apparently little changed throughout the ages. This anthropological approach, as we have seen, has not infrequently in the past led to very conjectural and unverifiable conclusions about the cultural origins and developments of early man, not least respecting religion. Therefore, it has to be employed with caution.

The Religion of Early Man

Considered archaeologically it would now appear that early man was concerned primarily with the most arresting situations with which he was confronted — those of birth, propagation, subsistence and death. These, in fact, have been the fundamental events and experiences in human society at all times, but especially under prehistoric and preliterate conditions. In the Old Stone Age when, in striking contrast to the paradisal picture of the Garden of Eden, life depended very largely on the hazards of the chase and the precarious supply of roots, berries and fish, the vagaries of the seasons, and so many other unpredictable and uncontrollable circumstances by the human means available, the emotional tension was endemic. To sublimate this a ritual technique was devised and developed to meet these requirements and to maintain equilibrium in an expanding social structure and religious organization where every scrap of creative intelligence and ingenuity, supported and supplemented by supramundane transcendental assistance, was urgently needed. This combination of human ability and the ritual control of natural processes and phenomena, especially on critical occasions, played a predominant part in the dawn and development of culture, and the mastery of early man over his environment. Indeed, the concentration on the pressure of events in the external world and in everyday affairs afforded little opportunity for speculation about the beginning and end of the world, still less of the universe and its operations. Ways and means

34

had to be found to enable man to cope with the ever-present perplexing and unpredictable problems confronting him in his terrestrial surroundings.

Prior to the transition from food-collection to food-production at the end of the Old Stone Age when after the Mesolithic interlude Neolithic civilization began to become established in the Ancient Near East in the fifth millennium B.C., the principal concern appears to have been centred in the food supply, propagation and the afterlife. As Frazer has said, "to live and to cause to live, to eat food and to beget children, these were the primary wants of man in the past, and they will be the primary wants of man in the future so long as the world lasts. Other things may be added to enrich and beautify human life, but unless these wants are first satisfied, human life itself must cease to exist."[1] Therefore, around an adequate supply of food and of offspring of man and beast the institutions of religion have found expression, apparently from Palaeolithic times.

Exactly when, where and how religion first emerged is conjectural in the present state of our knowledge, though there are unmistakable indications of a conception of the continuation of life after death in some form as early as the beginning of the Pleistocene geological period, or Quarternary Ice Age, in the deposits of the Dragon-bone caves in China near Peking, dated by Professor Zeuner "in the neighbourhood of 500,000 years' ago".[2] In Western Europe we know that ceremonial interment was practised in the middle of the Palaeolithic period, perhaps 200,000 years ago, at Le Moustier and La Ferrassie in the Dordogne, and at La Chapelle-aux-Saints in Corrèze in France and elsewhere. It was not, however, until the Upper Palaeolithic, after the arrival of the modern type of mankind distinguished as *homo sapiens* from his more primitive Neanderthal predecessors, at the end of the maximum glaciation, that attempts were made to revivify the dead with life-giving agents like shells and red ochre as the surrogate of blood. This is very apparent in the series of caves on the Italian Riviera at Grimaldi between Menton and Ventimiglia where the Upper Palaeolithic skeletons had been stained with iron peroxide (as also in the Paviland cave in South Wales) and equipped with vast quantities of shells as life-giving amulets, such as cowries; a practice that recurs at Les Eyzies and Chancelade in the Dordogne, at Brno in Czechoslovakia, and at Oberoassel near Bonn. The flexing of the body in the crouched position was adopted probably to prevent the ghost from "walking", but ceremonial interment and its tendance indicate care for the well-being of the departed rather than fear of the return of the dead as the primary purpose of the mortuary rites.

The extension of the revivification to the departed could hardly fail to bring the mystery of death into relation with that of birth and fertility. The projection of the religious consciousness into this domain found expression it would seem in the conception of a providential beneficence as the universal "good", or "bounty", upon which man depended for his sustenance, well-being and the continuance of the human race. Food and children became the tokens of a supramundane providence linking man with his terrestrial environment. To eat is to live, and to be fruitful and multiply, as the Yahwist writer of the Eden story affirmed, was both a necessity and a divine command. So early man adopted a ritual attitude to the production of food and offspring, doubtless for the same reasons and purposes.

This has now become apparent in the parietal and cave art that has come to light in the Upper Palaeolithic caves in France and Spain. The remarkable engravings and paintings frequently occur in the most inaccessible recesses, nooks and crannies, and difficult positions far from the light of day, often reached only with considerable peril. Thus, in the vast cavern at Niaux near Tarascon-sur-Ariège on the French side of the Pyrenees, the paintings are nearly a mile from the entrance, separated from it by a small lake often full of water. Among the designs a wounded bison with its legs drawn up has been depicted by skilfully utilizing three small cup-like hollows under an overhanging wall, and marking them with arrows in red ochre. In front of the expiring animal are circles and club-shaped representations of missiles. Here in a great subterranean sacred rotunda with side-chapels in the heart of the limestone mountain unquestionably magical rites were performed to control the fortunes of the chase on which the food supply depended, the wounded bison being only one example of the ritual at Niaux.

In the cave at Montespan in the Haute Garonne, very difficult of access, a number of clay models of felines has been found riddled with javelin wounds and broken in pieces, probably in a magical ceremony. On the floor the design of a horse has similar thrusts on the neck, as has a small figure of a bear on a platform in the centre, and on the breast of a lioness on the wall. Here the rites clearly were perpetrated to kill the animals being hunted in the chase by casting spells on them. Nearby in a small cavern at Marsoulas spear-markings one above the other were painted on the flank of fine polychrome designs of bisons, indicating that they had been employed for ritual purposes by successive generations in the Magdalenian period at the end of the Palaeolithic.

Indeed, the great sanctuary recently discovered at Lascaux near Montignac in the Dordogne, aptly called by the Abbé Breuil the "Versailles of Palaeolithic art", must have been a cult-centre for thousands of years from the beginning to the end of the Upper Palaeolithic period. Within its walls a great variety of rites must have been performed connected with hunting magic to control the chase.[3]

The most illuminating evidence, however, comes from the almost inaccessible cave on the estate of the Count Bégoüen near St. Girons in Ariège, entered with ingenuity by his three sons in 1914, and so appropriately called Les Trois Frères. Crawling through a vertical shaft not much bigger than a rabbit-hole they found beside quantities of engravings and paintings with arrowhead markings, the remarkable figure of a masked hunter or magician crawling along with bent knees seeking his prey. His face is enclosed in the mask of a stag with antlers, the eyes are those of an owl, the ears of a wolf, the claws of a lion, and the tail of a horse, but the legs are human. This may represent the figure of an embryonic god of the sanctuary controlling the multiplication of the species indicated, as the abbé suggests, but it seems more likely to represent a ritual expert engaged in a sacred dance to promote success in the chase, or the increase of the prey.

That fertility dances were held for this purpose is shown in the adjacent cave known as Tuc d'Audoubert which was first explored by Bégoüen and his sons in 1912. After hacking their way through a stalactite barrier at the entrance and scrambling along a narrow passage they discovered in a chamber two bison modelled in clay leaning against a block of rock, the female awaiting the male in a characteristic attitude of mating. In front of the models the interlacing imprints of human heels were made on the soft clay doubtless by those engaged in a sacred dance to make the bison increase and multiply. Therefore, it was not only to cast spells on the animals being hunted but also to maintain the food supply that these fertility rites were performed in the decorated caves. These included masked dances, representations of processions and holy persons engaged in the prescribed rites, aided with cult objects, charms, spells and amulets. Sometimes it seems that animals and human beings were brought together in a ritual action to establish a mystic communion with the providential source of bounty in a joint endeavour to conserve and promote the food supply and fecundity, as at Les Trois Frères.

The will to live as the primary urge was discharged by anticipatory rites giving visible and dramatic expression in response to concrete situations and current needs, supplying a vent to pent-up emotions and longings. These ritual techniques, which lay at the base of sacramental communion and sacrificial oblation, were efficacious not because "like produces like" but because a ritual resting upon urgent practical requirements established an *ex post facto* idea of sympathetic causation in the production of food and off-spring. The sacramental sign, or sacrificial victim, was regarded and treated in the same way as that which it symbolized because it had acquired the same qualities and powers. Hence the efficacy of the designs, disguises, masks, dances and other cult objects and actions employed by the ritual experts in their cultus. Thus, the blood of the victim was poured out to set free its life. As Loisy says, "Life issues from death, and death is the condition and means of life. To destroy in order to create, to liberate through death, the power that lies latent in a living being."[4] The ritual shedding of blood, and the manipulation of its surrogate red ochre, to establish beneficial relations with a god or totem, or to give renewed life to the dead, as we have seen, was a prominent feature in Palaeolithic ritual. It was not, however, until Neolithic times that an animal or human victim was offered as such for this purpose.

The Cult of the Mother-Goddess

Or, again, in the Upper Palaeolithic female figurines were sculptured with the maternal organs and their voluptous features greatly emphasized as fertility emblems to produce, preserve or renew life. The woman being the mother of the race, she was and must be always the life producer. Therefore, her generative organs and maternal functions were regarded as cult objects for this purpose, be they statuettes commonly called "Venuses", or bas-reliefs like the realistic figure of an obese female holding the horn of a bison carved on a block of stone in the rock-shelter at Laussel near Les Eyzies. Originally this relief, together with an associated sculpture of what seems to be an accouchement, was covered with red ochre to increase its vitalizing qualities and maternal potency. Between Laussel and Les Eyzies dancing figures were engraved for the same purpose on the walls of the cave of Combarelles.

Whether or not the mother-goddess was the earliest manifestation of the concept of deity, as has been suggested,[5] her symbolism has been one of the most persistent emblems in the archaeological record from the Palaeolithic Venuses, bas-reliefs, dancing figures and cowrie shells, to the statuettes and inscriptions of the cult of the mother-goddess in the Fertile Crescent, Western Asia, Baluchistan and the Indus valley, the Aegean and Crete, in the Neolithic and Bronze Age. With the adoption of agriculture and stock-rearing the figures and functions of the goddess became more clearly defined. With increasing concentration on the generative process in the maintenance of food production, from being the unmarried mother personifying the divine principle in maternity, she became united with the young god as her son or consort. In this dual capacity she was the dominant figure in the Babylonian seasonal drama with the sacral king as her obedient servant. In the Anatolian and Mystery cults she exercised supreme control over procreation, while as the earth-mother and the corn-goddess she was responsible for vegetation and the grain emerging from the soil, regarded as her fertile womb. As the syncretistic Magna Mater in the Graeco-Oriental world she was "the Goddess of many names". In this capacity her Mysteries differed from those of her male divine partner in that they were centred in birth and generation, in life issuing from life, rather than in death and rebirth, in life rising renewed from the grave. These interpretations were brought together eventually in Christendom and given a new mystical and theological content in terms first of the Church as the mystical Body of Christ, and then as the virgin mother of the incarnate Son of God — the Theotokos, or Madonna, with her own cultus. This unique position occupied by the goddess cult in the history of religion from Palaeolithic times to the Christian era, and still surviving in a variety of contexts, theological, devotional and in popular pastimes such as May Day celebrations, has acquired its dominance and significance because it has met not a few of the vital needs of mankind at all times throughout the ages.

Supreme Beings

The conception of deity, however, under Palaeolithic conditions is very difficult to determine. As we have seen, before the Neolithic transition from food-gathering to food-production, the religious consciousness was projected very largely on symbolic objects and emblems connected with fecundity, hunting magic and the cult of the dead. To what extent, if at all, this included an awareness of transcendent divinity, external to the world and controlling its processes, and the cosmic order, is still in debate. While the unilineal development of the idea of God from animism through polytheism to monotheism has been abandoned, the precise relation of "gods many and lords many" to one supreme being in prehistoric and preliterate society is by no means finally decided.

At the end of the last century Andrew Lang called attention to "high gods of low races" demonstrated by the evidence produced mainly by

A. W. Howitt and Mrs. Langloh Parker among the native tribes of south-east Australia. Supreme beings such as Daramulun in the Yuin coastal regions and Baiame in the Kamilaroi tribe, were established before missionary or other European influences were felt in New South Wales and the surrounding district.[6] Similarly, Atnatu, the all-father of the Kaitish tribe in Central Australia, stood aloof from the lesser spirits, totems and ancestors, having made himself, as it was believed, before "the dream time of long ago".[7] These supreme beings are thought to live in the sky and having inaugurated the tribal customs and beliefs they have been remote from mundane affairs, speaking only in the thunder and when the bull-roarers are swung at the initiation ceremonies.[8]

This evidence has now been confirmed in comparable states of culture where high gods have been found all over the world, largely through the exhaustive and laborious researches of Wilhelm Schmidt and his collaborators, who have shown that this type of supreme being is almost of universal occurrence.[9] Since very often they have been regarded as having existed before death came into the world it cannot be maintained, as Herbert Spencer contended, that the idea of God arose in ancestor-worship; or, as Tylor and Frazer asserted, as the result of an evolutionary process based on animism. These self-existent high gods have been thought to be independent of culture heroes and lesser divinities, standing head and shoulders above all secondary spiritual beings, and departmental gods, to whom popular worship usually has been offered. They are on a plane by themselves, and seem to represent the ultimate moral value of the universe, so far as such a reality can be conceived by the primitive mind.

Thus, Professor Evans-Pritchard recently has recorded that among the Nuerin Nilotic East Africa, God is pure spirit, Kwoth, because "like the wind or air he is everywhere and being everywhere he is here now". He is far away in the sky yet present on earth which he created and sustains. "Everything in nature, in culture, in society and in men is as it is because God made it so". Although he is ubiquitous and invisible he sees and hears all that happens, and being responsive to the supplications of those who call upon him, prayers are addressed to him and sacrifice offered to avoid misfortunes. Since he can be angry he punishes wrong-doing and as suffering is thought to be beyond human control, it is accepted with resignation because it is his will. But the consequences of wrong-doing can be stayed or mitigated by contrition and reparation, prayer and sacrifice.[10]

If this conception of deity has not been conditioned by Christian, Jewish or Islamic influences, it constitutes a remarkable example of a genuinely theistic response to the notion of the divine more fundamental than a unilineal development from plurality to unity. In any case, taking the evidence collectively, the widespread recognition of a supreme being would seem to be a spontaneous purposive functioning of an inherent type of thought and emotion; an evaluation of the *summum bonum* within the limits of the primitive mind; a religious response to the notion of providence, rather than speculation about souls and the universe. Indeed, when animation of nature is reflected upon and interpreted in terms of conceptual ideas about spirits and gods, the supreme being tends to be left vaguely in the background. Therefore, it has led to the peopling of natural phenomena with a multitude of spirits, departmental gods and culture heroes in such profusion that the high god has receded further and further into obscurity, having less and less interest in and dealings with the world and human affairs.

Nevertheless, exalted as are these all-fathers, occupying a unique status in the sky-world and the tribal community, it has to be remembered that it is within the very limited sense in which the qualities and functions assigned to them can be conceived in the states of culture in which they occur that they are believed to operate. "To go anywhere", or "do anything" and "to know everything", as is alleged of Daramulun among the Australian aborigines, can only be regarded as implying omnipotence and omniscience as these attributes might be applied to a powerful medicine-man. Similarly, their creative functions are comparable to those exercised by a great rain-maker, and are restricted to the very localized dimensions of the tribal perspective, while the problem of causation has little or no meaning beyond the powers possessed by a ritual expert. The all-father's control of the tribal ethic is confined to investing established custom with an inviolable sacredness seldom rising above the maintenance of the sacred sanctions governing the social order. Therefore, to say with Pater Schmidt that "the primitive religious beliefs that found expression in High Gods arose from the profoundest depths of a conviction of the person of the Supreme Being as the Universal Cause", is to lose sight of the fact that such a conception is and was as foreign to the preliterate, alike in the matter of personality and causation, as is the scholastic and metaphysical concept of creation *ex nihilo,* which he regards as an attribute of the original "revelation".[11]

Moreover, notwithstanding the elaborate culture-analysis he and his school devised to establish an alleged primeval revelation and subsequent "fall" at the threshold of the human race, the existence of a so-called *Urkultur,* or archaic substratum, now represented by the Bushmen,

Pygmies, Andamanese, Fuegians, Semang, and the native tribes of south-east Australia, remains purely conjectural. And among those who accept the hypothesis there are marked differences of opinion about the composition of the archaic substratum and its high Gods. The most that can be demonstrated is a progressive series of horizons within existing cultures, but however intensively and analytically modern surviving preliterate cultures are studied, they belong to the present and not to the past, and so cannot be shown really to be primeval. All have behind them a history extending over much the same length of time as our own, and native races can be regarded as "primitive" only in the sense that their long isolation in particular localities has caused them to retain many of their earlier customs and beliefs. While the universal recurrence of high gods among low races suggests a probability in favour of the belief being widely held by early man, to interpret it in terms of a primeval divine revelation raises more problems for theology than it solves, and goes beyond the limits of the available archaeological evidence.

Thus, the Palaeolithic data throw little or no light upon the problem. A few oval bone and stone pendants perforated at one end have been found at Creswell Crags in Derbyshire, similar in form to bull-roarers used by the Australian aborigines to produce, as is believed, the voice of the all-father. Attempts have been made to establish a Palaeolithic Bear cult in the Drachenloch caves in the Swiss Alps, in which a thank-offering is alleged to have been made to the supreme creative being for the bestowal of food, but neither the dating of the site nor the interpretation of its contents has been determined with any degree of certainty. Therefore, this is not a reliable source of information concerning alleged sacrifices to supreme beings in the last glaciation, while for pendants to serve the purposes of bull-roarers they would have had to be made of wood, and, therefore, doubtless, would have perished long ago.

The Sacred and the Secular

Nevertheless, as this conception of deity was so firmly established in Neolithic times it may well have been rooted in the history of religion prior to the great divide between food-gathering and food-production, especially in the Ancient Near East. Under Palaeolithic conditions, for the reasons that have been considered, the concept would seem to have been centred in a beneficent providence, as the transcendental Power embodying the universal good in the natural order and in human society, controlling its processes, sanctions, laws and institutions, just as it is among surviving preliterate peoples in similar states of culture. In the rudimentary stages of God-awareness, however undefined it may have been, the notion of providence combined with that of sacredness appears to have been fundamental. Out of it has emerged a great variety of beliefs, ritual techniques, social sanctions and organizations, all having a common source in which sacredness has been paramount. In pre-historic and preliterate communities they have been integral elements in an integrated structure at once social and religious. In recent times, not least in this country, religion frequently has been regarded mainly as "other-worldly" mysticism centred in a personal relationship between the individual and God on which the well-being of his immortal soul depends here and hereafter. This has been based on a dichotomy of two realms, the sacred and the secular, in line with the conception of the human organism as a duality of body and soul, and has been responsible for the spate of dualisms in Christendom and the modern world.

Thus, the religious reactions of preliterate peoples to the sacred order have been explained by an emotional approach in effective rather than in cognitive states—appetites and emotions instead of reason being represented as the motive force. Against this the French school of Durkheim and Lévy-Bruhl at the beginning of the century, in developing the theory that all rites are social in origin, maintained that in primitive society the universe is divided into the sacred and the profane so that the supernatural is the negation of the natural. The primitive is said to think in terms of "collective representations" in which objects are not divided from one another, everything being regarded as permeated with supernatural forces. Therefore, they are assigned to the sacred realm and given a transcendental significance. A thing thus becomes what it is not by the "law of participation", one and the same entity being simultaneously present in many places.[12] This is attributed to primitive people being in a state of pre-logical mentality completely immersed in a mystical frame of mind. It is not, however, lack of logic that characterizes their outlook but a particular attitude to the relation between the sacred and the secular, the natural and the supernatural, mind and matter, cause and effect. As Dr. Marett pointed out, "the savage has no word for 'nature'. He does not abstractedly distinguish between an order of uniform happenings and a higher order of miraculous happenings. He is merely concerned to mark and exploit the difference when presented in the concrete."[13]

The world is conceived as full of mystery and forces imperceptible to sense but intensely real. The entire universe appears as one great system of interrelated and inherent life, endowed with sacredness, with which man identifies himself sacramentally by ritual techniques. When the relationship is represented by a material symbol the symbol is treated in the same way as the spiritual entity it symbolizes, not because it is thought to be other than it actually is, but because it has acquired a spiritual quality which does not belong to it in its own nature, without changing its outward and visible form and character. This sacramental conception of symbolism based on the existence of an extra-mundane sacred order standing over against, and in a particular relation to, the phenomenal world is a fundamental assumption at all times and in all states of culture where these premises are accepted without contravening either logic or the "law of contradiction". In prehistoric and pre-literate society it lies behind the ritual control of natural processes and occurrences, and the socio-religious institutions like totemism, devised to facilitate what is called in the idiom of Lévy-Bruhl "mystical participation" in the order of the sacred. Thus, when a Palaeolithic ritual expert arrayed himself as a composite sacred species like the so-called "Sorcerer" in the cave of Les Trois Frères, he imitated its behaviour believing that he was establishing a sacramental relationship with the source of his food supply. Upon this providential Bounty man has felt himself to be dependent for his sustenance and well-being, and the institutions of religion have been the means whereby communion with it has been secured. In these precarious conditions emotional stress has been endemic, and myth and ritual have been the generally accepted way of dealing with the situation.

In modern secularized civilizations, while for the most part the hazards of the chase and of the the seasons have been now eliminated by the application of the scientific method to the means of subsistence, this has been done at the price of undermining to a considerable extent the foundations of the sacred stabilizing dynamic on which the social structure and its religious organizations formerly rested. Once the underlying ultimate reality at the base of all religions is invalidated, or rendered ineffective, so that its relationship with the secular order is dislocated or destroyed, the whole edifice is liable to collapse. Myth then degenerates into fiction and ritual into conventional traditional customs, quaint and picturesque, perhaps, but devoid of any serious meaning and vital significance. Having ceased to be an integral element in a living culture, they readily become unedifying superstitions like palmistry, crystal gazing, gambling and "luck".

To some extent, alas, this has befallen the Christian faith in the secular age which has now become the established régime, especially in Europe and America. In this contemporary situation God, freedom and immortality, postulated by Kant as the basic triad, are virtually discountenanced, and the established institutions, theologies and ideologies, sanctions and morals, are breaking up under the pressure of current events and ideas. Not infrequently this is camouflaged under the guise of a new theology or new morality justified on the supposition of meeting the needs of the times. Thus, to take the place of the former realities of the sacred order a new kind of mythology and cultus directed to nationalistic and political ends, and supposed religious and social demands, has arisen to give stability to Church and State in its various forms, leaving a dangerous vacuum. As Malinowski, himself incidentally a professed agnostic, pointed out in his Riddell Lectures at Durham in 1935, "a sound social life must be based upon a truly religious system of values, that is one which reflects the revelation to us of the existence of spiritual and moral order". This does not mean, as he explained, that "all the members of the society controlled by religious belief and ethics should be bigoted sectarians, or even practising believers". But it does mean, he declared, "the application of ethical principles and the recognition of spiritual values in public life and national policy." For, as he maintained, "if civilization and culture are to be preserved intact and enabled to fulfill their function for the common weal, the eternal truths of religion must be maintained because it is they which have guided mankind out of barbarism to culture, and the loss of which seems to threaten us with barbarism again".[14]

These eternal truths have been made known in divers forms and manners, often in those of myth and ritual as in the origin-stories in the book of Genesis, and in the annual enactment of the mysterious process of birth and death in the seasonal sequence, regarded as events of vital significance for the well-being and continuance of the cosmic and human orders and the stability of the social structure. Truth, however, can be ascertained by very many different methods, and can be expressed in a variety of forms and systems. Today scientific investigation by observation and experiment, and historical inquiry based on reliable documentary evidence, are very widely employed with great advantage and most valuable results. This is of particular importance in the commendation and defence of the Christian faith, based as it is on historical events and written records very deeply laid in the history of religion, in which the imagery and symbolism belong to varying states of culture and levels of thought and spiritual experience. Religious forms and systems, of course, inevitably tend to become effete and elusive with advance of knowledge and changing ways of life. But intellectual reason unenlightened and uninformed by spiritual understanding of the underlying truths all too easily obscures and destroys their transcendental values and realities, which lie beyond the finite conditions of mundane existence and knowledge.

Throughout the ages God has revealed himself in his ways and works transcending human observance and understanding; first partially in the religions of the world, more clearly in Israel, as the living personal Creator, and then finally and perfectly in the unique redemptive incarnation of Christ as very God and true man. It is this revelation, rooted and grounded especially in the ethical monotheism of the Old Judaic Covenant, that has to be seen and evaluated in this wider perspective as the consummation of all that has been divinely disclosed from the threshold of human history. In this context the emergence of the monotheistic conception of deity must now be examined in greater detail.

FOR FURTHER READING

Breuil, H., *Four Hundred Centuries of Cave Art,* 1952
Evans-Pritchard, E. E., *Nuer Religion,* 1956
Hick, J., *Evil and the God of Love,* 1966
Hooke, S. H., *In the Beginning* (Clarendon Bible, vol. vi.), 1948
James, E. O., *Prehistoric Religion,* 1957;
James, E. O., *The Cult of the Mother-Goddess,* 1959
Jensen, A. E., *Myth and Cult among Primitive People.* 1963
Lévy-Bruhl, L., *How Natives Think,* 1926
Luquet, G. H., *The Art and Religion of Fossil Man,* 1930
Marett, R. R., *The Threshold of Religion,* 1914
Schmidt, W., *The Origin and Growth of Religion,* E. T., 1931
Tennant, F. R., *The Sources of the Doctrines of the Fall and Original Sin,* 1903
Williams, N. P., *The Ideas of the Fall and of Original Sin,* 1927

Chapter Three

THE MONOTHEISTIC CONCEPTION OF DEITY

It is now apparent that monotheism cannot be regarded as the product of an evolutionary process from animism and polytheism along the lines indicated by Frazer and his contemporaries. Thus, the conception of divine providence, and all that this involved for early man, may have found expression in belief in a supreme being in Palaeolithic times comparable to that of "high gods among low races" today. Nevertheless, the fact remains that it was not until the rise of civilization in the Ancient Near East from the fifth millennium B.C. onwards, that the idea emerged of the existence of only one God to the exclusion of all other divinities. Even then in this crucial cradleland of the higher living monotheisms, Judaism, Christianity and Islam, it was a gradual and relatively late development, localized especially in the so-called Fertile Crescent from the Nile valley to Mesopotamia and Palestine, determined very largely by the physical environment in its earlier phases.

The Solar Conception of Deity in Egypt

In Egypt it was centred in the sun as the most conspicuous feature in the all-encompassing sky, rising anew every morning and descending, as it seemed, into the underworld in the evening, personified as the sun-god who bestowed light upon the dead, ripened the crops with his life-giving rays, and became incarnate in the occupant of the throne. Therefore, he was worshipped as the chief god in the pantheon at a very early period. Thus, in the texts inscribed on the pyramids in the fifth and sixth dynasties (c. 2580–2250 B.C.), the predynastic sky-god of the falcon clan, Horus, is represented as the source of life, the giver of rain and of celestial fire, symbolized as a hawk surmounted by the solar disk with outstretched wings, flying across the horizon as Re-Harakhte (i.e. "the Horus of the Horizon"). In the morning he came forth as the winged beetle Khepera, rising in the east, and setting in the west in the evening as the Heliopolitan god Atum. Eventually the numerous falcon-gods were absorbed in Horus the Elder as the sky-god *par excellence* soon after 3000 B.C. as a compound deity. The reigning Pharaoh then acquired a filial relationship with the sun-god as his incarnation under the influence of the Heliopolitan priesthood, thereby making the throne the unifying dynamic and cohesive centre of the "Two Lands".[1]

As the head of the pantheon, Re represented the sun in the fullness of its strength combining all the forces of nature, and identified with the great primeval cosmic god Atum, the self-produced father of the nine gods of the Heliopolitan Ennead, rising from the primordial waters of Nun; or in other theophanies regarded as born from a lotus flower, or from an egg by Ptah, the self-created god of Memphis. Thus, the sun-god in his corporate capacities and syncretisms personified the transcendent Creator of all things in heaven and on earth, including the gods, who at the beginning of time alone existed. From Re-Atum, with or without the aid of a consort, he begat the gods of the air and the atmosphere, the earth (Geb) and the sky-goddess (Nut), and their offspring Osiris and Isis, and Seth and Nephthys. The inclusion of the Osiris-Isis cycle in the Heliopolitan Ennead shows, however, that local divinities were given a place in the sun when they acquired eminence. Originally Osiris was the lord of the dead and the personification of the life-giving water of the Nile, renewing the fertile soil after the annual inundation, typifying the dying and reviving god brought into relation with the transcendent solar creator. Later, when with the establishment of the new kingdom Thebes became the capital, its local god Amon was united with Re and worshipped as Amon-Re at Luxor and Karnak with great magnificence as "the King of the gods". Indeed, by the eighteenth dynasty (c. 1546) he had inherited all the attributes, authority and functions, and the entire status of the supreme solar deity in the pantheon.

Thus, the ancient Egyptians arrived at a conception of a universal god without abandoning their polytheistic tradition, except for the abortive interlude between 1387 and 1366 B.C. when Amenhotep IV, subsequently known as Ikhnaton, established a solar monotheism centred in the ancient god of the air and of light, Aton, whom he proclaimed as "the sole deity of heaven and earth, sustaining all things, beside whom there is no other." Hitherto Re, Amon and Ptah had been regarded as self-created creators, instrumental in bringing the rest of their pantheons into existence together with the cosmos. Even the remarkable abstract theistic thought of the Memphite theologians made little or no permanent impression on the concrete solar theology when they tried to counteract the growing influence of Heliopolis by representing their god Ptah as the Creator of the universe and the source of all the gods. Therefore, when the princes of Thebes

48

about 1580 B.C. threw off the yoke of the Semitic invaders known as the Hyksos, they attributed their victory to their god Amon, whom they substituted for the Heliopolitan Re, thereby combining his life-giving functions with those of the solar creator-god.

Having acquired these attributes and this status in the new kingdom, Amon became virtually the first cause and the basis of all life, declared in a hymn, composed probably in the reign of Amenhotep II (c. 1450–1425 B.C.), as

> He who made herbage for the cattle
> And the fruit for men.
> And who made that whereon live the fish in the river,
> And the birds which inhabit the firmament,
> He who giveth bread to him that is in the egg,
> and sustaineth the son of the worm.
>
> He who made whereon the gnats live,
> The worms and the flies likewise.
> He who maketh that which the mice in their holes need,
> And sustaineth the birds (?) on every tree.[2]

While Ikhnaton may have derived his inspiration from this Cairo Hymn, substituting the solar disk, Aton, with its emanating rays, for the celestial orb, like Khnum, the potter-god of the cataract region, the maker of the gods and the fashioner of men,[3] his ephemeral movement, nevertheless, constituted a temporary heretical schism in the solar tradition. Unlike Amon-Re, the Aton, although originally an ancient designation of Harakhte crowned with the disk of the sun, was shorn of his earlier syncretistic nature as a blend of the deified sun, the horizon and the falcon. With all the iconoclastic zeal of a Somerset, his "beautiful child" Ikhnaton suppressed every vestige of the old religion. The temples of Amon-Re were closed, a new hierarchy was set up, the names of all the other gods were erased from the monuments, their images destroyed and the capital moved from Thebes to Amarna in Middle Egypt and renamed Akhetaton, "Profitable to Aton".

It is possible, as Budge has suggested, that this monotheistic movement owed something to the influences from Mitanni in Mesopotamia, introduced by his mother Tii and his wife Nefertiti, both of whom, together with his grandmother, the queen of Thutmose IV, may have come from north of the Euphrates.[4] But, although it was certainly the closest approach to the conception of a single supreme universal deity within Egyptian polytheism, it was essentially a form of sun-worship centred in the deified solar disk, if expressed in language and spiritual concepts not far removed from those of the psalmists in Israel. This is seen in *The Hymn to the Sun* recorded in one of the rock-cut tombs at El-Amarna:

> Beautiful is thine appearing in the horizon of heaven, thou
> living sun, the first who lived!
> Thou risest in the eastern horizon and
> Thou fillest every land with thy beauty,
> Thou art beautiful and great and glistenest, and art high above
> every land;
> Thy rays, they compass the lands, so far as all that thou hast
> created.
> Thou art Re, and thou reachest unto their end and subduest them
> for thy dear Son.
> Though thou art far away, yet are thy rays upon earth;
> Thou art before their face.[5]

Here the solar cultus is very definitely apparent with the dependence of the earth and its activities on the rising and the setting of the sun conditioning the life of the Two Lands. As soon as it rises men resume their labours and all cattle rest upon their pasturage, the trees and the plants flourish, the birds flutter in their marshes, and the sheep dance upon their feet. As the source of all life the Aton is extolled in much the same terms as is Yahweh in Psalm 104. 20–23, who is said to make "darkness and night wherein the beasts of the forest creep forth". The young lions seek their meat from him, and when the sun arises they lay them down in their dens, and man goes forth to his work until the evening. Both Aton and Yahweh are extolled respectively for their manifold creative works, it being asserted of the Aton in *The Hymn to the Sun;*

> How manifold are thy works!
> They are hidden before men,
> O sole God whose powers no other possessest.
> Thou didst create the earth according to thy heart,
> Whilst thou wast alone, cities, villages, and fields, high-ways
> and rivers.
> All eyes see thee before them.

As the Ikhnaton interlude coincided with the expanding imperial power of the State, the sovereignty of Aton was extended to cover foreign countries, Syria and Kush, as well as the Two Lands in the Nile valley. "Thou settest every man in his place", it is said, "thou suppliest their necessities." Indeed, his domain was not confined to the earth as it was he who made "the Nile in the Nether World and the Nile in the Sky, O how excellent are thy designs, O Lord of eternity."

This undoubtedly was the first attempt to establish an absolute monotheism in terms of a single all-embracing universal celestial Creator and sustainer of all things, notwithstanding its solar polytheistic setting. Ikhnaton declared himself to be the son of Aton who alone knows him. This, in fact, was true in so far as it was essentially a royal cult which had little or no influence on the populace, who continued to worship the sun in the sky in much the same manner as the earlier falcon-god in the horizon was venerated. Moreover, the Aton was too remote from mundane affairs and the everyday needs of mankind at large, too abstract as well as too confined to the youthful and ineffective Pharaoh and his family, to make a popular appeal. He was, therefore, destined to suffer the fate of most otiose high gods. For practical purposes the divinities of the solar cycle had to be brought into relation with the earth-gods of the Osiris-Isis tradition and the cult of the dead, so that through their agency the beneficence of the celestial realms might be bestowed upon the soil to cause it to produce with abundance corn and wine, and to give resurrection to the dead in the afterlife. Therefore, as Ikhnaton made no permanent or significant impression on the nation, as soon as he died in or about 1366 B.C., the Theban Amon-Re and his powerful priesthood were restored with added prestige, like the English monarchy at the Restoration in 1660. Henceforth in Egypt the syncretistic solar and Osirian polytheism held the field in which the indigenous gods with a local provenance retained their individualities and functions. Thus, in striking contrast to Yahwism in Israel, in which the prophetic movement in the eighth century B.C. established ethical monotheism which became the permanent faith of post-exilic Judaism, in Egypt the prevailing conception was that of a universal solar deity not very different from that of "the Goddess of many names" (e.g. Isis as the syncretistic Great Mother) in that he did not abandon his polytheistic attributes. Nevertheless, in all probability behind the many forms in which the Creator was manifest in the Nile valley — those of Atum-Re at Heliopolis, of Ptah at Memphis, of Thoth at Hermopolis, of Amon-Re at Thebes and of Khnum at Elephantine — was one supreme being regarded as the transcendent source of the creative process and the controller of the weather and the seasons. In view of the prominence of the sun in Egypt it is not surprising that it was primarily associated with the central luminary, asserted by Breasted to be the most insistent fact in the Nile valley.[6] But its remarkable fertility depended upon the conjunction of the life-giving rays of the sun with the vitalizing waters of the river which jointly made the desert blossom as the rose. Therefore, to fulfill these requirements the solar celestial gods had to be brought into relation with Osiris and his cultus equated with the Nile.

In Mesopotamia, the Sumerian and Babylonian civilization and its religion grew up in a different environment, the Tigris and Euphrates lacking the stability and predictability of the Nile. This had its influence on the conception of the gods as cosmic powers, under whose control was this precarious situation and the determination of destiny. It was not, however, a universal cosmic order vested in the monarchy as in Egypt, though the assembly of the gods in the heavens was recognized as the highest authority in the universe under the leadership of Anu, the supreme being whose name means "the sky shining brightly". But while he occupied an independent position controlling the universe and the course of human affairs in one version of the Sumerian cosmogony, it was his mother Nammu, who personified the primeval watery deep, who gave birth to heaven and earth, and fashioned all things.[7] The texts, however, are very incomplete, complementary and contradictory concerning the creation of the universe; and deeply involved in the process besides Anu and Nammu were the Storm-god Enlil, who is also described as "King of the gods" as well as "Lord of the winds", and Enki or Ea, "the Lord of the watery deep", dwelling therein.

Enlil being less obscure than Anu he became the head and leader of the Sumerian pantheon in the third millennium B.C. as "the father of the gods" who separated the heavens and the earth with his pickaxe. Therefore, he was virtually responsible for bringing the world into existence, making its soil fertile, sowing the seed of the land and providing it with trees, grain and cattle. Combining the violence of the prevalent devastating storms with the fructifying rain he sent on the earth, Enlil was regarded as the executor of divine power in its various aspects.[8] But as it was from the rivers, springs, canals, and wells that the life-giving waters were mainly derived, and they were equated with Enki, the Lord of the Earth, and of the waters, he was the source of fertility. Moreover, it was Enki who watched over the universe, taught mankind the art of writing and geometry, showed him how to build cities and temples and to cultivate the soil. Therefore, he became the god of wisdom and esoteric knowledge, having his temple at Eridu at the head of the Persian Gulf where the so-called "sweet waters" of the Tigris and Euphrates mingled with the "bitter waters" of the sea. There too the human race was fashioned from its clay by Anu, and all creatures were endowed with the breath of life by Enki. He transformed the marsh land into a veritable Eden, heaped up the granaries with corn and filled the canals with fish. Thus he was the giver of life, the patron of the arts and the creator of the fates.

Notwithstanding the power exercised by this triad of gods, Anu, Enlil and Enki (Ea), none of the Sumerian deities occupied the position of Re or Ptah in Egypt. Anu was a shadowy figure like so many supreme beings; Enlil was primarily lord of the earth; and Enki the lord of the waters and the god of wisdom, rather than universal creators. Furthermore, they were eclipsed in great measure by the rise of the younger god – Sin, the moon-god, Shamash the sun-god, and Adad the storm-god – before Marduk, the son of Enki, who became the hero of the Akkadian creation epic when Babylon was made the capital of the Empire of Hammurabi (1792–1750 B.C.). In times of great crisis, as for instance during the Deluge, the gods turned to Anu for succour, but their own status was dependent upon the vicissitudes of the cities or confederacies over which they presided. Even Marduk gave place to Ashur when Assyria rose to supremacy in Mesopotamia, in spite of the collective power of the gods having been bestowed upon Marduk after his victory over Tiamat. No god, in fact, had a permanently assured position. The honorific title of "Bel" as the Lord *par excellence,* which was conferred upon Enlil at Nippur when he was first recognized as the "owner" or "master" of the land, was transferred to Marduk and then to Ashur. The designation Bel, meaning "lord" or "master", was, however, applied to any owner, occupier, person, object or locality, as well as to divinities and their sanctuaries. In the Old Testament it is used in connexion with the indigenous Phoenician, Syrian and Canaanite gods who are called "Baalim". When Yahweh became the sole object of worship as the God of Israel their attributes and titles tended to be transferred to him without his becoming Bel in the Babylonian sense of the term. Thus, in Babylonia it was synonymous with Marduk when he became the Bel as the "lord of the land."

Babylonian Monolatry

The weakness of this monolatrous polytheism, in which one god was worshipped as supreme without denying the existence and functions of the other divinities, lay in each of the heads of their respective pantheons – Anu, Enlil and Marduk – being abstractions personifying the fulness of divine power in the universe but being subject to the changing fortunes of the political centres they represented, which were as variable as the behaviour of the Tigris and Euphrates. By the skilful reformulation of the Creation story, the prestige of a local god could be transferred from one deity to another when he became Bel. Thus, the mighty Enlil was replaced by Marduk and to complete the transference Enki conferred upon Marduk his name declaring "he shall be even as I am; Enki (Ea) is his name".[9] But this monolatrous syncretism was never really accepted or adopted in the ancient Sumerian cities in the south (Nippur, Erech, Ur and Kish), and outside Babylon Marduk had no temples or shrines. Even the assembling of the gods in his sanctuary there (the *Esagila*) was an ecclesiastical gathering of the clans rather than a demonstration of the lordship of Marduk. He was at most "a great King above all gods" to whom the other gods, like Anu Enlil, Shamash and Ishtar, had entrusted the direction of the universe so long as he reigned supreme in Babylon as its Bel.

Therefore, when in the first millennium B.C. the greater part of Western Asia came under the domination of Assyria, its own local god Ashur, who may have been of Sumerian origin, was raised to supremacy as "King of the gods, self-created father, maker of the sky of Anu and of the underworld, author of mankind who lives in the bright heavens, Lord of the gods, he who ordained men's fate." As the empire spread further and further afield, the sovereignty of Ashur was extended throughout the territory conquered by the Assyrian forces. Nevertheless, the remote Anu remained the supreme being, lord of heaven, and at times of crisis his former sovereignty automatically reverted to him, his universal rule having been only abrogated and delegated to his divine subordinates.

Baal and the Canaanite Pantheon

This was the nearest approach to a genuine monolatry in Babylonia and Assyria as Anu embodied all the qualities and attributes assigned to the other gods who still retained their own names and specific functions. In Mesopotamia the concept of deity was never that of a sole creator and ground of all existence, independent of the rise and fall of cities or nations. In Syria, Palestine and Asia Minor Baal, the most prominent divine being among the West Semites, was closely associated with fertility, the growth of the grain and with cattle, often appearing as the virile storm- and Weather-god bestowing the fructifying rain on the soil. Thus, in the Ugaritic text, recovered in 1930 from the archives at Ras Shamra on the northern coast of Syria, Aleyan-Baal occupied a position not very different from that of Marduk in Babylonia. With the aid of his consort and sister Anat he engaged in many conflicts with his divine antagonists, Mot, Yam and Prince Sea, personifying aridity, decline and decay in nature.[10] Thus, when he was killed by Mot, all vegetation withered until he was restored from the underworld by Anat. Then he released the rain-clouds to ensure the fertility of the parched ground so that "the wadis ran with honey"; an event probably celebrated at the annual autumnal festival.

In Israel, Baal frequently was identified with Yahweh as the controller of rain and the giver of fertility, in the early days of the monarchy when the two cults were often assimilated, especially in the northern kingdom in the time of Ahab and Jezebel. This is hardly surprising as Jezebel was herself a devotee of the Tyrian Baal, as were her two sons, Ahaziah and Joram and her daughter Athaliah. It was against this Canaanite influence that Elijah and his Yahwist successors took their stand, notably at the rain-making contest on Mount Carmel (I Kings 18. 9-19. 3). This may have been an ancient sanctuary of Baal and his consort Asherah served by a Tyrian priesthood. But in spite of their efforts to exterminate the cultus it persisted in Israel until the Exile in the sixth century B.C., the Josiah reformation in 621 being only a temporary expedient (I Kings 19. 14; Amos 2. 7; Hos. 2. 8, 4. 12 ff; Jer. 3. 2-4,6-13, 44. 15 ff, 20 ff.). While the Carmel struggle marks perhaps the dominance of Yahweh in Israel, so deeply ingrained was the fertility cult that either the attributes of Baal were attached to Yahweh or he remained a rival object of worship. This is shown by the frequent recurrence of the name Baal as a compound in the pre-exilic period (Judges, 6. 25 ff, 8. 33, 9. 4 ; II Sam. 6. 2; Deut. 4. 3).

In the Canaanite pantheon Baal, however, was a later incorporation who overshadowed the obscure high god El, the counterpart of the Mesopotamian Anu, whose abode was on Mons Cassius, the highest mountain in Syria. There on the Ugaritic Olympus he was supreme among the assembly of the gods, but as the old god he had lost his potency in spite of displays of erotic virility; the young god Baal having become "lord of abundance", the irrigator of heaven and earth, the controller of the destructive forces, combining the offices and functions of the storm- and weather-god.

The Pre-Mosaic Hebrew Concept of Deity

Nevertheless, there can be little doubt that El must have been a conspicuous figure in the Ugaritic cult before he was ousted by Baal and was compelled to withdraw from everday affairs in this world, like so many supreme beings who fell victims of senility. Indeed, the name El was a common designation of deity as a generic term throughout the Semitic world recurring in the Akkadian, Canaanite, Hebrew and Arabian pantheons. Thus, in the biblical tradition it appears as El Elyon, "the highest god", El-Shaddai, "the mountain god", El Olam, El Roi, El Bethel, in the pre-Mosaic narratives (Gen. 14. 18–24; 21. 33; 16. 13; 17. 1; 43. 14). Elohim, the earliest and common Hebrew word for God is a derivation of El, and its frequent use instead of El in the Old Testament may be to distinguish Yahweh from the rest of the Elim in the surrounding nations. When David captured Jerusalem and made it the new capital El was firmly entrenched, and doubtless there he was identified with Yahweh as the dominant deity.

The Hebrews being of Aramaean extraction, the patriarchs very likely may have worshipped their own particular manifestations of El in the theophanies at holy places such as Bethel, Beersheba, Hebron, Mamre and Shechem, in association with sacred stones, trees, springs, wells and in dreams. Out of these theophanies the national God of Abraham, Isaac and Jacob may have emerged at these ancient shrines. Unless there had been some confederation on a theocratic basis before the Exodus, Moses and Aaron could hardly have expected any response from the elders of the enslaved Hebrew tribes when they went to them with a message and mission from "the God of their fathers" (Ex. 4. 15 f.).

It seems to be not improbable that a supreme being called Yahweh, or some proper name compounded with *Yah* or *Yo,* occurred in Kenite tradition, though the origin and etymology of the designation are very obscure and uncertain. It is possible, however, that Moses had encountered the deity in some form or another before or after he married the daughter of Jethro, who was a Midianite priest apparently in his service. Indeed, the Yahwist document of the southern kingdom of Judah (commonly called J) uses "Yahweh" (traditionally rendered in English as "Jehovah") for "God" from the beginning. But if the chief deity of the Patriarchs was the mountain god Shaddai brought into conjunction with the exalted El Elyon, the northern Israelite document (E), and the later Priestly Code (P) in post-exilic Judaism, may be correct in employing Elohim (being a derivation of El) as the divine name of the God of Abraham, Isaac and Jacob before the disclosure of the enigmatic proper name to Moses at the burning bush (Ex. 3. 14 f.).

Though there is no conclusive evidence before the eighth century B.C. of the Tetragrammaton YHWH in the cuneiform script, from the second millennium *Yahu* or *Yah, Yawi-ilum* occur on Akkadian tablets, and *Ya Yami* in the Canaanite and Aramaean inscriptions.[11] While it cannot be said with certainty that these determinations can be equated with "Yahweh", they do suggest that there was a Western Semitic deity having a name with affinities with that said to have been revealed to Moses in the biblical tradition. That it was known to the pre-Mosaic Israelites, as the J narrative in Genesis asserts (2. 4–25; 4. 26) against the contrary statement in the E document (Ex. 3. 1–5; 6. 3 f.), may be, as Mowinckel conjectures that Moses only wanted some "control" evidence to convince the Hebrews that it was the God of their fathers who had sent him, presupposing that the name Yahweh was already known to them.[12]

Mono-Yahwist Monotheism

To what extent Moses was himself responsible for the introduction and establishment of absolute monotheism in Israel is still in debate. This problem is dependent upon how much of the evidence in the Pentateuch can be attributed to the Mosaic period, and which among the tribes were involved in the Exodus and the conquest of Palestine.[13] Unquestionably it was the Exodus which was the most prominent and significant event in the history of the nation, in which of course Moses was the principal figure and Yahweh the jealous God who alone claimed exclusive and universal allegiance from his "chosen people". The might of Yahweh exercised under the jurisdiction of his servant Moses was regarded as the consolidating force and dynamic centre of the desert Hebrew tribes introducing a new epoch in the history of Israel as a monolatrous theocracy based primarily on the covenant (bérith) established on Mount Sinai. It was this relationship with Yahweh that distinguished the nation from the rest of mankind as its most deeply laid and indelible conviction. Although he was not represented as the sole deity of the universe until much later, so far as Israel was concerned he alone was its God; the first condition of the covenant being absolute loyalty exclusively to him. If this was never realized until the dissolution of the monarchy it appears to have been inherent in the mono-Yahwist tradition from the time of the Exodus. Hence the perpetual conflict between Yahwism and the indigenous Canaanite sanctuaries (bamôth) and their gods, and the popular cults in the neighbouring countries.

While Yahweh acquired in pre-exilic Israel many of the characteristic features and attributes of Baal and his counterparts, unlike so many supreme beings the Holy One of Israel never became a shadowy otiose high god. It was he who was universally acknowledged to have brought the tribes out of Egypt, settled them in their "promised land" and given them victory over their enemies so long as they maintained their covenant relationship with him. Moreover, like a vegetation deity he also controlled the rain and gave them fruitful seasons and bountiful harvests. But, as in the case of the local storm-gods, he never ceased to manifest his wrath when his cultus was neglected, his "holiness" affronted, or his covenant broken. He destroyed his enemies in the Red Sea and in the marshes; by the desert wind, the earthquake, the devastating thunderstorms and volcanic eruptions, plagues, pestilences and wholesale massacres. Therefore, he was in very intimate contact with his people for good or ill, very far removed from a typical wholly transcendent all-father. His worship and its appointment in the Temple at Jerusalem was almost indistinguishable from that in the contemporary sanctuaries in Phoenicia and Egypt. Thus, it was approached in the porch by two bronze sacred pillars, Jachin and Boaz, and in the centre the Ark of the Covenant stood between cherubim with outstretched wings amid lions, pomegranates and date-palms on the walls. A brazen sea supported by bulls was placed at the right side for ablutions, representing perhaps the primeval waters as the source of life and fertility as in Babylonian and Canaanite mythology. It is hardly surprising, therefore, in view of the syncretistic and polytheistic nature of its background and cultus, that its erection as an adjunct of the royal palace was opposed by the mono-Yahwists, (I Kings 7. 21, 29; II Sam. 7. 7).

Prophetic and Post-Exilic Ethical Monotheism

After the Exile and the destruction of the Temple the ethical monotheism of the prophetic movement was definitely established in Judaism and it was in this milieu that the Temple was rebuilt and its sacrificial system and priesthood were restored as the focal point of the new theocracy. That this was accomplished after the Babylonian catastrophe is to be attributed very largely to mono-Yahwism having been the basic faith in the pre-exilic period in spite of the syncretistic cult. The prophets had revealed Yahweh as the one God perfect in righteousness, absolute in power, controlling the forces of nature, ordering the course of history, and omniscient in wisdom and knowledge, fufilling His purposes according to his will, hating iniquity and loving goodness, mercy and truth. His tender mercies were over all his works, but he demanded obedience to his commands and conformity to his standards of ethical conduct. Unlike the gods of the surrounding nations, whose existence was not denied, he was not sporadically beneficent when in a favourable mood and propitiated, nor was he dependent on the vicissitudes of competing cities, priesthoods and nations. The Hebrew monotheists saw behind the entire universe one creative, sustaining, omnipotent, omniscient will directing the course of events—that of Yahweh, the righteous controller of all things.

The remarkable triumph of ethical monotheism was the work of deeply religious men in Israel who were convinced that they were the recipients of a divine self-disclosure and unsolicited revelation of unimpeachable authenticity. They saw the truth in the same measure as they believed they had received it from the Holy One of Israel. They knew the mind and commands of the God in whose service they were enlisted, and so were able to differentiate between true and false prophecies. Therefore, they claimed to "speak that they did know and to testify that they had seen" and heard. And not only were they able to give utterance to their lofty monotheistic convictions, but also to keep alive in a minority of the nation the faith as they had received it until at length the entire community was transformed into a genuinely monotheistic people, maintaining that Yahweh was the God of the whole phenomenal world and the director of human history, demanding the allegiance of all mankind.

Unlike the Greek philosophers, the Mesopotamian monolatrists or the Egyptian priesthoods and Atonists, the Hebrew prophets did not derive their ideas of God from observation and reflection on nature, speculation about its operations, or through the agency of powerful priesthoods or pharaohs. They made no pretence at scholarship and profound metaphysical thought like Plato and Aristotle. They, in fact, maintained that they were just ordinary men distinguished from the rest of the community only by their consciousness of a projection of the divine personality of Yahweh within themselves when they delivered what they believed to be special messages vouchsafed to them from him. So they prefaced their declarations with the words, "Oracle of Yahweh", having been brought within his "corporate personality" as a living part of the divine Being.[14] Thus, they laid the foundations of the ethical monotheism which after the shattering experience of the Exile was carried on and developed in Judaism by the priestly and legalistic organization as the consolidating dynamic centre of the monotheistic theocracy, in which the prophetic and priestly traditions were combined effectively.

When the nation was re-established in and around Jerusalem in the sixth century B.C. on this firm basis, the greatly elaborated sacrificial system and ordinances were assigned a Mosaic origin in the desert to give them a supernatural sanction and authority. If the supreme importance attached to the Torah as a verbally inspired Word of God fostered a fundamentalist legalism, the prophetic ethical monotheism, nevertheless, was retained and maintained, based on the righteousness of Yahweh. Polytheism was completely eliminated never to be resuscitated, and by the time the last book of the Old Testament was admitted into the Canon of Holy Scripture the Jews had reached a stage of theistic development that justified the assertion of the Psalmist: Yahweh "hath not dealt so with any nation." (Ps. 147. 20).

Moreover, with their dispersion throughout Western Asia and the Hellenistic world, and subsequently in the Roman Empire and in Christendom, the sovereignty and worship of Yahweh in the traditional post-exilic setting remained the fundamental bond and unifying centre of Jewry. Until the destruction of the Temple in A.D. 70 he was believed to vouchsafe his presence on earth enthroned on the mercy seat in the Holy of Holies on Mount Zion. For those who by force of circumstances could not take part in the Temple worship, and this applied to everybody of course after A.D. 70, the Torah in its sacred ark in the local synagogue became the effective substitute, as the deified Word of God. Therefore, those who sought to know the will of Yahweh resorted to the scribes who sat in the seat of Moses in the synagogues. This mitigated the effects of the fall of Jerusalem and helped them to retain and consolidate the ancient belief in the theocratic significance of Judaism spread throughout the world.

Zoroastrianism

In a very different historical setting from that of Israel and the Hebrew prophets a universal monotheism arose in Iran under the inspiration of Zarathustra who in some respects resembled his Semitic pre-exilic counterparts. But the antecedents of the Zoroastrian movement, which arose in Persia in the middle of the first millennium B.C. (c. 620–551 B.C.), were deeply laid in Vedic India. Thus, the Aryan-speaking Indo-Iranians who established themselves on the Iranian plateau in the fourth millennium B.C. and gave their name, *Ariyana* (Iran), to the country of their adoption, were of Indo-European linguistic and ethnological stock and practised Vedic polytheism in which the good gods were called *devas,* "shining ones", and the demons *asuras.* In the Iranian Avesta this division of divinities was reversed, the devas becoming transformed into evil spirits while the asuras were beneficent deities. Mithra (the Vedic Mitra) was the god of light and of war, and Varuna the omniscient all-encompassing sky. These it seems were combined as the single wholly beneficent supreme being, Ahura Mazdah, the "wise lord", and sole creator of the universe. Haoma was the Avestan counterpart of the life-giving Indian king-god Soma, as the personification of the sacred beverage which was sacrificially crushed and sacramentally drunk, as priest and victim. In this sacerdotal capacity he was represented as the son of Ahura Mazdah, who offered himself to his heavenly father, and gave the elixir of immortality to those who partook of his divine substance in the *Yasna* ceremony.

Ahura Mazdah

This transformation of Vedic polytheism into Avestan monotheism was accomplished by Zarathustra who claimed to have been the recipient of a divine revelation when he had been driven from his homeland among the pastoral cattle-breeders and agriculturists by war-like tribes whom he called *dregvants*. They were "the followers of the Lie", the primeval spirit of evil, known as Angra Mainyu or the Druj, in opposition to Spenta Mainyu, the Good Mind, associated with truth and righteousness *(Asha)*. Each of these twin spirits had its respective demons and angelic forces in eternal conflict since the dawn of creation; the one bringing death and the other life into the world. Behind them lay a fundamental dualism, Asha and the Druj, Truth and the Lie, righteousness and evil, equated with light and darkness in the cosmic order, and on earth with the struggle between the followers of the two opposed rival spirits. They met, however, in the higher unity of Ahura Mazdah. Although they are not said to have been created by him since they existed before the world came into being, and the Druj was regarded as inherently evil from the beginning, in the earlier Gathas of the Avestan scriptures there would seem to be a latent dualism. It was not, however, until the later Mazdaean literature was compiled in the Sassanian period in the fourth century A.D., and in the Pahlavi books, that the Lie became Ahriman, the Evil One, coeval with Ormuzd, a combination of Ahura Mazdah and Spenta Mainyu. Then an absolute dualism emerged with two equally balanced opposed forces of good and evil representing light and darkness with good destined eventually to be established and evil ultimately destroyed when Ahura Mazdah would become all in all. To mitigate this dualism an attempt was made to introduce a primeval principle Zurvan, Infinite Time, from whom all things were said to have proceeded. As, however, the movement was declared to be heretical it was never given official recognition.[15]

Mazdaean Monotheistic Dualism and Eschatology

The Zoroastrian interpretation of the age-long struggle between

61

good and evil constitutes the first attempt in the history of religion to grapple with the problem within the context of ethical monotheism. Although it rapidly developed into a definite dualism and an ethic of self-salvation, nevertheless, evil at last was met on its own ground and conquered by the might of the spirit of goodness and beneficence, destined ultimately to triumph at the consummation of all things. Originally Ahura Mazdah seems to have been regarded by Zarathustra as the one and only creator, holy, righteous and true, the greatest and best, wisest and most perfect supreme ruler and controller of all things. Yet he was the author of good and evil. This left the problem of evil unsolved and opened the way for the Mazdaean dualistic solution. As in the Christian gospels, in the Avestan scriptures no attempt was made to explain how the two principles of good and evil came into existence, just as in the Eden story the machinations of the wily serpent were left undetermined. For practical purposes it sufficed to maintain that the elimination of evil could only be achieved by the prescribed ritual rules and duties, involving personal purity, honest and straight dealing, charity towards the poor, hospitality to strangers, care of cattle and the cultivation of the soil, the destruction of noxious creatures and the proper disposal of the dead. By these observances the powers of evil could be kept at bay. In principle this Zoroastrian ethic was humanistic, humanitarian and utilitarian, but it was based on the maintenance of a right relationship with Ahura Mazdah, the only wise lord. Essentially it was and has remained "the religion of the good life". In post-Avestan eschatology those who followed steadfastly the "path of righteousness" increased in strength power and wealth, and laid up a store of merit which would enable them to cross the perilous *chinvat* bridge, separating this world from the eternal world. This could only be accomplished by those whose good deeds in this life preponderated, and so secured justification at the final judgment when they would be recompensed in the renovated new creation.

To assume that the righteous would overcome the forces of evil merely by the inherent goodness of human nature was unquestionably to take a much too optimistic view of the situation. This may partly account for the resort to Magian magic and superstition to supply what was lacking in Zarathustra's lofty conception of the good life. Nevertheless, the fact remains that the evaluations were ethical inasmuch as the underlying principle was that of "evil for evil, good reward for the good, affliction to the wicked, happiness to the righteous". If the eschatology was crudely mundane, grim and anthropomorphic, fate was decided by Ahura Mazdah in strict justice determined by the deeds performed, works done, thoughts and intentions being assessed accordingly. To what extent it affected post-exilic Judaism is difficult to decide. But to some degree directly or indirectly it undoubtedly influenced Judaeo-Christian apocalyptic speculations and those of Islam. It also played a prominent part in Mithraic ethics and symbolism, being its Iranian prototype.

Parsee Faith and Practice

Eventually it became the state religion of Persia during the Sassanian Dynasty (A.D. 224–650) until the Arab conquest when Islam gained ascendance in Iran. Then the few who retained the Zoroastrian faith became known as Gabars, or "infidels", because they refused to accept the claims of Muhammad; and today Parsees (i.e. "people of Pars", the ancient Persia) number less than ten thousand in the cradle-land. The rest made their way to India in the seventh and eighth centuries A.D., and settled mainly in Bombay where they became a prosperous community of about 50,000 adherents. The same number were scattered about India, together with isolated groups all over the world, usually engaged in commerce and industry, and retaining their faith with its fire-cult and burial in "towers of silence", where this is practicable. At about the age of seven the children are initiated into the Parsee community by investiture with the sacred cord and shirt as "a Zoroastrian worshipper of God" pledged to "praise good thought, good words and good actions"; to uphold "the Zoroastrian religion which is holy, and which of all religions that have yet flourished, or are likely to flourish in the future, is the greatest, the best and the most excellent, and which is the religion given by God to Zarathustra." This confession of faith is repeated daily and practised by working out salvation by "thinking, speaking and doing nothing but the truth", and attending the prescribed fire rites in the temples as the sacramental means of approach to Ahura Mazdah. The chief of these are celebrated on New Year's Day which is the most important festival of the year when bathing and wearing new clothes are enjoyed. Though everywhere their dignity, aloofness and reserve have given the Parsees a position in the community akin to that of members of the Society of Friends in the West, they have tended to become agnostic or theosophic in outlook. Therefore, while the observance of the cultus has been mainly a mark of solidarity, ethical monotheism not infrequently has been abandoned.

This is in contrast to the remarkable adherence to rigid monotheism which has characterized Islam throughout its history and wide-spread diffusion. Taking its rise in an indigenous Semitic polytheism in Arabia, as a divine revelation vouchsafed to Muhammad through the angel Gabriel commanding him to proclaim Allah as the one and only God, it has spread throughout the world with amazing rapidity and permanence. In Mecca Allah was already known as the principal god of the Ka'ba, the central sanctuary and most sacred shrine in Arabia in which the Black Stone was the object of special veneration. There also three goddesses were worshipped — Al-Uzza, the feminine form of the moon-god; Al-Manet, the goddess of fate, fortune and destiny; and Allat, the Arabic designation of the goddess of fertility. *Al* and *Ilah*, in fact, mainly survived in compound names rather than as separate generic conceptions of Deity. Therefore, Allah was only recognized as a vague supreme being at the most in a polytheistic sanctuary until Muhammad proclaimed him as the sole living Creator of heaven and earth.

This doubtless explains to some extent the Meccans' rejection of his message to them that "there is no god save Allah", based on the authority of a divine revelation he claimed to have received on Mount Hera about A.D. 610. What perhaps is more surprising is that the Jews and Christians, with whom he sought an alliance, gave him no support although he maintained that his revelation confirmed the biblical record. This may have been partly because of his confused and inaccurate knowledge of the Judaeo-Christian scriptures derived from apocryphal and Syriac heretical sources, and from such late writings as the Talmud. Thus, in the Qur'an the legend occurs of Cain being shown by a raven scratching the ground how to dispose of the body of Abel; Abraham being thrown into the fire for refusing to worship idols; and attempts of Solomon to convert the Queen of Sheba to Islam. Most of the stories about the Madonna come from a Coptic "Life of the Virgin", while the assertion that Jesus did not die on the Cross, another being substituted for Him, came from Gnostic sources. Christians are said to worship God the Father, Jesus and Mary as three gods, and although the virgin birth, resurrection and ascension of Christ as the "Word of God" were accepted, he was said to be but a messenger of God, and the Holy Spirit the breath of God.[16] Therefore, he rejected the doctrine of the Incarnation and misconceived that of the Trinity, on the ground that they implied a division in the Godhead incompatible with his rigid monotheism. To confirm his own claim to be the prophet through whom the final revelation of God to man was given, he put into the mouth of Christ the words, "Verily I am Allah's messenger to you verifying the Torah which was given before me, and to announce the good tidings of a messenger who will come after me whose name shall be Ahmad" (Qur'an Sura LXI.6).

Nevertheless, the concept of deity in Islam unquestionably has affinities with that of the Hebrew prophets, except that while Allah was regarded as wholly transcendent, omnipotent, omniscient and all-willing, he was not fundamentally righteous; and such morality as he enjoined was based on the acceptance of his sovereign inscrutable will. This absolute submission was, in fact, his first requirement, coupled with the observance of the prescribed "Five Pillars", or duties, of Islam incumbent upon all Muslims. After Muhammad's conquest of Mecca and his establishment of the theocratic state at Medina his stress on forgiveness and benevolence was combined with unswerving acceptance of the despotism of Allah which, as in Calvinism, rendered retribution and predestination divine decrees.[17]

It was, indeed, this that appeared to the liberal scholastic range Mu'tazilite school of "seceders" as a travesty of divine justice, failing to satisfy the deeper spiritual needs and contrary to reason. In reaction to these juristic and rationalistic developments in Islam, coupled with the widespread luxury of the Caliphate, an ascetic movement arose about A.D. 800 among a small group of devout believers who wore white woollen garments called *suf,* and so known as the Sufi. Having come under Neoplatonic and Christian influences their purpose was to secure communion with God by mystical intuition. This, however, was foreign to the Qur'anic conception of Allah and, as has so often happened, it tended towards a pantheistic absorption of the soul in divine unity when it spread throughout Islam. Some of the Sufi, however, retained their orthodox belief in Allah as the transcendent living God of the Qur'an who had revealed his will and purpose most completely through his dislosures to Muhammad. The most influential adherent to the movement was Al-Ghazali in the eleventh century who combined orthodoxy with Sufi piety, and took up the cudgels against the Aristotelian philosophers (e.g. Avicenna, Averroes and al-Farabi). He, in fact, marks the end of this scholastic period in Islam, though a Neoplatonic movement arose in Persia and became prominent in the Shi'a sects prone to this type of thought. But it is significant that when Aristotelianism was making its way in the West, largely launched through these Muslim scholars, it was being suppressed in the Islamic world. Similarly, Sufi mysticism was losing its pantheistic trends.

The Qur'an may not be as faultless and infallible as Islam has consistently maintained, but it has been and still is the unifying dynamic of this great civilization. Always it has been "the religion of the Book", its special revelation having been not in Muhammad himself but in the message imparted to him freed from error. Thus, no peculiar importance was or ever has been attached to his birth, life or death, and he never claimed to work miracles. It has always been what he taught as divine truth that for his followers has made him the "seal of the prophets". He was the bringer of the Holy Qur'an and all that this has signified as the Word of God uncorrupted by human agency, and, therefore, uniquely true. In Christianity, on the other hand, it has been not so much what Christ said and taught as what he was and is that makes him unique. "God, having of old time spoken unto the fathers by the prophets by divers portions and in divers manners, hath at the end of these days spoken unto us in his Son, whom he appointed heir of all things" (Heb. 1. 1-2 R.V.). This was a genuinely new divine self-disclosure ratified by His death and resurrection. If it had not been for the rejection of this fundamental claim on which Christianity was and is irreparably established, Islam might well have become a Christian sect, or perhaps one of its "heresies". Here lies the unbridgeable gulf between the two faiths. Nevertheless, the former antagonisms are now undergoing considerable modification and a more "ecumenical" approach is becoming apparent, not least in the recent Vatican Council.

The Christian Conception of Deity

In the monotheistic prophetic tradition in Judaism, Zoroastrianism, Christianity and Islam there is a common element inasmuch as in all these theistic faiths God is accepted as the sole transcendent Creator and Sustainer of all that is, carrying with it a particular social and religious ethic. As Professor Malinowski has pointed out, "the dependence on higher powers implies further the mutual dependence of man on his neighbour. You cannot worship in common without a common bond of mutual trust and assistance, that is, of charity and love. If God has created man in his own image, one image of God may not debase, defile, or destroy the other."[18] Hence the supreme importance of the recognition of the loftiest conception of deity and of the eternal world that is humanly possible, for by it the religious, social and ethical life of man is determined. The Christian revelation fulfils these requirements because among all the higher living monotheistic faiths it alone has dared to claim and vindicate that the one, omnipotent, omniscient Ground of all existence has come within his creation in

66

the person of Christ as the Word made flesh. Dwelling among the human race with all its imperfections he has come to make known once and for all what God is like, and, aided by divine grace, to enable mankind to fashion his life accordingly. (St. John 1. 1–14; 14. 9). The Creator who is over and above the world is he who is everywhere, as has been dimly recognized it would seem, however obscurely, as far back as the available evidence throws any light on the problem. But instead of being a remote otiose Supreme Being, in the Christian revelation it is he in whom man lives and moves and has his being.

In the conception of divine Fatherhood in the Old Testament, the exaltation and nearness of God were recognized, but, as Dr. Montefiore admits, where Christ made a genuine departure was in his insistence on the constraining love of God in seeking the sinful and giving them a place in his kingdom, not of right or merit but solely as an act of grace.[19] This inaugurated a new idea of sacrificial self-giving redemption on behalf of the sinner by his complete surrender even of life itself. The Christian revelation was, in fact, a unique disclosure of divine love and forgiveness which lies enshrined in the heart of God at the very centre of the universe. For "God commendeth his own love towards us, in that while we were yet sinners, Christ died for us" (Rom. 5. 8). Love constrains because it has a stimulating magnetic effect in drawing the one loved towards the lover.

As "the image of the invisible God, the firstborn of all creation" Christ alone could say, "he that hath seen me hath seen the Father". And this has been the universal conviction of those who have come under the spell of his unique presence. Whether from the side of his humanity or from that of his Godhead, he represents the fullness of insight into the things of God and the climax of God's disclosure of himself to man. It has never been suggested, rightly, that God is disclosed alone in Christ, but that in him he was incarnate supremely and completely. As Baron von Hügel has said, "the divinity of Jesus can be wisely maintained by us only if we simultaneously remember that however truly God revealed himself with supreme fullness and in a unique manner in Jesus Christ, yet that this same God had not left himself, still does not leave himself, without some witness to himself throughout the ages before Christ, and throughout the countries, groups, and even individual souls whom the message, in fact, of the historic Jesus has never reached, or who, in sheer good faith, cannot understand, cannot see him as he really is."[20] But those who knew him most intimately while he was on earth, like all those countless millions since who have known him hardly less truly by faith and sacrament, are all agreed that he was and is so absolutely unique that he could not be other than the Christ, the incarnate Son of God.

FOR FURTHER READING

Breasted, J. H., *The Development of Religion and Thought in Ancient Egypt*, 1914
Budge, E. A. W., *Tutankhamen, Amenism and Egyptian Monotheism*, 1923
Frankfort, H., *Ancient Egyptian Religion*, 1948; *Kingship and the Gods*, 1948; *The Intellectual Adventure of Early Man*, 1947 (Pelican edition, *Before Philosophy*, 1949)
Gibbs, H. A. R., *Mohammedanism*, 1953
Gray, J., *The Legacy of Canaan*, 1965
Guillaume, A., *Islam*, 1954
James, E. O., *The Concept of Deity*, 1950; *The Worship of the Sky God*, 1963
Kramer, S. N., *Sumerian Mythology*, 1944
Kapelrud, A. S., *The Ras Shamra Discoveries and the Old Testament*, 1956; *Baal in the Ras Shamra Texts*, 1952
Lods, A., *The Prophets and the Rise of Judaism*, 1937
Masani, R. P., *The Religion of the Good Life*, 1938
Pedersen, J., *Israel, Its Life and Culture*, vol. ii., 1947
Rowley, H. H., *From Joseph to Joshua*, 1950
Söderblom, N., *The Living God*, 1931
Sweetman, J. H., *Islam and Christian Theology*, 1945 onwards
Zaehner, R. C., *Zurvan; a Zoroastrian Dilemma*, 1955; *The Dawn and Twilight of Zoroastrianism*, 1961

Chapter Four

ORIENTAL PANTHEISM

Though in the third millennium B.C. the three great cultural streams in western Asia, those of Mesopotamia, Iran and the Indus valley, proceeded from a common source on the Iranian plateau, with much the same conception of deity, the religious development in India was destined to take a very different course. At first the successive eastern waves of Indo-Iranians made their way from the Eurasian plains of southern Russia, where possibly the Indo-European languages may have evolved, across the Caucasus to the kingdom of Mitanni, and thence to the Hindu Kush, and north-west India. Another connecting link between west and east was through the hill villages of Baluchistan and Afghanistan to Sind and the Indus valley, where the great Harappa urban civilization arose about 2500 B.C. with its Iranian background. This homogeneous culture flourished until about 1500 B.C. in its forti-fied and carefully planned cities recently excavated at Mohenjo-daro and Harappa, practising an elaborate water cult, so prominent later in Hinduism, the worship of the mother-goddess of the Ancient Near East, and a male god with horns and three faces, seated in the attitude of yoga meditation — probably the prototype of the Hindu god Shiva, Lord of the Beasts (Pasupati), Creator and Destroyer — together with figurines and seal-amulets and phallic symbols.

Religion in the Harappa Civilization

It now appears that it was from this protohistoric substream that the fertility aspects and attributes of Hinduism were derived when the Aryan-speaking Indo-Europeans made their way into Sind and the Punjab between 1500 and 1200 B.C., bringing with them a common language, culture and religion, acquired apparently in their homeland east of the Caspian Sea. Thus, Shiva and his fertility cultus were foreign to Vedism in its indigenous form, and the sanctity of the cow was unknown in India either in the Harappa civilization, or when the Rig-Veda was compiled between 1500 and 1000 B.C. in honour of the Aryan sky-gods. In any case, as Sir John Marshall says, "the religion of the Indus people taken as a whole is so characteristically Indian as hardly to be distinguishable from still living Hinduism, or at least from that aspect of it which is bound up with animism and the cult of Shiva and the mother-goddess – still the two most potent forces in popular worship."[1] When the tall light-skinned pastoral people of Indo-European stock poured over the passes of the Hindu Kush mountains and settled in the Punjab in small village groups with their flocks and herds, and later moved eastwards into the Indus valley, probably they found the Harappa cities in ruins since they seem to have been destroyed by barbarians shortly before they arrived in the region. This breaking up of the solidarity of the static urban civilization opened the way for the welding together of a variety of cultures in a common religious tradition under the consolidating influence of Hinduism, with its polytheistic pantheon reflecting, doubtless, tribal struggles between rival chieftains and their alliances, transformed into the Vedic gods of the natural phenomena and their celestial counterparts.

The Vedic Pantheon

The most outstanding deities were Varuna, the all-encompassing sky, Indra the great warrior-god of thunder and battles, and Dyaus Pitar, the supreme being, with his consort Prithivi, the earth-goddess. They stand by themselves, the other gods being forms or manifestations of them. Later introductions were Vishnu and Rudra, and such lesser divinities as the Maruts, or storm-gods, with an underlying solar symbolism represented by Mitra, the god of light, who daily pursued his course across the sky in his seven-horsed chariot. In the collection of 1,017 hymns known as the Rig-Veda the gods tend to merge into one another, Dyaus Pitar and Prithivi becoming overshadowed by the more intimate and vigorous Varuna, Indra, Mitra and Agni, the sacred fire. Soma, the sacred life-giving plant, was sacrificially slain as the king-god in the ritual, and Rta, the divine power or cosmic order, governing the universe and the gods, endowed them with their supernatural qualities. Indeed, so fundamental was this cosmic conception of divinity that it assumed a pantheistic guise towards the end of the Rig-Veda period.

During the opening phase of Vedic Hinduism the changeless, impersonal divine Principle as the underlying unity gradually acquired an ethical significance under the guardianship of Varuna, who established heaven and earth and upheld the immutable moral law; while Agni was the lord of the ritual order, and Indra controlled the cosmic law. But so dependent upon Rta were the gods that they were constantly changing their places and functions in the pantheon. Thus, Agni is said to become Varuna when he strives for Rta, and as the sacred fire, carries the offerings to the sky by way of Rta. This was interpreted ethically in the priestly writings known as the *Brahmanas* where it is said "Right is the Fire, Truth is yonder Sun, or rather Right is yonder Sun and Truth is this Fire."[2]

It was Varuna, however, who as the transcendent head of the pantheon occupied a kathenotheistic role; that is to say, assuming all the divine characteristics distributed among the numerous gods in the pantheon without denying their existence. The sun was his eye, the sky his garment, the storm his breath, and the solar Mitra was his brother. He kept heaven and earth apart and established them on their foundations, regulated the courses of the celestial bodies, the clouds and the rainfall, and exercised supernatural and magical power *par excellence*. On him, and his sacrificial counterpart Agni, depended the right behaviour of all things, natural, ethical and social. He was the righteous Lord who protected the divine law. The sacred Fire was thought to be the charioteer of Rta who "harnesses the steeds and holds the reins of Rta, becoming Varuna when he strives for Rta". Once the sacred fire, the offering, Agni and Varuna had been equated with Rta it only required the cosmic principle to be made subject to the Brahmanic sacrifice to establish its complete supremacy and that of the Brahmins as its priesthood. As Agni had absolute control over the offering he became the mediator between heaven and earth, and the presiding priest, by erecting the fire-altar in seven layers of bricks in the form of a falcon, repeated, as it was supposed, the process of creation to restore its unity and the body of the Creator.[3]

By the end of the seventh century B.C. the Brahmins had relegated to themselves the key position of masters of the sacrificial ritual and the sole interpreters of the sacred knowledge embodied in the Veda, on which everything in heaven and on earth depended. By about 700 B.C. the voluminous Brahmanas had arisen as the sacrificial texts in the form of discursive and incredibly complex theological and liturgical treatises for the guidance of the meticulous performance of the prescribed rites, the secrets of which were in their possession alone. In these texts the most prominent figure was the god Prajapati who was at once the creator and creation. As the lord of production he personified the creative principle and fulfilled his office through the universal cosmic and moral order, Rta. This was accomplished by the restoration of his dismembered body from the several parts of which the universe had been created; Prajapati being virtually creator, priest and victim. Thus, in the Satapatha Brahmana it is affirmed that "the sacrificer is the god Prajapati at his own sacrifice". But in declaring "I will reproduce myself, I will become many"[4] he was giving expression to the pantheistic principle already inherent in the Rig-Veda, in Varuna pervading natural phenomena and human life as a ruler of macrocosm and microcosm alike. Through the control exercised over him by Rta he was a pantheistic process rather than a divine personality, being subject to a higher universal law. This monistic trend was further developed by the universe being equated with Brahman regarded as a neuter supernatural power operative in the sacrificial ritual which created the god.

In the Rig-Veda Brahman is used to signify the concrete expression of "holy knowledge" (Veda). Later in the collection of magical charms in the Atharva Veda, designed for popular use at simpler ceremonies, it was operative in spells and incantations to bring rain and heal diseases. It was, however, from the hieratic Rig-Vedic cult and its pantheon that Hindu thought primarily developed under the priestly influence, though the popular magical practices were also incorporated to a considerable extent without opposition or cleavage between the two approaches. But the movement was in the direction of an ultimate impersonal pantheistic Absolute and world-soul pervading the universe, as it is said, "without a second" (advitiyam). But by uniting the eternal energy which animated the human soul, called the *Atman*, with the Absolute or *Brahman* as the sum total of all existence, the Vedic gods and the Brahmanic sacrifice lost their significance and fell into the background. The eternal self (Atman) and the eternal ground of the universe (Brahman) were manifestations of the same universal principle understood as a pantheistic monism, or single all-pervading reality. But as the centre of interest moved from an external transcendental creator to the divine principle immanent in man and the universe, resolved into a fundamental first principle, a new synthesis emerged as the all-inclusive Ultimate Reality, neither Brahman nor Atman but transcending both. In short, God and the universe were regarded as identical.

The Pantheism of the Upanishads

This was achieved by a remarkable group of mystics who in the eighth and seventh centuries B.C. lived as hermits in the forests and compiled a number of treatises known as the Upanishads, a term meaning "sitting near a teacher" in the sense of a master gathering pupils around him to discover the eternal self in man and the eternal principle in the universe, and their essential nature and relationship. When this Brahman-Atman identification was accomplished, and the "way of knowledge" established, with the aid of the prescribed mystical exercises and techniques the goal was reached which is summed up in the equation *tat tvam asi*, "That art Thou, I am Brahman". Then, and only then, was release possible from the hampering conditions of phenomenal life in time and space, and the wearisome round of birth and rebirth (*samsara*).[5]

Thus, from the Vedic interpretation of the neuter Brahman as the vitalizing spirit which stirred within the poets as they sang and enacted their ritual hymns, the idea of an impersonal creative principle took shape. When this was equated with the immortal self, or Atman, and brought into relation with the pantheistic cosmic order as a monism, it acquired a moral significance based on the law of action and reaction known as *karma*. But if ultimately only Brahman and Atman in combination really existed the phenomenal world became virtually an illusion, as is indicated by the ambiguous term *maya*. At any rate that there was only one Reality, Brahman, was the opinion of Sankara, and it was this conclusion that was added as a corollary in the *Svetasvatara Upanishad*. Everything else was in the nature of a delusion. Therefore, besides the problem of the universe, in the Upanishads there was a desire to escape from the unreality and impermanence of existence under phenomenal conditions and limitations to that which alone is real and abiding. Ultimately when the cosmic cycle was complete all things must return to their origin and be absorbed in the source from which they emanated. But before the self could realize its true nature and destiny in terms of the Upanishadic equation, every vestige of karma had to be eliminated, as this had been accumulated by all temporal activities.

There was, however, a distinction in the older texts between Brahman as "noumenal" (i.e. intellectual intuition devoid of all phenomenal attributes) and Brahman as "phenomenal" (i.e. concerned with the phenomenal order and its processes). "There are", it is said, "assuredly two forms of Brahman, the formed (*murta*) and the formless, the mortal and the immortal, the stationary and the moving, the existent (*sat*) and the transcendental (*tya*)." The formless was the real whereas the formed was the unreal, the phenomenal and, therefore, illusory (*maya*).[6] Consequently, while the emphasis in the Upanishads has been on the Absolute, room has been found for the so-called "manifested Brahman" related to the world as its creator and ruler, and capable of assuming a physical body. Indeed, in the later Upanishads (e.g. *Isa* and *Svetasvatara*) it becomes virtually a personal all-seeing, all-wise, omnipotent, omnipresent and self-existent supreme being "having made all things well for ever".[7] In this new conception of deity the masculine Brahman was lord of lords and "divinity of divinities" from whom everything proceeds. He was at once transcendent and immanent, all-pervading yet over and above phenomenal existence; the beginning and the end

73

of the cosmic cycle; "the real of the real". At death the transcendental self in man was merged in him as a river is absorbed in an ocean, so intimate was the union of the soul with Brahman.[8]

In the relatively late *Brihadaranyaka Upanishad* "the Way of the Fathers" is distinguished from the "the Way of the Gods"; the first leading to mergence in Brahman by faith; the second to the offering of sacrifice and to good works such as almsgiving, charity and austerity. It is in this Upanishad that the first mention of reincarnation occurs in its Hindu form, although the belief was widely held among the aboriginal tribes in India. But its absorption was destined to assume great importance in the subsequent mystical development of Hinduism once it was brought into relation with the Hindu conception of metempsychosis. Being immortal the soul was independent of its perishable fleshy embodiment, and its release from its imprisonment in the body became the principal aim of the Indian mystic and sage in contracting out of rebirth (*samsara*) into a state of timeless being.

The Sankhya-Yogic School

Since this involves the removal of every trace of karma resort has had to be made to the discipline of Yoga, the Hindu system of ascetic practices, breathing exercises, mental concentration and intense meditation to secure the mystic condition conducive to liberation from the bonds of mind and matter. It is, however, essentially a non-theistic connotation, virtually, in fact, atheistical, and only once is it even referred to in the earliest Upanishads.[9] It was, indeed, as an antidote to the Upanishadic philosophy that the technique was introduced as a psychological device to produce the effects regarded as essential for the freeing of the soul from phenomenal existence independent of any theistic concepts. Thus, it arose in the so-called Sankhya analysis of reality in which the universe was divided into primeval matter (*prakriti*) and souls (*purusha*), as a reaction against the Upanishadic idealistic monism. Denying altogether the concept of deity, the Sankhyan duality of the soul and its materialistic matrix (*prakriti*) were regarded as uncreated substance which had existed from all eternity; differing from each other in their respective constitutions, compositions, content and duration. Against the Upanishadic quest of the Absolute, in the Sankhyan Way of Knowledge the search was for a principle (*prakriti*) in the form of primeval matter from which everything evolved. This included the subtle elements out of which the psychical organs and qualities have developed accompanying the *purusha*, or individual soul, in its cycle of existence from one body to another in the process of reincarnation.

74

Eventually, at the close of the world-age, all things were destined to return to their original state of primal matter and await the repetition of the cyclic process in the reproduction of a new universe, and individuals were to experience the realization of eternal being.

Then the *purusha* will have ceased to be a passive spectator of the pains and sorrows of the unemancipated existence of the world of appearances because it will have become aware of its true spiritual nature in complete isolation from its material integument and phenomenal environment. Therefore, in Sankhya salvation lies in the recognition of the fundamental and fatal mistake of not understanding the bondage of the soul, and of not securing its liberation, rather than in establishing the identity of the Atman with Brahman, as in the Upanishadic tradition. But this Sankhya-Yoga solution of the problem was fundamentally pluralistic and atheistic as it did not admit an Absolute, a World Soul, or an impersonal Brahman as a unifying or creative principle, the universe being inherently self-existent.

The Vedanta, on the other hand, was essentially monistic, and eventually under the influence of Sankara and Romanuja in the medieval period it acquired a theistic connotation. The adoption of the term *deva* for "God" or "Lord" in the *Svetasvatara Upanishad*[10] introduced a transcendent element in the Hindu concept of deity which embraced the Sankhya *purusha* and the Upanishadic Brahman-Atman equation. Behind these monistic conceptions of reality lay an ultimate first principle as the creative and unitary ground of all things with which personal relations could be established. Thus, in the conception of Atman the true Self was identified with Brahman as the Ultimate Reality, supreme, omnipotent, omniscient, the controller of the universe, the beginning and end of all existence. Indeed, in the Upanishads, while *deva* was sometimes called the Lord of all things, he remained one of the celestial beings as a breathing spirit far removed from Brahman, Atman or Purusha in the capacity of the supreme principle. Such, in fact, was the complexity of Hindu thought, be it monistic, polytheistic or pantheistic, that it is impossible to reduce it to a systematic course of development.

Bhakti and the Bhagavad-Gita

This became most apparent in the Mahabharata Epic which in its final form, probably in the fourth century A.D., embraced every aspect of Hinduism in its hundred thousand couplets compiled between 400 B.C. and A.D. 400. Within it is contained the immortal Bhagavad-Gita, "The Song of the Blessed One", in the form of an allegory in which the pantheistic monism of the Upanishads is united with the popular Vedantic theism. Centred in the fratricidal struggle between two families of cousins, descended from the same grandfather, Kuru, after eight days of bitter fighting the Kauravas section is represented as having been destroyed and their rivals, the Pandaras, established in the kingdom. On the eve of the battle Arjuna, the younger brother of their leader, hesitated to engage in warfare with his kith and kin. Thereupon his charioteer, Krishna, explains to him that his caste duty must be fulfilled and that he is as incapable of resisting this divine decree as he is of slaying the souls of those whom he kills in the conflict. The struggle must be left in the hands of the God who created and maintains the cosmos and demands from man absolute obedience.

Krishna is represented as the avatar, or incarnation, of Vishnu, a Vedic solar deity who had become the supreme being in the Bhakti phase of Hinduism with its monotheistic devotional trends combined with the Upanishadic conception of Brahman and the observance of caste obligations. In the Gita works, faith, and knowledge is each given its place in a monistic Way of Devotion in which the plurality of divine manifestation and intervention is centred in a higher theism personified in Vishnu, the awe-inspiring creator and destroyer of all that is.[11] Having shed his former solar attributes he assumed creative functions and incarnational appearances in his avatars as Krishna and Rama "for the protection of the good and the destruction of evil-doers, and for the establishment of *Dharma* (an indefinable term embracing the power holding all things together and governing their operations).[12] For these purposes Vishnu had appeared in the world from time to time in a variety of forms which included those of a fish, a tortoise, a boar and a man-lion, though supremely as the two principal figures, Krishna and Rama, in the Bhakti epics (i.e. the Mahabharata and the Ramayana).

Thus, in the Gita he is revealed both as the all-pervading eternal sole Brahman, and as omnipotent, omniscient, omnipresent, and transcendent, rather than as a pantheistic Absolute. In this capacity by becoming incarnate in Krishna the supreme being was brought into a vital relationship with mankind and the world, though not in the Christian sense of one unique act of incarnation and mediation in a redemptive process. As will be considered in the next chapter, Krishna was a very different figure from the Christ of the gospels and the creeds. As the avatar of Vishnu his role was that of a mythical hero who was one of the many embodiments of Vishnu in the endless repetitive cycles of birth and rebirth, of creation and recreation, moving towards an ultimate pantheistic goal. Nevertheless, the immense appeal of the Gita, sometimes described as the New Testament of Hinduism, has been largely due to its message going beyond the Upanishadic and Vedantic quest of liberation in a state of Brahman to union with the supreme being himself, notwithstanding the limitations and numerous incarnations of Vishnu. It retained some of the more sublime concepts of the Upanishads combined with the Sankhyan cosmology, identifying Krishna with the sovereignty of the soul of the universe as the source of all things and yet independent of time. The universal self is represented allegorically as at war with the five senses and their sins, a struggle symbolized by the great fratricidal battle in the Mahabharata epic. The Gita, like the medieval mystery play *Everyman*, is the story of every soul and its destiny, superimposed on the Vedanta, with all these very diverse and contradictory elements unified in a common devotion to Krishna as a saviour god.

Next in importance was the appearance of Vishnu as Rama, the seventh incarnation, as recorded in the Ramayana epic assigned to the poet Valmiki about 400 B.C., though its first and eleventh books are later editions at the beginning of the Christian era.[13] In the smaller Sanskrit epic the exile of Rama, the son of the king Dasaratha, with his wife Sita, is represented as the result of the jealousy of his stepmother. After living in the forest for fourteen years Sita was abducted and carried off in an aerial chariot to Ceylon, where she was rescued with the aid of the monkey clan and restored to her husband. As an avatar of Vishnu, Rama was represented as the type of victorious prince who voluntarily underwent suffering and persecution on behalf of struggling humanity, and Sita as the personification of the dutiful wife in perfection. When eventually Rama was fully deified in the fourteenth and fifteenth centuries, after having been venerated as the ideal of chivalry he was worshipped as the supreme being who saved those who clung to him as a baby monkey clings to its mother, or carries his chosen ones as a cat carries its kittens.

The Rise of Buddhism

Great as has been the devotional appeal of this epic, the Gita has remained unrivalled as the clearest expression in Hindu mysticism of the love of God for man, though this has been achieved largely in terms of the Buddhist conception of Nirvana in which deity originally had no place. Thus, it was from the Sankhya dualistic school of Indian philosophy that Buddhism, like its Jain predecessor, arose as a heterodox attempt to find a way of release from the phenomenal world with all its suffering and misery resulting from the law of karma and the consequential series of rebirths. Born in the middle of the sixth century B.C.

in an aristocratic family called Gautama, in the Sakya clan in Northern India of which his father was a chieftain and a member of the Hindu Kshatriya warrior caste, Siddhartha, commonly known by his family name Gautama (Gotama in Pali), was reared under conditions which have been described as not unlike those of a Scottish castle in the Middle Ages. At the age of twenty-nine he became so impressed by the travail of mundane existence, with its sickness, old age, death and rebirth, that he abandoned his wife and child and his luxurious way of life, donned the yellow robes of a Jain ascetic, and sought the guidance of two Brahmin recluses, but to no purpose.

After six years of rigorous asceticism in the company of five other ascetics who had joined him, he left them and followed alone a "middle way" between extreme mortification and luxurious living, adopting the vocation of a mendicant. Then when he was in his thirty-fifth year as he sat cross-legged in the yoga posture of contemplation under a pipal tree (Bodhi-tree) at Buddh Gaya, where the Mahabodhi temple now stands, he determined to remain until he attained enlightenment. Overcoming all the allurements and detachments of phenomenal existence, at length the long desired experience was achieved. In a flash of supreme knowledge (*Bodhi*) he became the Buddha, or Enlightened One, perceiving that the root cause of the universality of suffering (*Dukka*) was intense desire (*tanha*) arising out of the will to live and the will to possess. Having reached his goal he is said to have remained in the state of the passionless peace called Nirvana (Pali Nibbana). For the sake of suffering humanity, however, rather than remaining in this condition of bliss, he returned to Benares to "set the wheel of the Law" in motion by the enunciation of the "four noble truths" he had discovered. These consisted of the recognition of pain as the universal ill manifest in the craving for transient existence and pleasure involving birth, sorrow, disease, old age, death and rebirth, and all the desires of physical life. To remove the basic cause the eightfold path must be followed consisting of a right outlook, right resolve, right speech, right action, right occupation, right effort, right knowledge and right concentration.

The aim, therefore, of Buddhism and Hinduism is really the same, the question of questions for all Indian seers being liberation from the law of karma and the ever-recurring reincarnation it produces. Where Gautama differed from his predecessors was in the repudiation of the Hindu philosophic and mystical approaches, and for them the substitution of his all-embracing empirical Eightfold Path in which any concept of deity was rigidly excluded. Something more than abstract "right knowledge", or extra-mundane divine grace, was required to stop the wheel of continuous life, he contended. This he sought and

78

found in his "middle way" and its prescribed means of self-salvation, involving the renunciation altogether of the conception of selfhood (*atmanam*).

According to the Buddha, human personality consisted of five causally conditioned *skandhas*, or transitory "streams" of the life-impulse, collectively making up the person; namely, the body and its senses, feelings, sensations, perceptions, volitions, mental faculties and reason or consciousness. These took the place of the Hindu Atman, or "self", as an entity, no ego (*atta*) having any permanent or real existence in his anthropology. The skandhas being aggregates of five ever-changing elements and phases never the same for two consecutive moments, devoid of any permanence or continuity, the idea of reincarnation and transmigration, so fundamental in Indian pantheism and mysticism, was not easily fitted into this contention of *Anatta*, the unreality of the self as a conglomeration of unrelated parts. At the most it could be only an extra-temporal recurrence of sensations and ideas, which give some appearance of sameness and actuality, but in fact it is only the continuity of a sense of temporality, a *dhamma* lamp and its flame masquerading as a "self".[14] What transmigrates is karma as a stream of energy like the flame of a lamp, clothing itself in body and after body, craving for existence, and undergoing birth after birth. This goes on until *tanha* is overcome and its karma is destroyed by the adoption of the Buddhist *dharma* and its eightfold path.

The most that can be claimed for this non-atta, selfless, interpretation of human nature and its destiny is that of man in process of "becoming", as Mrs. Rhys Davids has contended, [15] rather than man-in-being. But in any case he is devoid of any abiding principle, and when the Pali scriptures were compiled in the first century B.C. the doctrine of Anatta was firmly accepted by the Theravada monastic orders in Ceylon, Burma and Thailand, where the original oral tradition was held to have been preserved. In this form it is almost impossible to maintain any real continuity between one new sentient being and the aggregate of skandhas that preceded it. As Dahlke says, "it is no persistent something that passes over; it is the individual tendency, the predispositions, the character, the consciousness, or whatever else one has a mind to call the value in potential energy represented by the I-process as its disintegration, that passes over by immediately taking effect, striking in, imparting the new impulse to the material to which it is *uniquely attuned* — the material that appeals to it alone of all that is present, and to which it alone of all that is present answers."[16]

But if the personal element is eliminated there is no obvious connexion between one birth and the next, or adequate reason for the

79

transference of the karma of one person to another in a continuous series of interrelated lives, likened to the flame returning to its pure invisible state in which it existed before it became visible as fire.[17] If this does not involve complete nullity it is at any rate a negative goal, Nirvana being regarded as a process of "becoming cool", or "blowing out", extinguished by lack of fuel (karma). Once the "five fetters" binding the individual to earth and rebirth have been finally broken for ever any form of conscious existence ceases.

In this Anatta-Nirvana concept the so-called "stream winner" at the end of the eightfold path attains transcendental peace in perpetuity as an *Arhant*, or "man perfected". Then "becoming" with all its pain and sorrow and rebirth is over for ever. No aspect of Buddhist thought is more puzzling to the Western mind however than this interpretation of the nature and destiny of man. While annihilation is denied, what persists in the "no-self" doctrine when the peace of Nirvana is attained is very difficult to ascertain. The reservoir of all things, the ultimate zero (*sunnya*) is the "void", "emptiness", "suchness" (*tathata*), regarded as the "indefinite", the "dissolved", the "no-thing", distinct from "nothingness" (*akincanna*) attained in meditation. This implies that at the source and consummation of Ultimate Reality there is no continuous change through growth and decay, birth and death; "no-becoming" This constitutes static being as a transcendental reality of "change no longer" beyond all empirical experience. Peace is only secured through the extirpation of the restless striving of conscious life with its round of birth and death.

Life may have seemed to be a passing series of becomings and vanishings conditioned by the empirical law of continuous change, and the world as worthless as it was illusory, but eventually a fundamental change was wrought. It may have been, as Miss Horner suggests, "because the arahan concept synchronized with some peculiar psychological upheaval in India, when men were prepared to stand upon their own feet with Self as the lamp, unafraid of falling; but when this wave in the history of religious ideas had rolled by, man was discovered cowering, unaware of his own strength, groping for a support, hoping that it would be found outside himself."[18]

Mahayana Buddhism

Already in answer to the negations of Jainism and Buddhism the Hindu Brahmins had developed a more optimistic approach based on the Bhakti movement, which in its turn had a profound effect on the subsequent development in Buddhism in the Mahayana, or "Great

Vehicle", in the northern half of the Buddhist world (e.g. Nepal, Tibet, China, Korea and Japan). This became apparent in India when after the reign of the great Buddhist emperor Asoka (269-237 B.C.), and the downfall of the Maury dynasty about 185 B.C., Buddhism lost its predominance in the sub-continent. Then the three ways of release from the law of karma–works, knowledge, and devotion – in Hinduism made a greater appeal than the negative nihilism of the Theravada "Little Vehicle" of monastic Buddhism (sometimes called Hinayana). By the beginning of the Christian era the Mahayana re-interpretation of the Dharma had become established in the north, leaving the Theravada in possession in the south, and in Ceylon, Burma and Thailand, claiming to maintain the original teaching of Gautama. Mahayana, on the other hand, affirmed that its basic ideas were inherent in the Dharma of the Buddha himself; stress being laid on loving-kindness and compassion rather than on the austere philosophy of life of the Little Vehicle, concentrated upon escape from mundane bondage to achieve nirvana. This not without reason was regarded in the Mahayana as incompatible with the emphasis on compassion assigned to the Founder in the Mahayana as the "Loving One". It appeared, in fact, a form of selfishness grounded in the self-salvation of the individual, notwithstanding the doctrine of Anatta. This conception of the no-self was combined with selfless giving and under Bhakti influences, reinforced perhaps subsequently by those derived from Christianity, an approach was made towards a doctrine of divine grace.

Thus, by the second century A.D. the northern tradition had adopted the cult of avatars of whom Gautama was the latest and greatest of a series of eternal Buddhas who had appeared on earth to spread the saving Dharma to suffering humanity. Indeed, "the realized Buddha", as an abstract concept, was thought to have lived always either on earth or in the heavenly sphere. Being virtually the Absolute at the heart of all existence the idea of Buddhahood penetrating the entire universe was not very far removed from a pantheistic principle with theistic aspects. It would appear in a variety of forms and persons, though it was in the historical Gautama that it was manifest supremely; and the Dharma he taught in its completeness after his enlightenment, notwithstanding the original atheism, was conceived in a quasi-theistic manner in the *Bodhisattva* ideal.

Thus, in Mahayana it was maintained that there were mythical heroes or Bodhisattva, who, following the example of Gautama, having attained perfect knowledge, refrained from entering upon the state of nirvana in order to help mankind by propagating the Dharma of the middle way. This magnanimous act involving the repetition of birth and death, and the pain and woes of mundane existence, was regarded with such admiration and veneration that it became the most potent converting force in central and east Asia at the beginning of the Christian era. It was, in fact, comparable in its devotional appeal to that of the Gospel in Christianity in spite of the enlightened ones being actually mythical saints. Moreover, they did not sacrifice their own lives, suffering with man for his redemption as in the Christian doctrine of the Atonement. Nevertheless, they became the characteristic feature of Northern Buddhism, and even spread to some extent in the Theravada school in the south. A fantastic mythology grew up around their exploits, and became very prominent in *The Lotus of the True Law*, which was one of the earliest sutras of Mahayana; a sort of "gospel" setting forth all that had been taught hitherto as in the nature of a *praeparatio evangelica* of the new movement.

The Buddha was deified as an eternal sublime being, the Father of the Worlds, appearing in human form as a celestial saviour of mankind by sharing in his compassion and love all the limitations and woes of earthly existence. In the form of a parable described as a dramatic performance of an undeveloped cosmic drama, the divine nature of the Buddha and future destiny of the universe are set forth in Mahayana terms and idiom, very different from those of the original Dharma and of the Theravada monks. Thus, the eternal Buddha is represented as displaying splendour and majestic power in speeches with his all-surpassing infinite wisdom, weaning humanity from its misery as a compassionate elder brother, manifesting himself by appearing on earth from time to time in his several forms and manners. Yet the earthly mortal Buddhas, called Sakyamunis, are not exactly divine beings since they are illusory. The true Sakyamuni dwells in his immortal grandeur omnipotent and omniscient on the "Mountain of Vultures" surrounded by bodhisattvas near Rajagritha, revealing to them the true law, like Allah imparting the Qur'an to Muhammad on Mount Hija. This revelation has been known in this world only very gradually, and Theravada is said to represent merely a preliminary phase of the whole "gospel". Therefore, it is regarded as the Lesser or Defective Vehicle (Hinayana) in preparation for the later disclosures of the Great Vehicle.[19]

The division between Northern and Southern Buddhism, in fact, was as fundamental as that between Catholicism and Protestantism in Christendom in the sixteenth century, and followed in some respects on much the same lines of distinction, the Buddha and Christ being respectively the unifying centre of an otherwise sharply divided duality. And corresponding to the ecumenical movement in Christianity today, in Buddhism attempts are now being made by a pan-Buddhist movement to bring together Mahayana and Theravada in a closer unity. Despite the marked cleavage in the two traditions the original pattern of the middle way has, in fact, remained virtually unchanged in respect of the nature and destiny of the individual, the law of karma and release from the pain, sorrow and disabilities of mundane existence. Nevertheless, in the Mahayana tradition the Buddha has become almost indistinguishable from the Bhakti conception of deity in Hinduism. Moreover, in the Pure Land sects in China and Japan a Western paradise has become at any rate a stepping-stone to nirvana for those who secured the necessary merit to enter this state of bliss. This is most conspicuous in the Great Sutra of the Endless Life (*Sukhavativyuha Sutra*) in which the Buddha is represented as extolling Amitabha, the Buddha of Infinite Light, and the indescribable joys of the Western paradise he has established, called Sukhavati, where there is "no withering and no change", and everything is in a state of perfection. The trees are of gold, silver, lapis lazuli, crystal and coral; the sands are of gold, silver or amber; the bathing ponds are filled with pure, clean and fragrant water; and in this pure land peace, harmony and brotherhood reign unmitigated eternally.

Amidism

Amitabha originally was a bodhisattva who, countless aeons ago, had accumulated such a vast store of merit during his progress towards Buddhahood, that he vowed to bestow on all who trusted in him with perfect faith and sincerity, an assured rebirth in his paradise far away in the western quarter of the universe by the simple device of constantly repeating the formula *Nama-Amida Batsu* ("Hail Amida-Buddha"). This was efficacious because he had willed that all men should be saved by attaining Buddhahood and ascending to his Pure Land. It only remained, therefore, for this exercise to be performed with the right dispositions and absolute faith in his inexhaustible merit, infinite compassion and unlimited power to save, to secure this state of bliss through his grace rather than as a result of self-salvation.

It is hardly surprising, therefore, that when Amidism as the "easy road" of faith was established in China by the seventh century A.D. it attained pre-eminence, especially in the north. By the ninth century in varying forms it permeated Chinese Buddhism everywhere, and in 1175 it was founded in Japan by Genku, better known as Honen, in the Jodo sect. There it made a widespread popular appeal and influenced Japanese art and sculpture to a considerable extent. His disciple Shinoran, who lived from 1173 to 1262, further developed its main tenets in the Shinshu sect, which is now the most important Pure Land sect in Japan, with ten branches. Requiring only simple faith in Amida without any ecclesiastical organization or cultus it has succeeded in securing a very considerable adherence of easy-going persons in search of an emotionally satisfying religion making little demand intellectually, ethically, or ascetically. Justification by faith alone sufficed.

Zen Buddhism

Against these free passports to a Western paradise, in the thirteenth century Nicheren instituted a sect based on the *Lotus Sutra of the True Law* as the only true doctrines of Gautama, the historical Buddha, dismissing the existence of a Pure Land as the vain imagination of a degenerate age. It was, however, in China in the Ch'an school that the foundations were laid in the sixth century A.D. of a movement for the return of the vigorous discipline and resolution to secure release from rebirth by the middle way revealed by Gautama the Buddha, and practised by the Theravada Lesser Vehicle. This reached Japan in the ninth century and became firmly established under the designation Zen by about 1200. At first the appeal was primarily felt in military circles where its austerity, discipline and chivalry were appreciated. But its temples as centres of learning, art and education, as well as of spiritual insight and contemplative mysticism, were frequented by cultivated people, while commerce and industry also were under their control.

In both the Rinzai and Soto schools of the sect the Zen masters devised and applied a technique to break down the conscious mind of its monks in order to produce an unconditioned consciousness, and the realization of a mystic state called *satori* (enlightenment). This was achieved in the Rinzai section as a sudden leap from thinking and knowing, from second hand to direct experience, producing immediate spiritual perception and intuitive awareness beyond the intellect and the senses.[20] The Soto section has adopted less sudden methods but the goal of enlightenment in both schools is the eternal peace of nirvana, paradise being found on earth as the eternal "now", or *satori*. The shock treatment employed in breaking down rational thinking includes the posing of insoluble problems by asking questions to which answers are impossible, and making ridiculous assertions, such as likening the Dharma-body of the Buddha to the "hedge at the bottom of the garden".[21] This however, is merely a device to elicit some basic reality rather like some of the parables and sayings of Christ in the gospels (John 3. 3–7; Matt. 19. 24, 18. 1–6; Luke 12. 1–8).

The aim of Zen being to penetrate into the depth of reality beneath the levels of conventional consciousness, thought and reasoning (*satori*), excluding divine grace, it is similar to some extent to that produced by drugs such as mescalin and marijuana (Indian hemp). In recent years this practice has become a vogue in the West, not least, alas, in Britain and America, as a way of escape from a materialistic world which for many young people of the so-called beatnik type has lost any ultimate meaning and significance. But the actual Zen *satori* experience is not readily perceived outside restricted circles in the West, and, as Professor Zaehner and Mr. Aldous Huxley rightly maintain, it is not a religious experience.[22] Nevertheless, in achieving a penetrating insight into the inner depths of consciousness and reality the way is opened, given the right religious conditions, for genuine mystical realization of union with God and the beatific vision, such as has been attained throughout the ages by Christian mystics.

Oriental Pantheism and Divine Immanence

In Christianity this is made possible by the Incarnation and the descent of the Holy Spirit as a charismatic outpouring of divine trans-cendence introducing an element of immanence which constitutes a bridge between the mystical and the non-mystical trends in oriental and occidental faith and practice. But whereas in Hindu and Zen mysticisms the purpose has been the realization of intuitive knowledge and insight of eternal being, for the Christian mystics the quest has been that of divine love in its fullness as revealed redemptively in Christ. This is appropriated sacramentally and by following the "unitive way" to its ultimate goal in complete personal union with the living God and the attainment of the beatific vision. In the Hindu Bhagavad-Gita the devotional way of becoming Brahman was, it is true, by loving, know-ing and following Krishna. Here the two approaches are almost identical, although in the Gita they are combined with the Yogic way of knowledge in liberating the soul from its fetters. Once this has been done its union with its ultimate source has been accomplished, ex-pressed in theistic terms, as distinct from absorption in Brahman as a monistic impersonal Absolute. The soul has a life and personality of its own, and so it cannot be either destroyed or merged pantheistically in Brahman. But if God is regarded transcendentally as a loving man, a personal quality is implied far removed from the Upanishadic, Yogic-Sankhya and Buddhist tradition, which is either monistically or dua-listically conceived, or definitely atheistic.

Although in the Indian mind belief in the existence of a personal God is obscured in both Hinduism and Buddhism, the primary aim of the liberation of the eternal element in man in nirvana transcends the purely rational, logical and materialistic interpretation of human nature and its destiny by making the ultimate goal essentially a spiritual state of being. In Bhakti Hinduism a *deus otiosus* in process of becoming a supreme being with personal and incarnational aspects, attributes and functions, can be discerned emerging from and rising above the underlying pantheistic substratum. This had its effects on Mahayana Buddhism notwithstanding its atheistic origins. Even the Buddha having revealed the way to attain nirvana by the four noble truths and the eightfold path was himself destined to become virtually deified, appearing in different forms and guises on earth throughout the ages with a Dharma-body. He was, in fact, regarded as the ultimate principle and the source of the cosmic order; though that God is love was and has remained quite unthinkable.

It is here that the Christian conception of deity and the relation of God to man are so widely separated from the Buddhist Dharma, though in the interior depths of the soul there is a common spiritual experience which runs through the oriental tradition and its Christian counterpart. Beyond the world of thought, sense and consciousness an ultimate reality is encountered however the experience may be interpreted theologically, mystically and philosophically. This becomes most apparent in the Gita where divine love and grace first appear in Hinduism. Bhakti, in fact, means "loving devotion to God" as against the non-dualistic (*advaita*) school of Sankara rejected by Ramanuja as a belief in God at all. For Ramanuja liberation was only a preliminary phase in the spiritual life prior to communion with God in a loving ecstasy of the beatific vision.

At this point the question arises, what is the real nature of the encounter of the soul with the ultimate source of reality in Christian and oriental mysticism? In Hinduism and Buddhism, as in Taoism in China, the relationship is one of identity of the self with the ground of all existence. In Christianity, God being at once transcendent and immanent, the soul is a divine creation, an inbreathing of the life of the Creator who is distinct from and stands over and against the world and its creatures. This is in contrast with the successive reincarnations for the purpose of the elimination of the law of karma, and the working off of its effects in binding the soul to a corporeal integument, rather than the forgiveness of sin as moral guilt rooted in human character and will. Even Ramanuja, with his insistence on a personal god, Isvara (the Lord), and the continuance of the relation between the soul and this concept of deity in the final state of bliss, could not escape from its being a "mode" of the divine being in a pantheistic identity.

In Christianity the doctrine of divine immanence finds expression in the indwelling of the Holy Spirit as the third person of the Holy Trinity who was operative in creation and responsible for the virgin birth of the incarnate Christ. It was he who descended upon him at his baptism, and upon the apostles at Pentecost. Subsequently he was believed to be manifest in the glossolalia, or "gift of tongues", in the Apostolic Church, and to be instrumental in the imposition of hands at Confirmation and Ordination. This conception of the work of the Holy Spirit escaped a pantheistic interpretation by its being coupled with divine transcendence, notwithstanding a pantheistic trend in the mysticism of Dionysius the Areopagite, Erigena, Nicholas de Cusa, Eckhart and Jacob Boehme. For a Christian there can never be identity of nature between man and God. The relationship is that of a living soul made in the image of his Creator and therefore capable of eternal union with him, and to some extent with the rest of creation, but transcendentally and immanently rather than pantheistically.

This creative sustaining divine power animated by the indwelling of the Holy Spirit bestowed upon mankind charismatically and sacramentally is distinct from the monistic denial of the reality of the phenomenal world. Nevertheless, it has much in common with the oriental conception of the experience of divine unity and of "cosmic consciousness" of the eternal, the infinite and the absolute. In its essence it is "insight" into the source of all being, a genuine mystical realization of the soul in its depth, brought into unitive relation with the divine, however the concept may be defined and understood. What is lacking in the oriental concept is a personal union with the hidden divine presence uniting the human and the divine in the One Christ as the ultimate reality in the Godhead. But both approaches to this common quest have much to learn from and give to each other. Unquestionably God at sundry times has not left himself without witness alike in the oriental and occidental search for him in divers modes and manners. Therefore, it can hardly be denied that Christ through the Holy Spirit has been operative leading those who throughout the ages have sought to attain the highest states of spiritual consciousness and development by different methods and techniques. Nowhere has this been more apparent than in Hindu India, and its outstanding contribution to the mystical tradition surely must be regarded as a *praeparatio evangelica* within the conditions of its milieu, historical background and outlook.[23]

This is not to lose sight of the uniqueness of the Christian revelation in which divine transcendence and immanence are brought into a relationship giving due emphasis to the two vital aspects of deity, with dimensions in both traditions yet to be realized by ecumenical contact, supplying what is lacking, correcting what is erroneous, imperfectly understood, or now outlived; and developing and perfecting that which is true and of permanent value and significance. Each with its age-long mystical tradition has its own experience of the interior depth of reality, and it is the recovery of this dimension of faith, insight and understanding, so manifestly diminished in this ultra-materialistic age, that is in urgent need of resuscitation. This can best be accomplished in the first instance by a determination of the agreement and differences in the Eastern and Western mystical approach to the notion of deity, and the evaluation in the ecumenical spirit of the affinities and divergencies underlying them.

FOR FURTHER READING

Barth, A., *The Religious India*, 1932
Bouquet, A. C., *Hinduism*, 1966
Conze, E., *Buddhism: its Essence and Development*, 1957
Déchanet, J. M., *Christian Yoga*, 1960
Edgerton, F., *The Bhagavad-Gita*, 1944
Eliot, C., *Hinduism and Buddhism*, 3 vols., 1921
Graham, A., *Zen Catholicism*, 1964
Horner, I. B., *The Early Buddhist Theory of Man Perfected*, 1936
Humphreys, C., *Buddhism*, 1951;
   Zen Buddhism, 1961
Keith, A. B., *Buddhist Philosophy*, 1923
Panikkar, R., *The Unknown Christ of Hinduism*, 1964
Piggott, S., *Prehistoric India to 1000 B.C.*, 1952
Pratt, J. B., *The Pilgrimage of Buddhism*, 1928
Smith, F. H., *The Buddhist Way of Life*, 1951
Suzuki, D. T., *Essays on Zen Buddhism*, 1927–33;
   Mysticism Christian and Buddhist, 1927
Watts, A. W., *This Is It*, 1961
Zaehner, R. C., *Mysticism, Sacred and Profane*, 1957;
         Hindu and Muslim Mysticism, 1960
         The Concise Encyclopaedia of Living Faiths, 1959

Chapter Five

SALVATION AND THE SAVIOUR GOD

WHILE the Indian mind sought a unifying pantheistic principle in the multiplicity of Vedic gods controlling the cosmic and phenomenal orders, in the Fertile Crescent and the eastern Mediterranean attention was concentrated mainly on the transcendental aspects of the sacral kingship and the concept of a saviour god. This was particularly apparent in ancient Egypt where Osiris as the culture hero and lord of the dead became the saviour god *par exellence* and his sister-wife Isis was represented as aiding and abetting him in this capacity in the work of "salvation". Thus, in the Texts inscribed on the walls of the royal pyramids in the middle of the third millennium B.C. Osiris was the most conspicuous figure, and in the liturgy of Unas, the last king of the fifth dynasty, the divine son (Unas) of the solar god Atum Re was described as Osiris, reigning as his posthumous son Horus who had been resuscitated by Osiris and Isis.[1] The rejuvenation funerary ritual in the Valley Temple and the Queen's Temple at Giza, and subsequently in the Mortuary Temple, was essentially Osirian, as were the reanimation ceremonies. These included the washing and purification of the corpse, its mummification and the so-called "Opening of the Mouth" rite, which may go back to predynastic times.[2] When later immortality ceased to be exclusively a royal prerogative, it was to the revival of Osiris that men turned more and more to escape corporeal corruption after death, and to attain a blissful immortality when they joined their Ka in the tomb or the cemetery. This, however, was accomplished by the correct performance of the prescribed ritual techniques whereby Osiris himself had been restored and reanimated by his devoted wife and sister, with the help of the funerary physician Anubis, rather than by justification by faith in the saviour god.

Isis the Saviour-Goddess

Although in Egypt Osiris was the principal and typical saviour god, Isis, nevertheless, was the "throne woman" personifying the sacral coronation stool charged with the mysterious potency of kingship.[3] So to some extent she was the source of the power and vitality of kingship, as well as the embodiment of the female creative principle. As early as the first dynasty the pharaohs were regarded as the "sons of Isis", and were represented as being suckled by her and sitting on her lap.[4] Therefore, in their divine capacity they stood in a very intimate relationship with her, and both she and they had soteriological features and functions. This became more apparent when it was believed that she was responsible for the collection, embalmment and revivification of the dismembered body of Osiris.[5] This gave her an important place and significance in the death and resurrection of the saviour god in the cult of the dead, and opened the way for her to become a mystery deity when her cult was Hellenized in the Graeco-Roman world. Then she became the syncretistic "Goddess of Many Names" depicted with the horns and solar disk with two plumes derived from the mother-goddess Hathor, surmounted by her hieroglyph, adorned with the feather of truth and holding the sign of life (*crux ansata*) with the uraeus over her forehead. Like the Virgin and Child in Christian iconography, she was often represented with Horus on her lap, and in the fourth century B.C. she was equated with the *magna mater* of western Asia in the Hellenistic world. There were, in fact, few goddesses of any importance with whom she was not associated in the Ptolemaic period, and in her great temple on the island of Philae at the head of the First Cataract she reigned supreme as the syncretistic saviour goddess of many names until her cultus was suppressed by Justinian (A.D. 527–565) and the temple converted into a Christian church by Theodorus (about 577).

In the meantime the cult had spread from Egypt and the eastern Mediterranean through Sicily in the third century B.C., and having become established at Syracuse and Catania, it reached Pompeii and Pozzuoli, the port of the Campagna, in the next century. It was not regarded with favour, however, by the Roman Senate, and several attempts were made to suppress it in the capital. On five consecutive occasions between 59 and 48 B.C. statues and altars of Isis on the Capitol were destroyed. Such was the popularity of the cult however, that in A.D. 37 permission was given for the celebration of the Isiac in a temple in the Campus Martius in Rome, and in A.D. 215 Aurelius Cavacalla gave the goddess a temple on the Capitoline hill.[6]

Nowhere is the emotion aroused in the initiates of this mystery more clearly and graphically demonstrated than in the curious romance of Apuleius in the middle of the second century A.D., known as the *Metamorphoses* (The Golden Ass), based on a Greek folk tale describing the adventures and experiences of its hero Lucius. Behind the story and its magic undoubtedly lies a camouflaged account of the actual initiation of Apuleius into the Isiac without divulging its esoteric revelations.

Thus, he is represented as having been encouraged by Isis to proceed through the darkness of Acheron in the nether regions (i.e. the experience of ritual death) to the Elysium where he adored her as his protector and saviour goddess. "Happy and thrice blessed is he who by the innocence and constancy of his former life has won so noble an inheritance from heaven, that he should be reborn and forthwith devoted to the service of the sacred rites."[7] During the experience he had approached "the borderline of death" and "beheld the Sun gleaming with bright light" and come into the presence of the gods whom he adored face to face. In the morning arrayed in the gorgeous vestments of an initiate he was presented to the people, and a year later admitted to the priesthood of Osiris, dedicated to the service of the goddess for the rest of his life.

Making due allowance for the fanciful character of the romance, unquestionably it was based on inner knowledge of his own initiation which involved undergoing "a voluntary death" to obtain the "hope of salvation", Isis being described several times as "the saviour of the human race" and her mysteries as "the purest of religions".[8] While it was not wholly without cause that in the first century B.C. her cult was suppressed as "a corrupting influence perversive of piety and moral behaviour",[9] abstinence from fleshly lusts, asceticism and ablutions in course of time acquired an ethical and spiritual significance. Indeed, Plutarch maintained that their aim was moral and practical, cleanness of body being conjoined with purity of heart.[10] It was, in fact, these qualities behind the observances that in the first three centuries of the era enabled those who embraced them to be assured of strength and renewal in this life, clearer spiritual perceptions, and in the world to come the hope of everlasting happiness through their Saviour goddess Isis and the immortal glory of Osiris.

While the appeal of the Isiac cult was primarily to women, it met the deeper needs of its initiates as did no other mystery in the pagan world. But it failed to make a permanent impression because like the other cults it could not free itself from its underlying mythology. Behind it lay the long history of the religion of ancient Egypt whence it sprang, and though it spread rapidly and assumed increasing importance at the turn of the era, despite its ethical and spiritual elements it could never get away from its ancestry and accretions. Essentially it was a product of the ritual and belief in which it arose, and when it came up against Christianity and its way of salvation in full force in the Roman Empire it proved to be unequal to the contest. Nevertheless, it played its part in the *preparatio evangelica* at a most important junction in the welter of religions which characterized the most crucial milieu in the opening years of what was destined to become the Christian era.

In the Mesopotamian background of Judaism, on the other hand, from which Christianity very largely emerged in the first instance, the situation was rather different. Thus, resurrection was never the focal point as it was in Egypt, and neither the goddess, Inanna-Ishtar, nor her son-spouse, Dumuzi-Tammuz, were ever clearly defined as dying and rising divinities. Although the texts are very obscure Dumuzi-Tammuz did not fulfil the role of Osiris any more than Inanna-Ishtar was the counterpart of Isis, notwithstanding certain resemblances between them. It is true that he was the suffering young-god associated with the decline and revival of vegetation but not in the manner portrayed by Frazer, as has been generally maintained, although he personified the generative force in nature. Similarly, the goddess, while like Isis she was bride and mother with many names and functions, her descent into the nether regions to secure the release of Dumuzi-Tammuz, and her subsequent release, raise a number of problems viewed in the light of the earlier Sumerian version of the myths.

As the goddess also was the incarnation of the fertility in the spring it was then that their nuptials were celebrated in Isin in the south of Mesopotamia in the third millennium B.C. when the reawakening of vegetation was apparent. Thus in the Sumerian version of the relevant text the release of Dumuzi from the underworld is now recorded by Kramer, thereby making it the prototype of the Akkadian account of the "Descent of Ishtar to the Nether Regions".[11] The sacred marriage of the king of Isin, Iddin-Dagan, to the Goddess was enacted at the New Year Festival at the spring equinox, her purpose in going down to the underworld being to secure the release of Dumuzi-Tammuz, as she appears to have stood in the same relation to Dumuzi as did Ishtar to Tammuz.

It was, however, the goddess who was the dominant figure in this act of renewal when and wherever it was celebrated. The young-god died annually and had to be rescued and restored from the land of the dead by her as his saviour resuscitating him, and by so doing reviving life in nature and in mankind. Therefore, in the last analysis Inanna-Ishtar was the source of regeneration while Dumuzi-Tammuz was her agent. She was the embodiment of creative power in its fullness; he was the personification of the decline and revival of vegetation and of all generative force. Jointly they were saviour deities but it was the goddess in her manifold aspects and functions who was primarily the creatrix, and originally she was probably responsible for the generative process as a whole. As other goddesses and their male partners emerged with more clearly defined positions in the pantheon as departmental divinities, she was to some extent obscured, but she always retained her earlier predominance in some measure. Thus, in the Tammuz liturgies and in the myth and ritual of the Annual Festival, it was she who released and restored her "resurrected child", with reciprocal effects on vegetation, the succession of the seasons and the well-being of the community. Throughout she took the initiative, the young-god and the king being the agents she employed as her servants in the bestowal of her gifts. Thus, it was she who invited the king to share her couch as her bridegroom in the sacred marriage[12] to enable him to exercise his beneficent functions, she being the active partner in the alliance. Therefore, she was essentially the saviour goddess.

Anat and Asherah in the Ugarit Pantheon

In the Ugaritic pantheon the work of salvation was distributed among Anat and Asherah as the leading goddesses, and Aleyan-Baal as the virile storm-and weather-god, "the lord over the furrows of the field", and the "rider of the clouds". In the background lay the Tammuz cultus adapted to the climatic conditions in Syria in which each of the deities maintained the rhythm of nature according to local requirements. This was personified in the perennial struggle between Baal and his allies, and his malign adversaries Mot and Yam, usually in conjunction with his consort, Anat or Asherah, the counterparts of Astarte and Ashtoreth. But notwithstanding the prominence of Anat in the Ugaritic texts, she never occupied the position of Inanna-Ishtar in Mesopotamia. Always she was overshadowed by her august husband, Aleyan-Baal, who remained the giver of life rather than the instrument employed by the goddess for this purpose. Whether she ever dominated the scene when she was the wife of the high god El cannot be determined as her original status is very obscure. Originally, however, she seems to have been a virgin goddess conceiving but not bearing offspring in contrast to Asherah who was "the creatrix of the gods", not their "progenitress", bringing forth her brood of seventy deities. But the goddesses seem to have struggled against each other to become the wife of Baal when he rose to supremacy, though at first Asherah was his bitter antagonist rejoicing at his death and trying to make one of her sons king in his stead. Neither of them succeeded in displacing the other, so they had to remain in joint possession of him, thereby never attaining a predominant status as a saviour goddess like Inanna-Ishtar.

93

In Hebrew tradition a different situation developed. There the bestowal of salvation was invested solely in Yahweh who, as we have seen, alone controlled the clouds, the seasons, fertility and the vicissitudes of history. As the Lord of creation he was wholly responsible for the course of nature and its operations, and this had the effect of his becoming equated with Baal to some extent after the settlement of Israel in Canaan. But so firmly established was the desert Sinaitic covenant tradition in the Hebrew confederacy that the two gods were never permanently assimilated, as is demonstrated in the account of the contest on Mount Carmel between Elijah and the priests of Baal, making due allowance for its having been written under mono-Yahwist influences (1 Kings 18. 19 ff.). It was, however, the Exodus that remained the most significant event in the life and religion of the nation, and upon it the idea of salvation with Yahweh as the one and only saviour god was mainly dependent. It was this great divine intervention in the history of Israel and its fortunes that afforded its never failing confidence in him: Yahweh is my strength and my song and has become my salvation (Ex. 15. 2).

Moreover, behind this great deliverance at the Red Sea lay the earlier dragon mythology in which he was represented as manifesting his strength and power by his victory over the forces of the deep (Têhom). Thus, the Deutero-Isaiah at the end of the Exile did not hesitate to call upon the God of Israel to awake and put on the strength of his arm "as in the ancient days" when he transformed the destructive waters and the dragonic denizens into life-giving rains and springs to nourish and fertilize the dry land and its creatures after his conquest of the primeval monsters (Is. 51. 9). Scattering his enemies with his mighty arm at the creation (Ps. 89. 10) he worked salvation in the cosmos and among his chosen people. He made a passage for Israel to pass through the Red Sea to the relative safety of the desert, it was contended, as he dried up the waters of chaos when he created the universe from the body of Rahab, cleaving it like Marduk fashioning an orderly universe from the body of Kingu after his contest with Tiamat. But in the Hebrew tradition Yahweh alone was the saviour god who exercised universal dominion by divine right, and delivered his creation and his people by his absolute sovereignty over all his works.

This is manifest in the liturgical commemoration of the enthronement of Yahweh as the Creator at the autumnal equinoctial annual festival known as the Feast of Tabernacles, or Booths (*Sukkôth*), held in the seventh month (Tishri) when the vintage had been completed.

Its connexion with the ingathering of the grape-harvest suggests a Canaanite rather than a desert origin for the observance in the pre-exilic agricultural community at the beginning of the rainy season (Ex. 23. 16, 34. 22; Hab. 3. 16 ff.). Behind it lay the ancient sacred drama of the dying and reviving saviour god, however much the theme may have been modified and transformed under Yahwistic influence to bring it into relation with the prevailing belief in Yahweh's lordship in the natural order as the sole transcendent deity, exercising divine control over the nation's vicissitudes and the rainfall. This is apparent in the enthronement psalms (93–99) which may have been an integral part of the rite celebrating the victory of Yahweh in the primeval creation conflict, the deliverance from Egypt, and the conquest of Palestine, culminating in a great invocation and thanksgiving to "the Lord of the heavens" to secure a fresh outpouring of re-creative power and deliverance at the New Year Festival.[13]

The Davidic Kingship

This was symbolized by the procession of the sacred ark to the temple where Yahweh was acclaimed as the universal sovereign lord of the universe, and by the renewal of the covenant (*berith*, i.e. cultus) with the House of David to secure his blessing on the forthcoming year in which rain and fertility were vital elements. The enthronement psalms unfortunately come from post-exilic sources though Psalm 81, which is parallel to Psalm 95, was in all probability composed for use at the Feast of Ingathering at the full moon in the month of Tishri in the autumn. In any case, they were employed in the synagogues as Sabbath Psalms, and, therefore, they were indirectly associated with the Creation story and with the Kingdom of God. Deliverance was regarded as coming from "the God of my salvation", and as being renewed continually from year to year (Hab. 3. 18), culminating in the divine intervention at the "Day of the Lord" when Yahweh would make known his salvation (Amos 9. 11 ff.).

The return of the remnant of the nation from exile in Mesopotamia in the sixth century B.C. raised hopes of the great deliverance at the Exodus being repeated by Yahweh as the saviour and redeemer. This went beyond the accomplishments of the saviour gods in the surrounding nations, who were concerned mainly with the preservation of the seasonal sequence, the food supply and the general well-being of the community in the natural order. Yahweh, however, was never a dying and rising vegetation god like Osiris and Tammuz. It is true that before the Exile the king was regarded as a sacred person, as the anointed servant of Yahweh, and David himself was described as the son of Yahweh (Ps. 89, cf. I Kings 8. 66–9. 36; 12. 16). But in Israel the king ruled only by divine permission and the monarchy was never regarded as the basic unifying centre of the theocracy like the throne in Egypt. On the contrary, it was viewed with the greatest suspicion by the mono-Yahwists, and even as an affront to Yahweh as an approximation to the sacral kingship in other nations (Hos. 13. 10 f.).

Therefore, after it came to an end with the fall of Jerusalem in 586 B.C., the royal office was reinterpreted in terms of the messiahship and acquired an eschatological significance. Zerubbabel on becoming governor of Jerusalem in 520 B.C. as a descendant of David was hailed as the deputy of Yahweh, and occupied a position in the cultus comparable to that assigned to "the Prince" by Ezekiel and his contemporaries (Ezek. 34. 24; 37. 25.), ruling in conjunction with the high priest (Hag. 2. 23). When his mission came to an end the civic and ecclesiastical functions were exercised by the high priest as the alleged descendant of Eleazar, the eldest son of Aaron, and he and his successors remained the focal point of the theocratic nation until its disruption in A.D. 70. Like the Maccabaean princes, who were not of the lines of Aaron or Zadok, their function was to bring "salvation" (i.e. "victory") to the people of God, and so to exercise what was virtually a messianic role as divine agents. But it was not only victory in battle and deliverance from the enemies of Yahweh in the surrounding region that was sought. The essential righteousness of the Holy One of Israel proclaimed in the ethical monotheism of the prophetic movement carried with it the idea of salvation from sin itself by a change of heart through repentance, Yahweh being both the saviour and redeemer of Israel. And this had a more personal application involving even an element of suffering (15. 49. 7 f., 26; 63. 8 f.).

It has long been a matter of debate among theologians, however, to what extent, if at all, the anointed Saviour was expected to fulfil his office through suffering and death. That the concepts of the Davidic Messiah, the Son of Man and the Suffering Servant of the Lord were distinct in post-exilic Judaism has been widely held, until eventually they were brought together in the Incarnate Christ in Christianity, though a few scholars have taken the contrary view.[14] The Isaianic Servant certainly seems to have been regarded as Israel as a nation, and its sufferings those that were endured by Jehoiachin and the exiles in and after 597 B.C., but, unlike the usual belief in the Old Testament, undeservedly suffering for the sins of others. It has been suggested, therefore, that the Servant was not intended to be Israel, or confined to a small faithful section of it, or to certain individuals (e.g. Moses, Hezekiah,

Jeremiah, Zerubbabel or Cyrus the Persian), including possibly the Deutero-Isaiah himself. This, however, is conjectural and could be associated with almost any outstanding figures having messianic possibilities, especially of a Tammuz nature as a dying and reviving saviour god. In any case, the Servant transcends the nation and unquestionably foreshadows the passion, death and resurrection of Christ in a remarkable manner, quite regardless of who the original figure may have been.

The Suffering Messiah

In Judaism the idea of a suffering messiah first appears in the Rabbinic Messiah ben Ephraim, in the post-Christian Targum of pseudo-Jonathan and in the Babylonian Targum. Later it recurs in the Targum of the Song of Songs. If it had been familiar when the Gospel tradition was in process of formulation the disciples of Jesus could hardly have been represented as being confused and bewildered by his announcement that in his messianic role he must suffer (Mark 8. 31–35). Neither the figure of the Davidic king nor that of the Son of Man could have been equated in their minds with the Suffering Servant, especially as portrayed in the 53rd chapter of Isaiah. If in fact Christ did apply to himself the role of the Son of Man, as is doubted by some commentators,[15] it did not suggest to his contemporaries the idea of suffering, nor prevent his followers from regarding his death when it occurred as the tragic end of their hopes and aspirations (Luke 24. 17 ff.). But once the significance of the Servant Songs was realized as messianic prophecy, it was the crucifixion and all that it involved and implied that made the most permanent impression upon the Early Church. Calvary then determined not only the nature and purpose of the messianic office but of the whole redemptive process. The functions hitherto attributed to the Davidic king were invested with apocalyptic glory in the supernatural Son of Man transfigured with suffering in the person of the defeated yet victorious saviour of mankind; he in his own messianic consciousness having applied the Servant prophecies to himself. But his disciples, like the rest of their compatriots, were looking for a very different Davidic messiah.

This to some extent may account for the *volte-face* of those who acclaimed Jesus with their cries of "Hosanna" when he made a triumphal entry into Jerusalem as the messianic king in the manner predicted by Zechariah, if they were among the crowd on the following Thursday evening who supported Caiaphas demanding his crucifixion as a bogus messiah. If the enigmatic Barabbas was an insurrectionary leader of one of the nationalistic groups who later were organized as Zealots, this would explain their demand for his release. In any case, since the passion was coincident with the Passover once it became the central redemptive event in the Christian conception of salvation, the crucified and risen Christ readily became equated with the Paschal Lamb. As the saviour god fulfilling all the prototypes, first in Judaism and then in the Graeco-Roman world, he had inaugurated a new era in which all mankind were brought into a covenant relation with God. This was proclaimed and enacted at the institution of the Eucharist on the night of the betrayal, the sacred elements being identified with his broken body and poured out blood, and destined to become the central act of Christian worship in perpetual commemoration of his sacrificial death "till he come" (I Cor. 11. 26; Mark 14. 25; Matt. 26. 29).

In the messianic tradition in its Christian setting the Davidic king, the Son of Man, the Suffering Servant and the saviour god not only had a common pattern of thought and theology but also a common theme, motif and liturgical expression deeply laid in the sacral kingship of the Ancient Near East as well as in Judaism. Thus, in the suffering saviour god and the mourning goddess weakness and strength were combined in the defeated yet virile young-god triumphing over death and the powers of evil to secure renewed life and vitality in a declining natural order. In its Christian setting it was transfigured and reinterpreted in the Johannine apocalypse in terms of the conquering Christ under the apocalyptic symbolism of the lamb slain from the foundations of the world to ensure the final triumph of good over evil, of life over death. The malign forces were personified in the dragon and his host, and their destruction was celebrated by the sacred marriage of the victor as the prelude to the reign of universal peace, prosperity and righteousness. The messiah as "the lion of the tribe of Judah", and the lamb restored to life after conquering death, represented the final vindication of the saviour god amid universal celestial rejoicing and the symbolism of the sacred marriage (Rev. 19. 1–9).

Behind this imagery lay the complex mythology derived from Mesopotamian, Egyptian and Iranian sources, but however much the Christian doctrine of Messiah may have been influenced by current and more remote apocalyptic tradition, Jewish and pagan, it was unquestionably the historic Jesus who in the first instance produced by what he was and did, perhaps more than by what he said and taught, the conviction of his messiahship among his intimate followers. The Johannine apocalypse was compiled at a time of persecution, probably in the reign of the Roman Emperor Domitian (c.A.D. 95), addressed originally to the seven churches of western Asia in which no doubt the cult of the sacral kingship with its ritual combat, heavenly man and sacred marriage was not altogether unfamiliar, Emperor-worship being the predominant issue at the moment. Whether or not the symbolism was actually borrowed from the underlying mythology, it was around the sublime figure of Christ the King and the triumphant Saviour that the Christian conception of redemption was set forth to encourage faithfulness at the approach of impending persecution. The demonic forces are represented in all their might being overcome by those of the victorious saviour god, those who have remained loyal and steadfast to the faith giving their lives, perhaps as martyrs, thereby attaining salvation in the New Jerusalem. These are they who have washed their robes and made them white in the blood of the Lamb, and so they stand before the throne of God and minister to him continually day and night in his temple, as a priestly community offering their worship to him (Rev. 7. 14 f.).

Notwithstanding all the nonsense that has been written in attempts to interpret its contents, imagery, predictions and chronologies in respect of present and future personages and events as a sort of historical and eschatological "Old Moore's Almanack", ranging from the papacy and Lutheranism to Napoleon and Nazism, the symbolism is of very considerable religious value. As a record of unfailing faith in the purpose of God and the final triumph of righteousness, it is unsurpassed even in the Zoroastrian Avesta, or in any of the contemporary apocalyptic eschatologies. Salvation is based more on works than on faith, martyrdom being their highest expression and the most efficacious means of securing redemption and its rewards. The Church though facing severe persecution, even extermination, was represented as indestructible, and this, in fact, has proved to be true in the light of history. Thus, where Nero made "torches" of Christians to illuminate his garden by night now stands the Vatican and the great basilica under the patronage of St. Peter whom he is alleged to have put to death on that very hill. And everywhere it is "the Lamb" in conflict with Babylon and "the beast" who has prevailed. If the predictions often have not been fulfilled it may be, as Dodd has affirmed, that "the God of the Apocalypse can hardly be recognized as the Father of our Lord Jesus Christ".[16] But nowhere is Christ held in such honour and esteem as the Saviour god interpreted through apocalyptic imagery.

The theme of salvation is centred in the victory of the lamb whose blood was shed on behalf of the redeemed, overcoming the fatal effects of the Fall by destroying the serpent's reign of evil on the earth. Those whose names were written in the Lamb's Book of Life, and who in the heavenly Jerusalem ate of the fruit of the Tree of Life and drank of the Water of Life, proclaimed that by virtue of this sacrificial immolation of life through death "now is come the salvation and the power and the kingdom of our God, and the authority of his Christ" (Rev. 12. 10 R.V.). In the final vision of the new heaven and the new earth death, pain, sorrow and evil are eliminated for ever, the Tree of Life from Eden is to be transplanted by the banks of the river of the water of life in the centre of the city, yielding twelve manner of fruit every month for the healing of the nations, reserved for those who have been victorious in the struggle against evil (Rev. 22. 1). Thus, the Eden symbolism and that of the Phoenician Garden of God with its magical precious stones and metals (Ezek. 33. 13), were combined in the Johannine apocalyptic conception of salvation in the glorified city and its mystic equipment, reversing the initial catastrophe at the threshold of history.

This, therefore, was basically a Judaeo-Christian approach to the concept and its theme though the imagery was derived ultimately very largely from Near Eastern and Graeco-Oriental mystery sources and their death and resurrection myth and ritual. It was, in fact, to a blissful Elysium with idealized terrestrial conditions that those who were initiated into the pagan mysteries hoped to attain. As Sophocles affirmed "thrice blessed are those mortals who having seen these rites depart for Hades; for to them alone is it granted to have true life on the other side. To the rest all is evil." Only they know "the end of life and its god-given beginning" (*Frag.* 719; Pindar *Frag.* 102). Substantially this is identical with the purpose, setting and conditions of the Johannine apocalyptic cultus and its message of hope for the "saved", and of woe for the "damned". The crying need, indeed, always has been relief from a sense of the disabilities of life in time and space and the bestowal of a spiritual dynamic which transcends death and endures throughout eternity.

Demeter and the Eleusinian Mysteries

In Greece this was secured in the Eleusinian Mysteries by protracted ritual purifications, fastings and ablutions under the guidance of a *mystagogue*, ending with the drinking of a sacred gruel, or *kykeon*. Three days later the Greater Mysteries opened in Athens in the autumnal month Boedromion (September-October). After the initiates had been scrutinized and addressed by the Archon-king and the Hierophant as the principal officiant, they bathed in the sea, each carrying a small pig. A number of obscure rites were then performed and a procession was assembled to proceed along the Sacred Way to the sanctuary of the goddess Demeter at Eleusis, carrying a statue of the young divinity Iacchos, later identified with Dionysus-Bacchus. On arrival dances were held in her honour at the sacred sites connected with her legend in the so-called Homeric hymn. These included the well of Kallichoron, where Demeter was alleged to have met the daughters of the king, Keleos, and where eventually her temple was built. After again bathing in the sea and roaming about the shore with lighted torches enacting the search of Demeter for her abducted daughter Kore (Persephone), the neophytes repaired to the Hall of Initiation (*Telesterion*) for the climax of the rites. There in darkness and absolute silence, adorned with wreaths and ribbons, they beheld sacred sights accompanied by utterances which might never be disclosed to the uninitiated. Whatever may have been the precise nature and significance of these esoteric disclosures, unquestionably the experience in the Telesterion aroused intense emotions and numinous reactions in the mystai having the effect of a rebirth to newness of life, which it was believed endured beyond the grave.

At first initiation in all probability was confined to Eleusinians and Athenians, but later it was extended to all who could speak and understand Greek, until eventually it was opened to all Roman citizens as well as to all Greeks. Demeter thus became a widely accepted saviour goddess in the Hellenic world, and behind her mysteries lay a long history going back to ancient rustic observances in the annual sequence of ploughing and reaping. While her name suggests an Indo-European origin, its meaning is very uncertain and could be rendered either as that of the corn-goddess or of the earth-mother. In any case, in association with the ancient goddess Kore, or Persephone, who at Eleusis became her daughter, Demeter was regarded as being responsible for the growth of the fruits of the earth, particularly of grain. It is not improbable, as Nilsson has suggested, that her mysteries arose out of an agricultural festival in October celebrating the bringing up of the corn that had been stored in jars or subterranean chambers (silos) after the threshing in June. During the four summer months when the grain was below ground and the fields in Attica were barren and desolate before the autumnal rains commenced, the corn-maiden, it is suggested, was alleged to be in the realms of the god of wealth, Plouton, later identified with Pluto, the god of the nether regions. When the silos were opened in October and the seed-corn was sown in the newly ploughed fields, her release was celebrated at the Greater Eleusinian Mysteries.[17] Be this as it may, they appear to have originated in pre-Hellenic Mycenaean agrarian rites to promote the fertility of the corn, and of vegetation in general, before they acquired their esoteric mortuary and mystery significance to secure newness of life and a blissful immortality. Therefore, their origin, purpose and background were fundamentally different from those of the death and resurrection liturgical drama and its imagery in Christianity.

It is not improbable that some kind of dramatic performance took place in the Telesterion at Eleusis at the climax of the initiation rites in which the life and sufferings of Demeter as the *mater dolorosa* were depicted, and an ear of corn may have been reaped in a blaze of light before the wondering eyes of the mystai, possibly including the announcement of the birth of the divine child Iacchos or Brimos. These, however, remain conjectures of post-Christian writers in their endeavours to discountenance the pagan rites. All that can be definitely asserted is that the initiates did undergo a mystical experience which gave them the assurance of salvation achieved by magico-religious revelations. To this extent, but only within these limitations, can the rites be regarded as a prototype of the Christian mysteries, any resemblance to a conception of redemption being conspicuously absent. As will be considered later, this also applies to the alleged sacramental meal in the preliminary rites. It was essentially in the vegetation tradition that the Eleusinian ritual was operative, and when it was extended to procure a blessed afterlife, in the Homeric background lay the shadowy shades in the gloom of Hades, whereas in the Judaeo-Christian apocalyptic imagery the prophetic Sheol had become abandoned in post-exilic Judaism. The most that could be hoped for in the Homeric age was for initiates to be accorded the Elysial bliss comparable to that of the heroes in the *Odyssey* in their Isles of the Blest (Od. iv. 56 ff.).

The Dionysiac and the Orphic Way of Salvation

In contrast to this essentially Hellenic mystery the orgiastic rites of the worship of Dionysus which made their way into Greece from Thrace and Phrygia in the sixth century B.C., introduced an ecstatic conception of salvation which eventually acquired a mystical significance. The Thraco-Phrygian wild revels continued however to be held on Mount Parnassus after the Dionysiac had been sobered when it secured a place in the Olympian tradition. Under the restraining influence of Apollo and his ancient oracular shrine at Delphi, it was transformed into an allegorical eschatology in terms of the Orphic doctrine of reincarnation leading to the Elysian fields. Indeed, as Plutarch remarked, at Delphi Dionysus was at home no less than Apollo, and it was he who inspired the frenzied Pythian prophetess seated on her tripod above a vaporous cleft in the cave below, situated as it was supposed at the *omphalos*, or naval-stone at the centre of the earth.

There too Orpheus, the prophet and hero of the Dionysian cult, and priest of Apollo, found a place in the oracle. Thus, a more serious element was introduced into the quest of release from the innate evil Titanic inheritance associated with the mortal body in which the Dionysian divine soul was incarcerated, until it was liberated by the Orphic *teletae* (initiation rites) through the series of rebirths and deification leading to eternal bliss. But the orgiastic ecstatic tradition was never wholly repressed, notwithstanding the philosophic content introduced by Plato in his *soma-sema* doctrine of body and soul relationship in the context of pre-existence and reincarnation attaining its ultimate goal in Elysium (*Phaedo*, 64, 66). He did not hesitate to pour scorn on Orphic "quacks and soothsayers" though he recognized that the Orphic life was intended to promote ethical uprightness and moral righteousness (*Republic*, 364 D). As Jane Harrison says, "the grace sought by Orpheus was not physical intoxication but spiritual ecstasy, and the means he adopted not drunkenness but abstinence and rites of purification".[18] The votaries were not begotten anew by a god or goddess. They were made immortal and divinely pure by the prescribed way of life in a succession of existences until at length the Dionysian soul became "god instead of moral".

On the Orphic gold tablets discovered at Patella and at ancient graves in southern Italy and Crete, dating from not later than the fifth century B.C., "the child of earth and the starry heaven" who had flown out of the sorrowful weary wheel and "paid the penalty of deeds unrighteous" by virtue of his initiation and adoption of the Orphic life, is depicted as having become divine on the Isles of the Blest, like the emancipated souls on the Apulian vases in the museum at Naples. These scenes show, whether or not they were actually "Orphic", as Nilsson has said, that "there exists in every man, however humble his station, a dormant desire to enter into communion with the divine, to feel himself lifted up from the temporal into the spiritual. This form of ecstasy found its herald in the god who, with Apollo, impressed himself most strongly upon the religious feeling of the age-Dionysus."[19] And the Orphic conception of salvation constituted the first really serious attempt in the Graeco-Oriental mystery tradition to make human destiny depend upon character and conduct in the present state of existence, with the subjective aspect of sin being given greater prominence than the objective approach. While the divine soul was incarcerated in the mortal body it was conscious of its defilement inherited from previous incarnations. To restrain the divine life from which the soul had fallen, the ritual prescriptions, rules of conduct and of ethical behaviour were directed.

It was the expression of a genuine religious and moral need when social life was undergoing profound disturbances in the Hellenic world, and neither the Homeric heroic chivalrous virtues, nor the Hesiodic values of temperance, fair-dealing and industry, met the situation. A widespread disillusionment with life among the cultivated section of the community in Ionia produced a heightened sense of sin and resort to ritual purity and asceticism as the way of salvation based on the Orphic and Pythagorean conception of the good life. The Olympian gods and heroes had failed to supply the need because transcendentally they had little or nothing to offer, as they only differed from mankind in having superior knowledge and power in degree rather than in kind. Ethically their weaknesses and shortcomings were the same as those of mortals, being merely glorified men. Orphism provided a means whereby its votaries surmounted the barrier which separates man from the supernatural world, and enabled them unconditionally to surrender themselves body and soul to those mighty powers that transcend time and space, and the personal life of men here and hereafter. Thus, they were translated to the timeless spaceless realm of the eternal. Having taken the kingdom of their god by force, breaking through the outer defences, they found salvation in that divine union which is the goal of all mysticism. In Orphism the wilder elements were sublimated and brought into relation with the doctrine of metempsychosis, finding expression in an ethical interpretation of rebirth and expiation in Tartarus. It was there that the liberated souls were destined to dwell in the nether regions when they left the body, until they were reincarnated in a new physical integument, be it human or animal, and at length the cycle of generations was completed. In Tartarus retributive justice would be meted out to the righteous and the unrighteous, while those who occupied an intermediate position between the "saved" and the "damned" were punished for a millennium and then returned to earth to live a series of good lives on both sides of the grave. But ultimately the soul would be purged and acquire divine status in the Isles of the Blest (Pindar, *Olympian Odes*, 129 ff.; *Olympia*. II. 55 ff. 62 ff., *Frag.* 133).

These hopes and fears were not specifically Orphic but they were inspired and developed by Orphic faith and practice, which represents in Greece an advance in the moralization of human destiny, especially when it came under Platonic influences. Therefore, Orphism prepared the way for the Christian conception of salvation notwithstanding its very different and much less edifying background in the Dionysiac and its Bacchic frenzies. Nevertheless, it did offer a way of deliverance by a god regarded as "Lord and Saviour". As Farnell says, "it familiarized the world with the conception of the element in the human soul, with the sense of kinship between man and God. It quickened this sense by means of a mystic sacrament whereby man's life was transcendentally fused with God's. It raised the religious emotion to a pitch of ecstasy and rapture far above the Hellenic scale. It strongly marked the antagonism between flesh and spirit and preached with insistence the doctrine of purity, a doctrine mainly ritualistic but containing also a spiritual idea of purity of the soul from the taint of sin. It divorced religion from the State, making it the pre-eminent concern of the individual soul and brotherhood. Finally its chief aim and scope was otherworldliness, its mission was the preaching of salvation, of an eschatology based in the dogmas of posthumous retribution, purgatory and of a succession of lives through which the soul is tried; and its promised immortal bliss obtainable through purity and the mysterious magic of a sacrament. Alien in origin, alien to the earlier spirit of Hellenism, and always working in the shadow—for none of the later influential schools of philosophy adopted it—it must be reckoned as one of the forces that prepared the way for the inauguration of a new era and a new faith."[20]

Mithras as Mediator

To what extent this applies to Mithraism is not at all clear. Being, as we have seen, a Vedic-Iranian cult in origin when it became established in the Graeco-Roman world at the beginning of the Christian era, with the Isiac already in possession to a considerable extent. It may have become the most effective challenge to Christianity in the empire in the second century A.D. This, however, is open to question. Nevertheless, it did make a strong appeal, particularly in military circles, as has been pointed out, not least because it offered a way of salvation in the struggle with evil both for its votaries and for the world at large, ensuring the eternal well-being of those who were initiated into its mysteries. In the Mazdaean-Iranian conflict between light and darkness Mithras was regarded as the mediator between the supreme being (Ormuzd) and the source of evil (Ahriman). But when the mystery reached the Roman Empire Mithras was primarily the giver of life and light. This he achieved through his sacrifice of the primeval bull, the first creature, thereby bringing abundance upon the earth.

It is this which is displayed in the *tauroctonus*, the well-known bas-relief at Heddernheim in Prussia, where he is represented slaying the bull with a dog springing towards the wound in its side and a serpent drinking his blood to vitalize the vine. But unlike most saviour gods he did not himself pass through death to renewed life. His function was that of the regeneration of the world by his sacrificial act, thereby also imparting immortality to his initiates, who were enabled by his aid to ascend through the seven celestial spheres to the heavenly Empyrean, to a state of beatification free from all the trammels of mundane existence. It is not improbable that behind this symbolism of the tauroctonus there may have been a primeval renewal myth and ritual in which deliverance was wrought by the sacrifice of the primeval bull. But in any case, however permanently efficacious this may have been regarded, it was not repeated in the mysteries. Mithras as the god of light became identified with the *sol invictus*, the Unconquerable Sun, who gave victory to kings, being himself unconquered in his struggle with darkness. As the mediator between heaven and earth, he was the helper of mankind in the destruction of the forces of evil. Thus, he was destined to become the centre of a syncretistic world-religion which acquired a soteriological significance meeting the spiritual needs of its diverse and widespread votaries.

From Persia the cult passed to Asia Minor in the Hellenistic period and accumulated numerous elements in the course of its diffusion. This is apparent in the frescoes and bas-reliefs in the Mithraeum at the ancient city of Dura-Europos on the right bank of the Euphrates between Aleppo and Baghdad, brought to light by the expedition of Yale University and the Academie des Inscriptions between 1929 and 1937, revealing an advanced stage of syncretism. In the bas-relief in the niche at the east end of the narrow hall with its customary benches, dated at about A.D. 168–170, the birth and exploits of Mithras are depicted round the niche together with his conquest of the sun and the banquet of reconciliation. At the top are Kronos and Zeus, and around the inner niche the signs of the Zodiac. In the centre of the bas-reliefs is the killing of the bull, and on the lateral sides are rather later scenes (third century) representing Mithras hunting wild beasts. Proceeding by way of Asia Minor to Rome the cult became further Hellenized, Mithras being identified with Hermes, Apollo and Helios, as well as the dispenser of the nimbus, or *Hvareno*, derived from the heavenly light.[21] But in all the mithraea the tauroctonus was the focal point concentrating attention on his mediatorial functions, and the source of divine grace, waging ceaseless and victorious warfare against the hosts of darkness.

At the end of the second century A.D. emperors in Rome after the reign of Commodus (A.D. 180–193) assumed the surname *Invictus* (invincible), hitherto reserved for Mithras. But while after his initiation governors of provinces, high military officials and prominent members of the public services followed the example of Commodus, and Mithraea were then established everywhere in the ports and along the military and trade routes from Ostia to Hadrian's wall, there is, however, no evidence of the mystery having been at all widely adopted by the common people. Its appeal seems to have been confined almost entirely to the ruling and official classes, and to members of the forces in their campaigns. Indeed, in the third century, when it was at its height, its popularity was due very largely to imperial patronage, and, unlike Christianity, its soteriology was based on Iranian mythology rather than on historical foundations within recent memory and capable of verification in the light of reason.

The scenes represented on the Mithraic monuments often are of a miraculous or mythological character, such as the hero emerging from a rock in a cavern sanctuary adorned with a serpent and adored by shepherds who offer him the first-fruits of their crops and the firstlings of their herds. In other cases he is shown springing from a tree like a vegetation divinity. The neophytes are depicted in acts of devotion, and ascending to the celestial realms, as has been mentioned. There they are represented as being invested with the sun by Mithras and partaking of the heavenly banquet in the solar paradise. This is in contrast to the contemporary Christian iconography in the catacombs in Rome where the figure of the Good Shepherd and the monogram of the first two letters of the name of Christ in Greek predominate.

As the unconquered warrior who never grew old or lost his virility, Mithras, however, was by no means an uninspiring mediator and hero though devoid of high ethical standards and genuine soteriological claims. At his best he was but a member of a polytheistic hierarchy originally primarily concerned with his victorious struggle with the demonic powers of darkness. His mystery escaped persecution and received imperial patronage because it found no difficulty in taking its place in the rest of the pagan cults. This, however, could not save it from extinction because of its inherent weakness and background, notwithstanding its adoption of certain Christian ideas and practices. Therefore, in the fourth century when it met the challenge in full force, the unconquered Mithras fell before the all-conquering Christ whose sign was adopted by the young Illyrian soldier Constantine when he became master of Rome in 312. "*In hoc signo vinces*" was the symbol of the saving act whereby the new world-order was initiated. It is not without significance that the most impressive surviving example of a Mithraeum now lies beneath the lower church of the Dominican basilica of San Clemente in Rome, erected in the time of Constantine. In an earlier level dating from the imperial period the remains of the house of St. Clement may occur. The abortive attempt of the Emperor Julian (A.D. 332–363) to revive paganism, himself a votary of Mithras, failed because it was a spent force as he was compelled to recognize when possibly he asserted, "Thou hast conquered O pale Galilean".[22] Whether or not he actually uttered these words, they sum up the outcome of the prolonged struggle between the two opposed religions in the empire at the beginning of the era.

Salvation in Hinduism

Mithras as a mediator was too much of an abstraction confined almost exclusively to a restricted male congregation of adherents to make a permanent universal appeal as a saviour god, especially as he was not himself a sacrificial victim on behalf of mankind. In Hinduism and Buddhism, again, the stress has been on deliverance from phenomenal existence and the cycle of metempsychosis resulting from the law of Karma rather than from sin as a moral concept requiring for its removal repentance, forgiveness and atonement in a process of redemption. The methods employed for the attainment of emancipation from bondage to the sequence of rebirth have varied considerably, but the underlying cause has remained the same, as has the final goal in the unity of the soul with the Absolute and the passionless peace of nirvana. Escape from the sufferings of conscious existence by a variety of methods and systems has ranged from the Upanishadic conception of the liberation of the soul from all things mundane, and the rationalistic Sankhya dualism, to the Bhakti devotional personal theism of the Bhagavad-Gita incorporated in the great Mahabharata Epic (see chap. IV).

In this remarkable allegorical dialogue all the current ways of salvation have been combined in relation to Krishna as the mythical saviour god; one of the many incarnations of Vishnu, the supreme being. These are by no means reconcilable even when they are unified in the principle of loving faith and personal devotion to Krishna as the saviour of all who surrender their heart, mind and soul to him. Nevertheless, the popular appeal has had a ready response because it has met the deeper spiritual needs liberating the soul from the trammels of karma and rebirth by divine grace. "Give thy mind to me," said Krishna, "be devoted to me, sacrifice for me, honour me. Thus shalt thou come to me, truly do I promise it unto thee for thou art dear to me, I will liberate thee from sin, therefore be of good cheer." By loving, worshipping, reverencing and coming to him salvation is attained (Gita, XVIII. 66).

Nevertheless, the approach and setting of the Gita is essentially Hindu. In striking contrast to the Christian conception of salvation by divine grace and union with the living God, all the ways in which deliverance can be obtained in Hinduism are combined together with the duties of caste, which are exalted above all other obligations. Moreover, Krishna is regarded as a descent, or avatar, of Vishnu who had manifested himself in at least ten sub-human forms to deliver the world from dangers, while in Chapter V of the Gita, which may be a Brahmanic interpolation, no mention of Krishna occurs at all. In the Mahabharata, except in the Gita, he appears only as the Pandara chieftain, and in the later Vishnu Purana he is represented as a gay youth brought up by a cowherd engaging in all kinds of pranks to the despair of his foster-mother and her neighbours. The unruly boy often let loose their calves, and when reproached burst into rude laughter, defiantly snapping his fingers at them. In their absence he drank up their milk, greedily ate their curds, and carried away the rest for the monkeys in the forest who were his friends. Such was his sporting instinct that he chased wild bulls, vicious cows, ferocious wolves and howling jackals, soaring up trees and plunging into the river beneath to scare girls bathing in it; or having stolen their clothes watching their dismay when they see him concealed in the branches with their garments on his arm. All this was harmless enough in a Puck-like youth full of the *joie de vivre*. But the amorous young cowherd attracting to himself in dark-eyed passion sixteen thousand glamorous milk-maids by the ravishing airs he is said to have played on his flute, to say nothing of his relations with Radha his favourite mistress, is scarcely such an innocent and inspiring figure. But this is the Krishna of the popular cult of the Puranas who became the object of erotic devotion and crude pictorial representation in the shrines, very far removed from the sublime revealer of Bhakti in the Gita, and still more so from the incarnate Christ as perfect God and true man, who in the presence of his enemies dared to say "which of you convinceth me of sin?".

Bodhisattva and Buddhahood

To what extent Bhakti was subject to Christian influences is largely conjectural but in any case it was well established long before they were felt in India. Indebtedness to Mahayana Buddhism certainly is apparent in the Bhagavad-Gita, and to some extent in the doctrine of *moksa* (or release). Indeed, it is the combination of Mahayana and Bhakti that approximates most clearly to the Christian conception of salvation, especially in the interpretation of the saviour god in the two faiths. Thus, when the Hindu concept of avatars was brought into relation with that of the Buddhist Bodhisattva, who on behalf of humanity has delayed his attainment of Buddhahood, Krishna and the Buddha both acquired a status and function which proved to be what was lacking in their earlier respective schemes of self-salvation. The Buddha, in fact, as we have seen, then became virtually himself an eternal avatar appearing on earth from time to time to spread his saving Dharma to suffering humanity, in contrast to the southern Theravada denial of anything in the nature of divinity or divine grace playing any part in the attainment of nirvana. Even in the very different milieu of the northern Great Vehicle, the adoption of a transcendental attitude to nirvana and a Pure Land, or Western paradise, was a long process of development and adaptation. This involved the renunciation of the bliss of passionless peace in order that the knowledge of salvation might be spread throughout the world in a manner very different from that originally proclaimed by Gautama after his enlightenment. Something more positive then was required, as in theistic and Bhakti Hinduism, but it was not until the third century A.D. that the Buddha was recognized as a quasi-divine avatar who came to earth out of compassion for mankind as its "elder brother" in a variety of forms adapted to the new environment in China, Japan and Tibet, often incorporating the indigenous gods, ancestors and heroes as Buddhas.

Although Mahayana unquestionably met a very real need as a missionary faith in the Far East, in so far as the doctrine of salvation is concerned it was primarily release from all that was believed to be the cause of the ills to which humanity is heir in the four noble truths. Thus, it was ignorance (Dukka) not sin in an ethical sense that has to be dispelled, though the Buddha is said to have defeated the principle of evil (Mara) at his enlightenment under the bodhi-tree, and in Buddhist legend Mara assumes a personal role. But this can hardly be compared soteriologically with the victory of Christ over sin and death in the Christian doctrine of the Atonement. Nevertheless, as Professor Smart says. "the concept of Mara illustrates clearly the centrality of contemplative insight in the Theravadin tradition".[23]

In Mahayana, however, the representation of the Bodhisattvas as compassionate beings who in their loving-kindness for humanity had postponed their release from suffering, death and rebirth for the welfare of mankind, was nearer to the redemptive self-offering of Christ than the Theravadin ideal of self-salvation through mystical experience, right knowledge and the prescribed techniques to produce "emptiness" (advaya). But the doctrine of "emptiness" was by no means excluded from the Bodhisattva ideal, both the Greater and Lesser Vehicles being agreed about the ultimate goal of liberation from the bondage of the law of Karma and phenomenal existence. The difference between them lay in how this was to be achieved. Was it confined to personal effort in the practice of the Dharma disclosed by the Buddha, or was it with the aid of earthly Bodhisattvas and celestial Buddhas effecting union with the divine? In the Pure Land sects in China and Japan this involved the recognition of the Buddha as a divine being with whom communion was possible and necessary. Thus, in Amidism, as we have seen, Amitabha Buddha was worshipped as a saviour god who bestowed his merits on those who sought his saving power and grace in complete faith expressed in the repetition of his sacred name, thereby enabling them to be reborn in his paradise.

This, however, is so far removed from the original tenets of Buddhism in which the Buddha was regarded as a saviour only in the sense that he had opened the path to liberation along which all must pass to attain nirvana by their own efforts, that it has produced the inevitable reactions of which Zen is an outstanding example. Viewed from the Christian standpoint, while the Mahayana interpretation of soteriology has some analogies to the doctrine of redemption entirely absent in the Theravada conception of self-salvation, nevertheless, the distinction between Christ and the Bodhisattvas or celestial Buddhas is fundamental. The Buddhist "saviours" are innumerable, running into thousands, and the historical Gautama was only one of many, with others yet to come. These semi-divine saints with vast stores of merit were ready and eager to help the faithful to attain Buddhahood. Nevertheless, behind them nirvana remained the ultimate goal even when a Pure Land was a transitory stage in the process of release with the doctrine of karma taking the place of sin.

The Christian Conception of Salvation

In Christianity the perfect self-offering of the saviour is conceived as the source of all saving grace once and for all through the incarnation and sacrificial death of the redeemer. This secured deliverance from sin and restored communion with the living God resting on the merits of Christ alone. In Buddhism and Hinduism there is nothing at all comparable to this conception of salvation. Nevertheless, since in Christianity Christ always has been accepted as the one and only mediator between God and man, the universal and unique redeemer, apart from whom there is no salvation (Ephes. I. 3–14; Col. I. 10–22), what he has accomplished has been regarded as all-embracing. In the biblical doctrine behind the establishment of the covenant with Abraham lay that with Noah, which is represented as a renewal and ratification of the divine plan of salvation going back to the threshold of human history

(Gen. 1. 28; 6. 18; 9. 8 ff.; 17. 1 f., 7 f.). Therefore, from the beginning man is conceived as standing in some sense in a covenant relationship with the Creator at all times and all over the world. This was given a particular application in Israel where when it was broken through human frailty it was re-established continuously, as, for example, at the Exodus, in the time of the Judges, after the Exile, and eschatologically in the Messianic hope. In Christianity this reached its culmination in Christ as the mediator of the New Covenant (Heb. 9. 15-22) summing up all the previous dispensations, God having created man for union with himself and willed that all should be saved. The whole of creation being rooted and grounded in Christ (Col. 1. 16 ff.), the redemption which he wrought once and for all was of universal relevance. The manner of its mediation often may have been obscure but its reality has been none the less efficacious; the Kingdom of God being co-extensive with the entire world and Christ inherently the hope and fulfilment of all man's strivings for salvation.

FURTHER READING

Brandon, S. G. F. (ed.), *The Saviour God*, 1963. see especially Chapters I (Bleeker); IV (Bruce); V (Conze); VI (Smart); XV (Zaehner).
Cumont, F., *Mystères de Mithra*, 2 vols, 1899
Farnell, L. R., *Cults of the Greek States*, vol. iii, 1907
Frankfort, H., *Kingship and the Gods*, 1948; *Ancient Egyptian Religion*, 1948
Franks, R. S., *History of the Doctrine of the Work of Christ, 1918*
Green, E. M. B., *The Meaning of Salvation*, 1965
Grensted, L. W., *A Short History of the doctrine of the Atonement*, 1920
Guthrie, W. K. C., *Orpheus and Greek Religion*, 1952; *The Greeks and their Gods*, 1950
Johnson. A. R., *Sacral Kingship in Ancient Israel*, 1956
Kramer, S. N., *Sumerian Mythology*, 1944
Manson, W., *Jesus the Messiah*, 1943
Nilsson, M. P., *A History of Greek Religion*, 1925
Pallis, S. A., *The Babylonian Akitu Festival*, 1926
Rashdall, H., *The Idea of Atonement in Christian Theology*, 1920
Rowley, H. H., *The Servant of the Lord*, 1952

Chapter Six

SACRIFICE AND SACRAMENT

WHILE salvation has been and is a universal quest which in Christianity is centred in Christ as the unique redeemer, the normal means of the dispensation of this divine saving grace always has been in and through faith in the incarnation, death and resurrection of Christ and the sacramental channels ordained and instituted for this purpose. Here again, however, the sacramental principle is by no means confined to its Christian manifestations. On the contrary, as we have seen, in essence it goes back to prehistoric times, and has been a recurrent feature in most of the higher religions both ancient and modern. This is not surprising inasmuch as they have arisen in an attempt to establish and maintain right relations with the transcendental Powers upon whom man feels himself and his physical environment to be dependent and secure from the forces of evil.

The Sacramental Principle.

Etymologically "sacrament" is an ambiguous term interpreted by St. Thomas Aquinas as "the sign of a sacred thing in so far as it sanctified man", and in its Christian application it is applied to rites usually directly or indirectly ordained by Christ as effective pledges of the bestowal of inward and spiritual grace. In Roman law, however, the word *sacramentum* was used to describe a legal and religious sanction, or an oath of allegiance taken by soldiers to their commanders. In the Middle Ages in Western Christendom its scope was narrowed down to seven rites—Baptism, Penance, Confirmation, Holy Orders, the Eucharist, Matrimony and Extreme Unction—while any ceremony or object endowing a person or thing with a sacred character was given the title of "sacramental", though not instituted by Christ, or held to convey grace *ex opere operato*. At the Reformation in the sixteenth century the term was further confined by the Protestant Reformers to the two rites, Baptism and Holy Communion, of Dominical institution. In the history of religion, however, the sacramental principle has a much wider implication and significance.

Taking the word in its broadest sense as the material sign or symbol conveying something "hidden" and "mysterious" spiritually perceived and made efficacious, as the Greek *mysterion* suggests, almost any person, object or event, set apart and surrounded with ritual prohibitions because it belongs to the sacred order, tends to acquire a sacramental character, as indeed, St. Thomas Aquinas recognized.[1] But it is in the intercourse between the human spirit and a personal deity in an I-Thou relationship that this is most apparent. The universe as the expression of the divine, acting dynamically and immanently in all the processes of nature, is a sacramental conception inasmuch as it assumes divine action and control through material forms and agents to effect some cosmic purpose and determine a spiritual reality. But it is in human nature and its relations that a divine principle in the universe is apprehended most clearly and completely. Therefore, the action of the divine upon man has been conceived more readily as an influence of a person upon a person rather than as the impact of a pantheistic immanental principle upon things.

The self is immanent in the body because it transcends it, and it transcends the body because it is immanent in it. When God is regarded as supra-personal revealing himself to and acting upon mankind sacramentally, the "inward" and the "outward" experience meets in a higher unity which guarantees for the latter its full validity, so that the purposive order holds its own against the merely casual. In this context no hard and fast distinction can be drawn between the "inward" and the "outward". Natural phenomena, human experience, cosmic events and divine activity are interrelated in an I-Thou relationship like that between subject and object, operative through a ritual technique in which the outward elements perceptible to the senses are the embodiment of spiritual reality and the instruments of divine grace and power. Thus, in Christianity it has been generally agreed that the body and blood of Christ are conveyed sacramentally to the believer in some manner in the Eucharist. But it was in the sacrificial context of the Passover and the inauguration of a new covenant by the shedding of the blood of the Redeemer "for the remission of sins" that the ordinance was instituted. Therefore, sacramental communion and sacrificial oblation were brought into a vital relationship.

The Institution of Sacrifice

In his *Lectures on the Religion of the Semites* in 1899 Robertson Smith, in fact, based the institution of sacrifice on a communal meal in which the god and the worshipper together eat the sacred flesh of a "theanthropic animal", at once god and kinsman, to absorb its nature and life.[2] Now it is undoubtedly true that the eating of sacred food, like the pouring out of the blood of the victim, has been the means whereby life, strength and other similar qualities have been bestowed in order to establish a bond of union with the sacred order or with a specific divinity. But Robertson Smith's totemic interpretation of the origin of sacrifice encounters the initial difficulty that the totem, or sacred ally in the form of an animal or plant, eaten under ritual conditions in a common meal by members of its clan, has never been a sacrificial victim. Totemism, moreover, is a specialized institution which certainly has not been of universal occurrence, and it is very doubtful whether it was ever practised among the Semites. Nevertheless, sacrifice in one of its aspects is a *communio* by virtue of the mystic power inherent in the victim by its consecration when it is destroyed in the immolation by the priest and consumed by the offerer sacramentally, establishing a communication between the sacred and the profane.[3]

This, however, is by no means the only or the primary purpose of the institution of sacrifice. In its basic and broader interpretation "sacrifice" (Latin *sacrificium* from *sacer facere* "to make holy") involves the destruction of a victim to maintain or restore a right relationship between man and the sacred order by effecting a bond of union with the divinity to whom it is offered; or to "cover", "wipe out", neutralize or carry away evil and guilt contracted wittingly or unwittingly. From these primary intentions secondary aims have arisen such as the desire to secure the favour of an offended god by the offering of bribes on the utilitarian principle *do ut des*, "I give that thou mayest give"; or as a freewill thank-offering made in recognition of benefits received. These two principles are very closely related. Thus, the offering of the first-fruits of the crops, the firstlings of man and beast, and many other gifts of a similar nature, though conceived as honoraria are not far removed from bribes. The *do ut des* notion, in fact, is seldom entirely absent in any piacular sacrifice however refined and sublimated may be the form in which it appears.

The Piaculum

The very deeply rooted belief that blood is the seat of vitality *par excellence*, or soul-substance, capable of ritual transference from one person or animal to another, is the principle underlying the blood-offering as a piaculum exercising expiatory functions in the removal of sin or evil in its various forms. This is very clearly shown in the Hebrew conception of the *nephesh*, or principle of life, the elimination of which constituted death (II Sam. 1. 9; I Kings 17. 21). Thus, the *nephesh* of the flesh is said to reside in the blood which is poured out on the altar to make atonement because of its indwelling vitality (Lev. 17. 11). Therefore, the Mosaic covenant had to be ratified by the sprinkling of the blood on the altar as a peace offering, and on the congregation of Israel in the Hebrew ritual (Ex. 24. 6-8), thereby effecting a blood bond between Yahweh and his chosen people on a vital relationship, like that of the common meal. Similarly, the rite has atoning value because the sacrificial outpouring of the blood has a piacular efficacy as an expiation for wrong-doing "covering up", wiping out or purging uncleanness, defilement and pollution, or removing evil by transferring it to a "sin-carrier", as in the Day of Atonement very primitive ritual in which all these methods of expiation occur (Lev. 16).

Here, again, the purpose was to re-establish the vital union between God and the nation upon which the welfare of the community and its individual members depended. The piacular victim combined the sacred and the profane by virtue of its inherent potency through its consecration, and so by its destruction rendered harmful influences innocuous. Sin, sickness or death in the piaculum was met with a fresh outpouring of life, and atonement for the evil contracted or misfortune incurred was made by an act of expiation and propitiation. If divine hostility has been aroused by an offence committed deliberately or inadvertently, a victim has to be offered to expiate the fault or error. When the evil was in the nature of a pollution contracted by the breach of a taboo or by contact with something defiling or sacred, such as a corpse, a woman in childbirth, or an unclean animal, cathartic methods or expulsion might be sufficient. Generally, however, they were employed in conjunction with the sacrificial piaculum, the victim having been set apart as a substitute for the offerer with whom it was identified by its consecration.

The piaculum, therefore, has a dual purpose. It may be an attempt to make a fresh start by driving away the accumulation of evil hindering divine benevolence, or the means whereby vitality and strength, spiritual or physical, may be secured by healing the breach. In its primitive modes of expression it has been devoid of any moral qualities in the ethical sense. Nevertheless, as sin under these conditions has been regarded as a ritual defilement, once the taint has been removed by an act of expiation right relations with the sacred and the social orders have been restored. This has been accomplished by the piacular efficacy of the inherent life in the blood of the victim poured out sacrificially to effect expiation and atonement (Lev. 17. 11). Thus, in Hebrew tradition the blood-offerings of the firstlings of the flocks and herds were thought to be more efficacious to this end than those of the fruits of the ground, as is demonstrated in the Cain and Abel story. Even the first born of mankind had to be redeemed (Ex. 20. 22–23. 33; Deut. 16. 1–8), and it is not improbable that this practice had behind it an earlier grim requirement before human victims were replaced by animal substitutes.

Human Sacrifice

Of all blood-offerings the most efficacious in the ancient civilization were those connected with the sacral kingship regarded as the divine embodiments of the god of vegetation. Thus, when their vigour began to wane, or after a reign of a fixed number of years, or when the crops failed, kings were put to death because weakness in the sovereign had reciprocal effects on life in nature. To prevent this calamity, as soon as these symptoms appeared in the occupant of the throne, he or his son, or his substitute, often a prisoner of war, was sacrified. This reached its height in Mexico where it has been estimated that not less than twenty thousand victims perished annually on Aztec and Nahua altars in the calendrical ritual in the fourteenth century A.D. That human sacrifice, especially of children, was widely practised in Palestine is shown by the numerous bodies of infants and young children discovered in the foundations of buildings to strengthen the walls of cities and houses. In Israel children were "passed through the fire" in the valley of Hinnom to Moloch before the Josiah reformation in 621 B.C.,[4] and again just before the Exile. Similarly, the king of Moab apparently did not hesitate to offer up his eldest son as a burnt offering on the wall to propitiate the god Chemosh (II Kings 3. 27). That such sacrifices were thought to be acceptable to Yahweh is clear from the account of the vow of Jephthah in the offering of his daughter (Judges, 11. 30 ff.) and the annual commemoration of its fulfilment. The story of the offering of Isaac recorded in the eighth century midrash with great literary skill (Gen. 22. 1–14) to show that the ancient requirement was not in fact executed was doubtless based on a legend of a sanctuary where human victims were offered; the concession in this case being represented as a reward of faith.

The Day of Atonement

To replace a human victim by an animal was an easy transition when animals were thought to share with mankind the same life principle which was liberated when the blood was poured out sacrificially to nourish, revive or propitiate the deity, or to make atonement for the sins committed or the evil contracted. In Israel originally it would seem that at the annual expiation on the tenth day of the seventh month atonement was made by the high priest for himself and the priesthood by a sin-offering of a bullock and a burnt-offering of a ram. Then two he-goats were "set before Yahweh" and lots were cast over them to determine the one to be a sin offering and the one to be presented to Azazel, a desert goat-demon. Yahweh's victim was slain and upon that for Azazel was heaped all the guilt of the nation as the sin-receiver, or "scapegoat", rather than as a sacrificial victim. It was then dispatched to the desert carrying with it the pollution of the sanctuary and its servants. In its present form three stages in the development of the annual purification can be detected in the Levitical narrative. The first appears to have been a simple expiation instituted in the middle of the fourth century B.C. confined to the offering of a bullock and a ram and the two goats (Lev. 16. 3–10). This was subsequently elaborated and transformed into a cathartic atonement ritual with censings, the manipulation of the blood of the bullock in the Holy of Holies and on the altar, together with the transference of the iniquities of the people to the "scapegoat", the carcasses of the victims being destroyed by fire in a void place (Lev. 16. 11–28). Finally, a note was added ordaining the Day of Atonement as a "high sabbath", set apart as a fast on which "no manner of work should be done", and the people were to "afflict their souls" (Lev. 16. 29–34a).

This very primitive ceremonial based on evil as a miasma removable by purifying agents and expulsion by a sin-receiver was interpreted in post-exilic and Rabbinical Judaism in terms of ethical and spiritual concepts, the piacular being represented as a demonstration of repentance. The violation of the law and of the commandments of Yahweh was an affront to his holiness requiring genuine penitence and amendment involving a clean heart and a broken spirit. Without these essential qualities the blood of bulls and the ashes of a heifer could not avail, and so in the later literature as the daily sacrifice was held to expiate unintentional breaches of the Torah (the Law), the Day of Atonement removed sins committed with a "high hand" when the observance was accompanied by true repentance.[5] Moreover, when the Temple was destroyed in A.D. 70 and the sacrificial worship inevitably came to an end, the provision made before the catastrophe for special confessions of sin and prayers for forgiveness in the synagogue liturgy for the Diaspora, and all those who were prevented from attending the Atonement rites in the Temple at Jerusalem, tended to place the emphasis on the deeper significance of the cathartic ritual.

It is not surprising, therefore, that in the Early Church with its own particular conception of sacrifice and priesthood centred in the vicarious self-offering of Christ, in an age saturated with sacrificial ideas, its interpretation was related to the Day of Atonement ceremonial and theology. Therefore, the victorious ascended redeemer exalted as a prince and a saviour offering his eternal sacrifice in his priestly mediatorial capacity was likened in the Epistle to the Hebrews to the Jewish high-priest in the Holy of Holies exercising his sacerdotal function on behalf of Israel. But whereas he failed to make perfect those who drew near, Christ beyond the veil alone, it was contended, was "able to save to the uttermost those who came to God through him," because he had removed the barrier of sin that separated man and God by his own sacrificial death (Heb. 5. 6 ff; 7. 25; 9. 24; 10. 1, 4).

Unlike the Aaronic Levitical priesthood and its sacrificial system in the Old Covenant, which according to the author of the Epistle to the Hebrews were only copies, or Platonic shadows, of eternal realities (Heb. 9. 23), the high priesthood of Christ, after the order of Melchizedek, was eternal belonging to the "age to come" in the heavens. By his incarnate life, death, resurrection and ascension he had opened a new and living way to God so that those who were united to him by faith and sacrament partook of this eternal life while still pursuing their earthly pilgrimage. That which was dimly foreshadowed by the entry of the transitory Levitical high priest into the Holy of Holies on the Day of Atonement became an accomplished fact and timeless reality in the self-offering of Christ on the Cross; his blood-shedding having atoning efficacy because by it "he entered in once for all into the holy place, having obtained eternal redemption" (Heb. 4. 3; 9. 12, 24).

The Eucharistic Sacrifice

This interpretation of the death, resurrection and ascension as a priestly oblation of supreme value and validity involved the perpetuation of the offering in the heavenly sanctuary with its mundane counterpart in a cultus on earth. If the sin offering had been made once and for all, the eucharistic thank-offering remained to be offered "until he come" at the Parousia. The sacrifice on the Cross was thought to have made divine grace operative in redeemed humanity as a "royal priesthood" offering "spiritual sacrifices", the eucharist being brought into relation with the corporate life of the Church. The last gathering of the apostolic company on the night of the betrayal constituted the nucleus of a liturgical rite which, whatever may have been the original intention, could hardly fail to become the *anamnesis*, "showing forth" sacrificially the drama of redemption analogous to the Jewish paschal memorial, once the death of Christ had acquired a sacrificial significance. Thus, in the Early Church the eucharist was closely related to the perpetual sacrifice of Christ in heaven, the offering of the gifts of the consecrated elements on the altar on earth symbolizing their heavenly presentation by the eternal high priest on the altar on high. Therefore, a sacerdotal hierarchy was established in line with the Levitical priesthood in Judaism but tracing its descent not from Aaron but from Christ and his apostles.[6]

That the sacrifice of Christ was regarded as a blood-offering is clear from the institution of the eucharist in the sacrificial context of the Passover, and the reference to the shedding of his blood as a New Covenant "for the remission of sin" (Luke 22. 20; Mark 14. 24; I Cor. 11. 25). This did not require repetition annually, or at fixed periods, as in the Jewish prototypes, the eucharist being interpreted as the unbloody commemoration and continuation of the sole redemptive offering for the sins of the world, instituted by Christ himself at the Last Supper. Once he had been slain as the priest and victim his liberated life could be immolated in a ritual sacrifice and made available for all mankind for all time under the sacramental signs of his broken body and poured out blood. The eucharistic memorial is unbloody because it is made by means of the sacramental elements as the efficacious symbols of the all-sufficient sacrifice on the Cross.

Since in the institution of sacrifice it is not the death of the victim that is the essence of the oblation but the surrender of its life,[7] in the dual capacity of priest and victim the risen and ascended Christ is represented as laying down his life in order to take it again, and bestow it in all its fullness in and through the appointed channels in his mystical body, the Church. Having abrogated the Passover with the eucharistic memorial, the New Covenant in his blood shed upon the Cross was sealed, whether or not in fact the institution occurred at a paschal meal, and apart from anything that had been said at it about the repetition of the rite, it became the central act of worship in Christianity as the New Israel. Around it developed a theology and liturgiology which has constituted a new departure in the spiritual and symbolic significance of the sacrificial blood offering.

This, of course, has been a matter of considerable controversy in Christendom, but the doctrine briefly summarized and approved by the Lambeth Conference in 1930 is in general accord with that now widely held in the liturgical movement, affirming "we continue a perpetual memory of the precious death of Christ who is our Advocate with the Father and the propitiation for our sins, according to His precept, until His coming again. For first we offer the sacrifices of praise and thanksgiving; then next we plead and represent before the Father the Sacrifice of the Cross, and by it we confidently entreat remission of sins and all the other benefits of the Lord's Passion for all the whole Church; and lastly we offer the sacrifice of ourselves to the Creator of all things which we have already signified by the oblations of His creatures. This whole action in which the people has necessarily to take its part with the Priest, we are accustomed to call the Eucharistic Sacrifice."[8] Regarded in these terms the doctrine is quite definitely in line with the essential meaning and purpose of the institution of sacrifice in its sacramental setting as it has been conceived and practised in theistic religions throughout the ages.

Sacraments and Symbols

Similarly, the sacramental principle has a much wider range than the sevenfold system of the medieval Church, reduced by the Reformers to the two Dominical ordinances of Baptism and the Eucharist, as it embraces the deepest emotions, experiences and evaluations in every state of culture and in most religions where, as we have seen, rites obtain in which the "inward" and the "outward" meet in a higher unity. Mental and spiritual activity is only known as embodied, the embodiment being effectual sacramental signs of that which it confers, effecting what it signifies. As Edwyn Bevan has pointed out, symbols are of two kinds. There are those which as visible objects stand for something of which we have direct knowledge such as the Union Jack or the Cenotaph in Whitehall. These are national emblems indicative of certain patriotic qualities without giving any specific information about the nation or its role in the world, unlike those symbols which convey hitherto unknown knowledge to those who see them, or to "what is beyond the range of human experience."[9] It is to the latter category that the sacramental principle belongs. As "no man has seen God at any time", the deity and the things of the divine order can be visualized and made actual under temporal conditions only by signs and symbols. Certain rare souls with unusual mystical gifts or occult powers may be able to reach a perception of the timeless, spaceless presence of the transcendental without these material aids. Hindu mystics, however, usually resort to the techniques of Yoga exercises in the contemplation of the Infinite, while in Western Christendom those who reached the heights of mystical experience, such as St. Teresa of Avila, St. John of the

Cross, St. Bernard of Clairvaux and St. Thomas Aquinas, had regular recourse to the sacraments of the Church.

As human beings are normally accustomed to think symbolically and to make mental or pictorial images out of the materials presented to the senses, ultimate reality in its various aspects and modes of expression is perceived phenomenally by means of effectual signs through the instrumentality of matter. These may be pictorial or plastic images or aniconic objects, such as trees, rivers, springs, mountains, stones or rocks, often bearing some resemblance to a supernatural being believed to be the source of the sacred power of which they are the vehicle. Therefore, they have been duly venerated and treated in a ritual manner like the menhir anointed by Jacob at Bethel after the nature of the sanctuary had been disclosed to him by its divine "owner" in a dream, interpreted in terms of a Yahwistic theophany (Gen. 28. 10–12). Behind the story was the ancient practice of incubation, or sleeping at shrines and sanctuaries in order to obtain dream-oracles from the divinity localized at the sacred place, regarded as a sacramental visitation conveying knowledge of certain events, or seeking guidance and aid in that which lies ahead. Similarly, the animals drawn in the decorated Palaeolithic caves to control the fortunes of the chase and promote their propagation, were executed in the belief that the sacramental treatment of the representations would have beneficial effects on the food supply.

In agricultural society the first-fruits may have been regarded as sacred because they were thought to embody the soul-substance, or vital principle, of the vegetation spirit, and so were dedicated to the god controlling the harvest. Being in consequence taboo the crops could be eaten as ordinary food only after they had been desacralized, and the malevolent forces of evil, equated with famine and pestilence, overcome. Hence the performance of sacramental rites having as their purpose the establishment of a bond of union with the benevolent powers to secure a fresh outpouring of vital potency, and the expulsion of malign influences. Thus, for example, among the Ainu in Japan the new millet had first to be eaten ceremonially by the old men in the form of sacred cakes identified with and addressed as the cereal divinity, thanking him for the good crops and beseeching him to nourish the people. They then solemnly partook of the cakes in much the same way as they killed with profuse apology and ate a bear cub at the Bear Festival at the end of the winter.

In Mexico during the May festival in honour of the war god Uitzilopochtli, the Aztecs fashioned an image of him in dough in which a quantity of beet seed and roasted maize was mixed and moulded with honey. It was then covered with a rich garment by noblemen and placed in a chair on a litter. Accompanied by maidens in white and young men in red robes, both crowned with garlands of maize, it was carried in procession to the foot of a pyramid-shaped temple. There amid strains of music of flutes, trumpets, cornets and drums it was taken to a shrine filled with roses and venerated with reverence and awe. The young men laid at the feet of the image pieces of paste made of beet and maize in the shape of its large bones which were consecrated to transform them into the actual limbs of the god. Human victims were then offered to him and the image was broken into small fragments and given to the people fasting as his flesh and bones. Portions of the sacred food were taken to the sick in their houses by their relatives. Similar rites were repeated at the winter solstice when the heart of an identical dough effigy of the same god, fortified with the blood of children, was pierced and cut out by a priest and eaten by the king, the rest of the image being consumed sacramentally by the male members of the community.[10]

To dismiss these widespread and numerous illustrations of symbolic images and their sacred meals in varying states of culture as "the heathen in his blindness bowing down to wood and stone" is to misconceive the underlying sacramental principle as an integral element in the history and comparative study of religion. It is because the figures have undergone what is believed to have been a fundamental change by their consecration that they have become the channels of the divine life and its qualities inherent in them, establishing thereby for those who partake of them a bond of union with the sacred order. It is, in fact, to complete the identification with the source of transcendental power that the sacramental link (*communio*) is forged, and when this is done in a communal ceremony the life of the entire community is believed to be renewed by communion with the beneficent Powers. It is only on the rationalistic assumption that there is no reality at all corresponding to the outward and visible signs that they can be dismissed as valueless nonsense. But nowhere has this unreality been accepted by those who have seriously practised such rites. Thus, in Hinduism the *arca*, or consecrated cult-object as the embodiment of Vishnu, is regarded and treated by the Vaishnavas (i.e. the worshippers of Vishnu) as the god himself. Therefore, it is given the same tendance sacramentally. It is not until this relation of the god to his material vehicles is abandoned that sacramentalism becomes idolatry, the symbol having then lost its symbolic reality for the votaries.

In Hebrew tradition the situation is confused and contradictory because both attitudes were maintained in pre-exilic Israel. When the desert tribes settled in Palestine, so firmly established was the Canaanite cultus that its images continued to be venerated by the Hebrews, often in association with the worship of Yahweh. This was most apparent in the great sanctuaries in the Northern Kingdom, such as Bethel, Dan, Gezer, and Taanach, where bull-worship flourished with asherim, statuettes, teraphim and the ephod (Judges 17–18; I Sam. 19. 13; 21. 9). It was this, coupled with the adornment of the Temple in Jerusalem with similar symbolic representations, that led the mono-Yahwists under prophetic influence to denounce the pagan gods and their images as worthless idols devoid of reality, and to claim, therefore, that their worship and their outward signs were an affront to the god of Israel. Hence the prohibition in the decalogue against the making of any graven image, or the similitude of Yahweh, on the ground that unlike the indigenous Canaanite gods, and those of the surrounding nations, he was incapable of being symbolized in any animate creature or inanimate object. Therefore, in post-exilic Judaism all divine representation was strictly forbidden, and even his holy name was not allowed to be uttered lest it should be taken in vain (Ex. 20. 4; Deut. 5. 8).

In Christianity the Incarnation introduced an entirely new and different conception of the sacramental principle and its symbolism. Once it was recognized and accepted that God had in fact become visible in the world in human nature and had instituted and ordained a sacramental system as the appointed means of grace, it was no longer possible to maintain this attitude to signs and symbols. Therefore, in the second century paintings began to be executed in the catacombs, and sacred images played an increasingly prominent part in the cultus when the persecutions came to an end in 313. These often took the form of Christian symbols such as the monogram of Christ, a dove, fish, anchor or olive-branch. In the Eastern Church icons painted in oil on wood, or rendered in mosaic, ivory and other materials, in representation of Christ, the Madonna and the saints in Byzantine styles were venerated.

At the end of the seventh century, however, a movement arose against the worship of these holy pictures, partly on account of superstitious uses, but also in antipathy to presentation of divinity in any medium, stimulated by Muslim influences. This was vigorously pursued by the Monophysites who maintained a single divine nature in the person of the incarnate Lord. Therefore, declaring them to be idolatrous, efforts were made to prohibit their use in the Byzantine empire, until the case for images was decided in favour of their adoption at the second Council of Nicaea in 787. Already Gregory the Great, about 600, had commended them as having their value for the instruction of the illiterate. While the Eastern Orthodox Churches banished statues, they retained and encouraged the treatment of icons with reverence; in

Western Christendom no such distinction was recognized. Henceforth the didactic employment of images and pictorial art was widely adopted, reinforced by a decree of Charlemagne, which incidentally modified the Nicaean decisions.[11]

The controversy being so very intimately associated with its Christological background, the making and veneration of pictures and images were determined to a considerable extent by the attitude taken to the doctrine of the Incarnation and its sacramental expression. In the defence of their use for the instruction and the stimulation of the devotion of the faithful, particularly the unlearned, now generally conceded alike by both Catholics and Protestants in some form or another, a distinction was made between the worship (*latria*) that might be offered exclusively to God, and the veneration (*dulia*) paid to saints and cult objects. This differentiation was complicated by the closely related sacramental value believed to be inherent in material and pictorial representation, though it covered the prohibition of making any image of God the Father, which has been generally maintained.

The Incarnation, however, placed the second person of the Holy Trinity in a very different position. His dual nature, human and divine, taken in conjunction with the divinely ordained sacramental system, afforded adequate grounds, as has been pointed out, for a corresponding interpretation of image-worship, while excluding so far as possible idolatrous and superstitious aberrations always liable to occur in this form of devotional practice. This was done in Western Christendom by recognizing the lawfulness of having pictures or statues of Christ and the saints, but limiting the cultus associated with them to the reverent regard commonly shown to sacred places and occasions; such as removing the hat in church, on passing a war memorial or funeral, or at a graveside. The gesture is one of respect shown to the person represented, or to a hallowed acre, as a symbol of the presence of whoever or whatever the image symbolizes rather than to the object itself. But St. Thomas Aquinas maintained that since Christ is adored with the worship of *latria* it follows that the adoration directed to his image is an act of *latria*.[12] Be this as it may, it is only when, as in the Byzantine Church, icons were worshipped in their own right that there has been a danger of their becoming, at any rate officially, the recipients of the worship alone reserved for the triune Godhead as such.

Sacramental Sacrifice

It was, however, when the sacramental principle was brought into relation directly with the institution of sacrifice that it fulfilled its purpose most clearly inasmuch as then the aim always has been to establish communion with the benevolent powers on which man depends for his well-being. In Christianity the sacraments have been centred in the Incarnation instituted to perpetuate the union of God with man in the historic person of Christ as the Word made flesh, in and through a visible organization, the Church, regarded as his mystical body. In Vedic India, on the other hand, where sacrifice was quite as fundamental, it acquired a pantheistic setting and significance. Even so in the first instance it was regarded as the means whereby the gods obtained heaven, and were enabled to exercise their benevolent functions in sending rain, causing "the sun to return at dawn to ripen the harvest", as well as that by which man existed and acquired wealth and hidden knowledge of the inner mystery of being.

The Vedic Offering

As the masters of this all-sustaining sacrifice the Brahmins brought under their own control every aspect of creative supernatural power in heaven and on earth. This, as we have seen, was facilitated by the conception of the pantheistic cosmic principle, Rta, beyond the gods, governing alike the transcendent and mundane order and associated with Varuna as the regulator and protector of the moral laws of the gods and the universe, together with Agni, the lord of sacrifice (see chap. IV, pp. 71). It only required this basic principle to be made subject to the control of the Brahmanic ritual as "the womb of Rta" to establish the complete supremacy of the priestly offering, the priesthood usurping the position formerly held by the sacral kingship when it was declared that "the Brahmin is entitled to this universe by his superiority and his birth."[13] As in the Brahmanas "the sacrifice is the god Prajapati at his own sacrifice", in this capacity the priest became Prajapati renewing the creative process, inaugurating the social organization and ensuring the continuance of the cosmic order and the prosperity of the community.[14] The victim also represented the universe in its several parts, the body of the Creator (Prajapati) being broken anew and restored for the conversion of the world.

As in Vedic India all things were vitalized and sustained by the sacrificial cultus, the Brahmins held the secret of the universe in their grasp because they alone had a correct knowledge of the ritual texts and techniques. Moreover, this was brought into conjunction with the sacramental principle when the king-god Soma, as the fermented plant originally equated with the royal deity, was thought to be slain as the sacrificial victim when he was crushed to extract his life-giving sacred ambrosia to revivify those who partook sacramentally of this nectar of immortality.[15] This was essentially a priestly action like the fraction of the consecrated host in the sacrifice of the Mass, though differing from it in that the Vedic manipulation governed the world of the gods as well as the world of man. In the Brahmanic tradition apart from the rite the gods had no independent existence or functions as personal beings so that all individuality was submerged in the priestly office and its offering until at length existence was reduced to the universal sacrifice of the primal man Purusha and Prajapati, whence everything emanated. It was against this absolute sacerdotalism that the Upanishadic movement reacted, substituting for the Brahmanic sacrifice, its metaphysical mysticism based on a new theory of the universe[16] distinct from that which lay behind the ritual order of the Brahmanas, and opening the way for the more radical refutation of the claims of the Brahmins and their offering by Mahavira, the founder of Jainism, and by Gautama the Buddha, both of whom belonged to the rival Kshatriyas (princes and warrior) caste. In the Vedic rite, however, all the sixteen priests had to partake of the Soma, the two principal Brahmins imbibing very large quantities, like Indra the chief warrior-god, who quaffed vast amounts of it, becoming highly intoxicated and thereby gaining power over his enemies by its divine exhilaration.[17]

The Iranian Yasha Ceremony

This orgiastic aspect of the sacramental Soma cult underwent considerable modification when it was introduced in the Yasna Haoma ceremony as the central rite in Zoroastrianism, without losing its original sacrificial and sacramental qualities as the source of spiritual efficacy. Acquiring a personality of its own it then became deified, and the sacrificial immolation of the Haoma, the Iranian counterpart of Soma procured from the Elburg mountains in the Caucasus was symbolized by its pounding in a mortar to extract its life-giving juice in order to confer immortality on the worshippers who partook of it. In the Avesta, Haoma is at once a prophet (*Duraosha*), a plant (*Zaire*) discovered by him, and a heroic figure. As a god he was the son of Ahura Mazdah who became the first priest of the cult, immolating himself so that from his body broken perpetually the divine essence streamed forth.[18] Thus, the dying plant-god has been represented as bestowing his own life sacramentally and sacrificially upon his votaries, and he also has effected the regeneration of the universe.[19] So potent and efficacious was the mystic plant believed to have been that Angra Mainyu, the Evil Mind, was said to have created a lizard to destroy it, but it was prevented by ten fish continually protecting it in paradise so that it remained the sacramental earnest of everlasting life.

The Mystery Cults

This is an outstanding example of the anticipation of the central rite of Christianity since Haoma was regarded as both god, priest and victim incarnate in the sacred plant and pounded to death in perpetuity to confer immortality on those who drank the life-giving juice proceeding from him. Its historical background, of course, was very different from that of the eucharist, being essentially Indo-Iranian, and although the resemblance between the principal doctrines of Zoroastrianism and Christianity is remarkable, the relation of the two faiths to each other is by no means apparent. It was in the sacerdotal aspect of Mithraism rather than in Christianity that the Haoma cultus found a place and significance, both Mithras and his initiates, when they attained the degree of "Lion", participating in a sacramental banquet in which wine was substituted for haoma.

To what extent, if at all, plagiarism is to be detected in these rites is very conjectural, though it is not improbable that it occurred on the Mithraic side, at any rate in respect of the sacramental meal. But apart from the bread, wine and water in the initiation rite, parallels with the Christian eucharist detected by Justin Martyr[20] are relatively slight, while its mythological setting is definitely solar. Thus, the celestial banquet of Mithras was with the sun-god and his heavenly allies, just as in another scene he is represented holding a drinking-horn in the left hand receiving a bunch of grapes from Ahura Mazdah. Moreover, unlike the Haoma ceremony, it was confined to the initiation of the neophytes rather than being a perpetual sacrificial memorial of historic events culminating in a supreme act of self-offering; the killing of the primeval bull, as we have seen, having a very different significance from that of the redemptive sacrifice on Calvary on behalf of all mankind.

In the other mysteries which were current in the region in which Christianity took its rise at the beginning of the new era, the parallels are even less apparent. Thus, the sacred meals and lustrations were never a prominent feature in the Graeco-oriental rites, notwithstanding their sacramental appeal as a means of attaining a blissful immortality. It was upon this end that the cultus was concentrated, thereby supplying an urgent need absent in the official religion of the Hellenistic age and the Roman Empire. In the Eleusinia, for instance, while the mystai underwent numerous preliminary ablutions which included bathing several times in the sea, and partook of a kind of barley porridge (*kykeon*) at this stage in their initiation, there are no indications that the lustrations were sacramental, effecting a rebirth, or that the *kykeon* contained the divine substance of Demeter. That the goddess was a corn totem is an unwarranted conjecture on the part of Jevons, as is the suggestion that her worshippers "annually partook of the body of their deity, i.e. of a cake or paste or posset made of the meal and wheat and water."[21] Farnell says, "the drinking may have been sacramental in a less mystic sense; the worshipper drank the cup that the Goddess had drunk of, and shared in her sorrows, but there is no trace of the idea of transubstantiation, and the fullest communion at Eleusis was obtained not by eating or drinking sacred food, but by seeing a sacred sight."[22]

This applies equally to the Thraco-Phrygian Attis-Kybele cult where again, according to Clement of Alexandria and Firmicus Maternus, at some point in the initiation the votary "ate out of the timbrel (drum), drank out of the cymbal, and went down into the bridal chamber (*pastos*)",[23] but for what purpose is not explained. It is true that in his liturgy Attis is called "the corn-stake", but to say with Farnell that it was a sacramental communion of cereals and fruits with bread eaten "as the very substance of the body of the divinity of Attis",[24] is as conjectural as that of Jevons' contention respecting the Eleusinian evidence, there being no adequate reason to suppose that Attis was the mystic bread in a sense which Demeter is never found to have been. More plausible is the suggestion of Hepding that in some cases there was an actual ritual burial as part of the ceremonial, the initiate rising from the grave with the divinity to a new life.[25] This has been a prevalent custom in initiation ceremonies, and the procession to the bridal-chamber commemorating the death of Attis would naturally suggest the rebirth of the mystai from the cave-sanctuary of the goddess. Firmicus Maternus, in fact, viewing the situation from the Christian standpoint, suggests that "death is the sequel to the pagan meal as an antidote to which is the bread and cup of Christ giving the true food of life." But such an allegorical interpretation would of necessity be a post-Christian attempt to contrast two sacred meals without throwing light on the original nature and purpose of the custom.

When the ecstatic rites of the Anatolian Magna Mater Kybele were introduced into Rome from Asia Minor at the end of the Hannibalic war (205–4 B.C.) they were limited to her temple on the Palatine Hill until the restrictions were relaxed by Claudius in imperial times. Then at the spring festival, the death and resurrection of her youthful lover Attis was celebrated from March 15th to 25th as a ritual renewal of nature which reached its climax at the Hilaria on the 25th with rejoicing, banqueting and libations. This was followed on March 28th by the gruesome *Taurobolium* at the sanctuary of the goddess (the Vatican phrygianum) on the Vatican Hill in the second century of the present era. It was apparently to these initiations that the formulae quoted by Clement of Alexandria and Firmicus Maternus refer. If this were so, it was the Attis votaries who engaged in a ritual meal, eating from the drum and drinking from the cymbal, in the Antonine period (A.D. 138–161), before they descended into a ditch. There crowned with gold and wreathed with fillets they stood below a grating over which a bull (or ram) was stabbed to death. Drenched in its blood the neophyte emerged reborn for twenty years, or as a late inscription records, perhaps under Christian influences, he was *renatus in aeternum*.[26]

This crude ritual regeneration originated in Asia Minor before it made its way into the West from Cappadocia or Phrygia in the second century A.D. In the next two hundred years it was widely adopted, spreading through the Empire from Rome to Gaul, Spain and North Africa, in association with the worship of the mother-goddess. To what extent, if at all, it was adopted and practised by Mithraism, as has often been asserted, is difficult to determine, but in any case it belongs essentially to the cult of Kybele. On those who underwent the ordeal doubtless it made a deep impression, though in the earliest inscriptions it is said to have been practised on behalf of the emperor and the empire. But since the neophyte was fed with milk like a new-born babe at the vernal equinox, according to the Neoplatonist Sallustius,[27] it would seem that it was regarded as a sacramental process of rebirth in the fourth century A.D. (when it was especially popular) like the Hellenistic Isiac and the Sarapis cult with its sacramental meal in the Sarapaeum.

In the orgiastic Dionysian *omophagia*, when the frenzied Thracian votaries are said to have torn to pieces a live bull embodying the god Zagreus (or Dionysus) in order to devour its sacred flesh, [28] this savage attempt of the *Maenads*, or *Bacchae*, to become possessed by their god did not commend itself to the sober and unemotional Greeks. Nevertheless, ecstasy is infectious, and in the sixth century B.C.: the Dionysiac with its sacramental eating of the bull in some manner gained very considerable popularity in Greece despite its unhellenic character. The orgies, in fact, may have found a place in the Orphic mysteries notwithstanding the efforts to restrain or eliminate them, but in becoming a mystical movement, based on the story of the Titans having killed and eaten Dionysus, while some of the wilder rites may have survived, they became repellent. Indeed, the Orphic ban on killing and eating animals may have been to some extent to eliminate the *omophagia* inherited from the Dionysiac. Anyway, before the Christian era the wilder escapades had been repressed and sublimated in Orphism without removing the Titanic background of the mysteries, substituting for them a more spiritual conception of release from reincarnation and the attainment of union with the divine by purity of life.

The primary purpose of the Orphic ritual was to raise the soul to its native divinity through sacraments which conferred divine life on the recipient, and so enable him to gain immortality. This was accomplished by a ritual regeneration which retained the ancient Bacchic conception of sin as ritual impurity, and of man becoming divine by a series of rebirths, but recognizing that "the grace sought was not a physical intoxication but spiritual ecstasy, the means adopted not drunkenness but abstinence and rites of purification".[29] The aim of initiation was to free the Dionysiac soul from its fleshly bondage and secure union with the divine nature rather than absorption into and unity with the Absolute as the ultimate zero of existence, as in the Indian conception of Brahman and nirvana. Orphism, however, did introduce oriental categories into the West, preparing the way for the welter of oriental mystery cults into the Graeco-Roman world after the conquests of Alexander the Great in the fourth century B.C. And it certainly played its part in the Christian *praeparatio evangelica* inasmuch as it introduced an ethical element in its sacramental approach to the deeply laid struggle between good and evil, however vitally different the two interpretations of sin and salvation may have been.

This, indeed, applies to all the Graeco-oriental mystery cults. As a background of faith and practice they provided a death and resurrection symbolism though in none of the cult-legends was it suggested that the death and resurrection symbolism of the divinity was the self-offering of a *historical* person at a particular time and place. Sacred meals not infrequently occurred but they were not the culminating point in the cultus, while rebirth tended to be either a reincarnation in another body or a renewal, rather than a fundamental regeneration in this life in union with the risen and ascended Saviour enduring in eternity. Behind all the mysteries lay an esoteric polytheistic myth and ritual from which they were never able to extricate their sacramentalism.

Christianity, in fact, became virtually a mystery religion when it broke away from its Jewish moorings at the end of the first century, and had to render its own theology and worship explicit in the Roman Empire. But this was accomplished in complete independence of the pagan cults. Its conception of deity remained firmly based on Judaic ethical monotheism, reinterpreted in terms of its own Trinitarian faith, in which divine transcendence and immanence were brought into conjunction, centred in Christ as the Lord of the universe and the Saviour of redeemed humanity. This was perpetuated in the eucharist in its paschal sacrificial setting, combined with a sacramental efficacy which cannot have been derived from either the Mystery religions or Judaism. The New Covenant was established and sealed in the blood about to be shed in the supreme act of Atonement, recalling the Sinaitic Mosaic offerings and those of the Temple worship. They had no counterparts, however, in the pagan mysteries, for which incidentally St. Paul and the early fathers of the Church had nothing but contempt and repudiation. Equally unthinkable for the Jews was the idea of partaking of the blood of the Covenant, as abhorrent as eating food sacrificed to idols was for St. Paul (I Cor. 8. 4). Therefore, the Eucharist occupies an independent position in sacramental sacrifice, standing apart from either the Jewish or the pagan parallels, fulfilling all that was of permanent value and significance in them.

Judaism, as St. Paul contended, was our tutor to bring men to Christ (Gal. 3. 24), and the mystery cults were not without their influence in preparing for the acceptance of the faith as a sacramental drama, offering to all who embraced it the promise of a blessed afterlife, and an inner mystical experience calculated to quicken their spiritual life for all time. When it became a catholic movement in the civilized world, it had to formulate its theology and express its worship in accordance with the requirements of its Gentile environment. Therefore, it moulded itself on the pattern of the mysteries as a way of salvation through symbolic rebirth and mystical sacramental union with God, raised to the ethical plane and removed entirely from the setting of the ancient seasonal drama and its polytheistic associations. As it was in the eternal order of reality that Christ was claimed to have conquered, redemption and renewal of spiritual life were offered, unknown and unattainable in any rival system or cult. Therefore, Christianity ultimately prevailed because it constituted the culmination of man's spiritual pilgrimage and provided a different gift of life from that obtainable in any other religion.

FURTHER READING

Angus, S., *The Mystery Religions and Christianity*, 1925
Bevan, E., *Symbolism and Belief*, 1935; *Holy Images*, 1940
Cumont, F., *Oriental Religions in Roman Paganism*, (Chicago), 1911
Gavin, F., *Jewish Antecedents of the Christian Sacraments*, 1928
Gayford, S. C., *Sacrifice and Priesthood: Jewish and Christian*, 1925
Gray, G. B., *Sacrifice in the Old Testament*, (Oxford), 1925

Guthrie, W. K. C., *The Greeks and their Gods*, 1950; *Orpheus and Greek Religion*, 1935
Hicks, F. C. N., *The Fullness of Sacrifice*, 1930
James, E. O., *Sacrifice and Sacrament*, 1960
Kennedy, H. A. A., *St. Paul and the Mystery Religions*, 1913
Leeming, B., *Principles of Sacramental Theology*, 1960
Marett, R. R., *Sacraments of Simple Folk*, 1933
Nock, A. D., *Conversion*, 1938
Oesterley, W. O. E., *Sacrifice in Ancient Israel*, 1937
Quick, O. C., *The Christian Sacraments*, 1952
Smith, W. R., *Lectures on the Religion of the Semites*, 3rd. ed., 1937
Stone, D., *A History of the Doctrine of the Holy Eucharist*, 2 vols., 1909

Chapter Seven

THE HOPE OF IMMORTALITY

THOUGH the hope of immortality is by no means peculiar to Christianity, having, in fact, constituted one of the most universal and integral elements in the history of religion, nevertheless, it has acquired a fundamental and characteristic significance in Christianity from the belief in the resurrection of Christ and all that this has implied in the work of redemption. Indeed, without this affirmation as an historical event the Christian religion would cease to be Christianity to all intents and purposes. Behind it, however, lies a variety of interpretations of the cult of the dead and of the afterlife, which require more detailed consideration if the specifically Christian doctrine is to be assessed in its several aspects and its conceptions evaluated. These go back to their dim beginnings in the Old Stone Age when Neanderthal man first attempted to answer the question of questions, "If a man die shall he live again?" From then onwards death has been regarded as such an intrusive and disruptive event in the natural sequence of ever-renewing life that it has called forth a combination of deeply seated emotions, hopes and fears, respect and veneration, which have found expression in the attitude adopted towards the corpse and its disposal, and its ultimate destiny.

Death and the Afterlife

At first it sufficed to protect the body from molestation and to recover any bones that were missing or disturbed, though sometimes it was tightly flexed perhaps to prevent a revengeful ghost from returning and wreaking vengeance on the survivors. More often, however, judging from grave goods interred with the deceased which included food offerings, weapons and artefacts, sometimes in profusion, it was to provide for his well-being and necessities in the future life, after the mortal remains had been revivified by the aid of such vitalizing agents as blood, or its surrogate red ochre, shells and other amulets. Generally the next life was envisioned as in some sense a continuation of earthly existence though on a different plane of being, making it possible for things to be done in a new manner; sometimes as a sort of "looking glass world" where the normal order is reversed. But food, drink, tools, weapons and warmth usually have been required, including an amazing quantity of priceless funerary furniture in ancient Egypt and in the royal tombs at Ur in Mesopotamia, recently excavated by Sir Leonard Woolley, belonging to the third millennium B.C. (c. 2700–2500), in which a wholesale interment of courtiers, attendants and soldiers has been revealed, who accompanied their sovereign to the afterlife to continue their service to him and his queen.[1] These spectacular graves, however, are very difficult to explain as the Sumerian and Babylonian funerary equipment elsewhere was so very meagre compared with that of dynastic Egypt, and nowhere have any indications of human sacrifice been found in Mesopotamia.

Egypt and Mesopotamia

In pre- and proto-historic times the contemporary civilizations in the valleys of the Nile and Euphrates appear to have developed along more or less parallel lines in respect of mortuary beliefs and customs, until they diverged in the third millennium B.C., perhaps on account of their different climatic and geographical conditions and social structures. Up to the third dynasty in Ur (c. 2100 B.C.), apart from the splendour of the royal obsequies, the graves contained relatively simple offerings and goods. Then came a diminution in the furnishing of Sumerian interments, whereas after the union of Upper and Lower Egypt the immense power of the divine kingship in the Nile valley found expression in the construction of the royal mastaba tombs, culminating in the gigantic superstructures in the form of the pyramid, which have led to the old kingdom being known as the Pyramid Age (2700–2200 B.C.).[2] In these "everlasting habitations" of their royal occupants, their glorious afterlife is described and extolled in the Pyramid texts or inscriptions inscribed on their walls. In them are portrayed the Elysian fields located in the northern part of heaven, where they were destined to dwell for ever in idealized conditions of perfection in their mummified and reanimated bodies which had been rendered imperishable, and in some cases become one of the circumpolar stars which never set.

In Mesopotamia, on the other hand, the gods had decreed that immortality should be withheld from man when they created him to keep them supplied with life-giving offerings. Therefore, in Babylonia the inevitability of death was accepted, though the continuance of the earlier disposal of the body and its tendance suggests that some conception of a conscious existence beyond the grave survived. In what it consisted, however, was so obscure and unattractive that it afforded little or no opportunity for reflection or speculation. Thus, in the available texts (e.g. the Gilgamesh epic, the myth of Adapa, and the Descent of Inanna-Ishtar to the nether regions) the afterlife is represented as a shadowy existence in a sombre land of no-return (Irkalla) beneath the earth, ruled by the goddess Ereshkigal and her husband Nergal. This house of dust and darkness is surrounded with huge walls and carefully guarded gates with bolts and bars, and in it dwell rulers and commoners alike without distinction; irrespective of age, class, status or ethical behaviour. Sometimes it took the form of a hollow mountain into which the Apsu, or watery deep, flowed, unless the entrance was in the west across the sea reached by a ferry. But wherever it was situated its denizens were huddled together in dust as dismal shadows in a semi-conscious condition destined to wither away like the vegetation in the devastating heat of a Mesopotamian summer.[3]

The Hebrew Conception of the Afterlife

Much the same mortuary procedure obtained in Palestine both before and after the arrival of the Hebrew tribes in their "promised land". Nothing persists like funerary customs and beliefs, therefore it is not surprising that the firmly established Babylonian and Canaanite cult of the dead survived among them. Thus, the Palestinian custom of interment with food vessels, amulets, jewellery and other ornaments, sometimes in caves when they were available, remained little changed after their occupation of the country at the end of the Bronze Age and the beginning of the Iron Age (c. 1200–1000 B.C.). The death taboo, the sacredness of the corpse, and the customary mourning ceremonies were observed, while Abraham purchased the cave of Machpelah at Mamre (Hebron) from Ephron the Hittite, in accordance with Hittite laws and feudal duties, to make it secure as the patriarchal family vault where its members could be "gathered to their fathers". (Gen. 23; 49. 29, 31). But grave furniture became less abundant after the Israelite settlement in Canaan, preoccupation with the afterlife being of little importance in the Israelite monarchy. Cave burial then ceased, a few of the kings having been buried in multichambered shaft-tombs in association with the mortal remains of their predecessors. Family graves usually were located in the native town of the occupants as near the house as possible, the underlying belief being that of funerary fellowship and the consolidation of kith and kin rather than of a communal afterlife.

These customs and cult practices and their survivals suggest that the pre-prophetic beliefs of the Hebrews about the dead and their requirements beyond the grave were much the same as those that had always prevailed in Palestine and in the rest of western Asia. It was, however, by the Babylonian attitude to the afterlife that the Deuteronomic pre-exilic legislation was determined, denouncing the earlier beliefs and customs and prohibiting necromantic intercourse with the dead through oracles, divination and spiritualistic seances with their mediums. Thus, in the early days of the monarchy attempts were made to put away out of the land those who had "familiar spirits and the wizards" because this traffic with the departed was incompatible with the absolute sovereignty of Yahweh over both the living and the dead. The popular belief, however, was firmly entrenched that the deceased in the capacity of *elohim* were in possession of superior divine knowlege and supernatural power. Therefore, they continued to be consulted surreptitiously, and Saul, who had issued decrees for their suppression, did not hesitate to pay a clandestine visit to a medium at Endor when he was at the end of his tether in his campaign against the Philistines, in the hope of obtaining occult knowledge of the fate of the forthcoming battle on Mount Gilboa. In response to his request the *nephesh* of Samuel was thereupon made to appear from his subterranean abode as a ghostly figure wrapped in his familiar cloak, and confirmed his fears of the results of the fatal conflict on the morrow (I Sam. 28. 7 ff.).

From this graphic account of that ominous night it appears that at the beginning of the monarchy in Israel, making due allowance for the narrative having been compiled under Deuteronomic influences, it was still believed that the dead could be materialized and invoked by the mediums, and that they were then recognized and were *au fait* with contemporary situations and their outcome. As Samuel was represented as engaging in dialogue with Saul, and as passing sentence of death upon him, clearly he was regarded as living a conscious life in the nether regions. It was to bring the practice to an end that the Deuteronomic conception of Sheol was adopted as a land of no-return, and its denizens as shadowy shades devoid of consciousness, surviving in a state of silence and forgetfulness as *rephaim*, or "powerless ones", rather than *elohim* (i.e. "divine beings") (Ps. 87. 11 ff; 94. 17; Job. 26. 6; 28. 22; Is. 14. 9 ff.). Moreover, they were regarded as being outside the jurisdiction of Yahweh who was solely "the god of the living" concerned only with his chosen people and their fortunes in the land in which he had placed them in this world. Therefore, in Sheol they were remembered no more and cut off from communion with him (Is. 7. 19; Ps. 6. 5; 30. 9; Deut. 14. 1 ff.).

Though the earlier belief in a continuance of conscious existence was never eradicated, so long as the Deuteronomic attitude prevailed the only hope of survival was in the descendants in the family, and, if a man died childless, by his brother marrying his widow to raise up seed to him (Deut. 25. 5 f.). It was the *nephesh*, or breath-soul, that was withdrawn at the dissolution, the indwelling breath of life (*ruach*), breathed into Adam and repeated at every subsequent birth, being merely a shadowy ghost-soul and replica of the living organism. After the Exile it was conceived as an impersonal effluence capable of existence as an independent entity after the body had returned to the dust of which it was made, preserving some continuity of identity with the individual.

The Homeric Hades

In the Homeric literature in Greece a similar conception of Hades recurs in the idea of the *psyche* as a breath-soul escaping from the body in the last gasp of the dying person. Though it was regarded as a shadowy double of the man it was completely disembodied and devoid of consciousness like the Hebrew *rephaim*. In its gloomy realm in Hades it was merely an insubstantial phantom without emotions or perception (*nous*); a witless feeble shade flitting about like a bat, incapable of joy or sorrow. The mother of Odysseus gazed vacantly at her son and only when she drank dark blood did consciousness momentarily return to her.[4] Nevertheless, as Rhode has pointed out, the description in Homer of the offerings at the obsequies of Patroclus are inexplicable if the soul immediately upon its dissolution "flutters away insensible, helpless and powerless, and, therefore, incapable of enjoying the offerings made to it."[5] Though the account may have been to some extent a piece of ostentatious barbarism on the part of Achilles, it is more likely, as Nilsson says, to have been a carry-over from the rites formerly performed at the tomb of the prince of Midea near Dendra in Pre-Homeric times.[6]

Afterlife in the Mystery Religions

Moreover, as in post-exilic Judaism, the conception of the dead as impotent shadowy shades devoid of consciousness could not be the final verdict on the nature and end of the human species. Annihilation might be a conceivable alternative to a progressively conscious and active afterlife in some way related to and determined by mundane existence, but not a phantasmal meaningless impotence in a cul de sac harbouring inert shadows, except for a privileged few of quasi-divine celebrities in inaccessible Isles of the Blest. It is not surprising, therefore, since the Homeric Olympian gods with their permanent gulf between mortals and immortals had nothing to do with the dead, that it was to the mystery divinities and their esoteric cults that recourse was made, because they were able, as Cicero affirmed, to teach men not only "to live in happiness but also to die with high hope."[7] Their main purpose, in fact, was to secure for their initiates a happier lot beyond the grave, for the words of Plutarch, "death and initiation clearly closely correspond, word for word and thing for thing. At first there are wanderings and laborious circuits, and journeying through the dark, full of misgiving where there is no consummation; then, before the very end, come terrors of every kind, shivers and trembling, and sweat and amazement. After this, a wonderful light meets the wanderer; he is admitted to pure meadow lands, where are voices and dances and majesty of holy sounds and sacred visions. Here the newly initiated, all rites completed, is at large."[8]

This, as we have seen, was attained at Eleusis by whatever happened in the Telesterion at the culmination of the rites in the sanctuary of Demeter to identify the mystai with the saviour-goddess through a mystical death and resurrection ritual. Thereby they were redeemed from a shadowy existence in the subterranean regions of darkness and inertness, and destined to enjoy for ever the delights of walking in the meadows of Persephone. There beyond the grave awaited them the supreme joy of basking in the golden sunshine in the flowery fields beside streams of living water beneath trees laden with delicious fruits, shaded by thickets of myrtle and cooled by gentle breezes, singing and feasting, and listening to the sublime strains of the Elysian choir. But attractive and reassuring as was this hope of salvation and eternal life for the Eleusinian initiates, it failed to give any ethical significance to the hereafter.

It remained for the more barbaric and orgiastic Thraco-Phrygian Dionysiac, after it had been sobered under Orphic influences, to introduce a moral content into the Mystery afterlife by making the destiny and condition of the soul beyond the grave dependent upon its conduct on earth. Being essentially divine by virtue of its Dionysian origin; through incarceration in a body (soma) as in a tomb (sema) corrupted by its inherent Titanic nature (see. chap. V, pp. 103 f.), immortality consisted in freeing the soul from its prison-house by the adoption of the Orphic way of life. But such was the impurity clinging to it from its

Titanic inheritance that notwithstanding the grace and strength received by its observances deliverance required a succession of reincarnations before the soul could pass to the Isles of the Blest as its final Elysium.

Pre-existence and Reincarnation

This hope of immortality and eschatology combined with the doctrine of metempsychosis and the assurance of eternal blessedness, though in one form or another very influential in both Platonic and Orphic speculation, was by no means a new or isolated phenomenon. On the contrary, the doctrine called "Orphism" had a very wide currency before it was introduced as an intrusion in Greece, and given an ethical interpretation by Pindar, Plato and Virgil, far removed from its earlier ritual observance and Olympian mythology of the Homeric tradition. Indeed, behind it lay the very ancient and widespread idea of the pre-existence and reincarnation of the disembodied soul going back to its animistic manifestations almost everywhere in primitive cult with no ethical significance; and predominant in the great oriental pantheisms where interminable successions of lives were believed to be required to reach their goal in "communion with the whole universe", as Radhakrishnan has described nirvana. The doctrine of metempsychosis and its law of karma in its Upanishadic guise in Hinduism, however, cut across the earlier conceptions of a blissful immortality spent in the Vedic paradise ruled over by Yama, and it was not easily reconciled with its conception of the afterlife and retribution beyond the grave. In the Upanishads man is represented as continually determining his own destiny during his present life, the law of karma being an operation of natural causality in which divine intervention and redemptive suffering had no place or significance. In each rebirth expiation is made for the deeds done in a previous existence, deliverance being secured through Vedantic knowledge, or in Buddhism by the enlightenment attained by Gautama and made accessible by the Dharma he devised. Every action performed had its intrinsic consequences for good or evil, though, as we have seen, in the Anatta interpretation of the process there is no obvious connexion between one birth and another, or any adequate reason for the transference of the karma of one organism to another.

The cycle of births in successive lives was never explained by Plato in his ethics of existence and metempsychosis. The aim was to become as like God as is humanly possible, while "the true penalty of wrongdoing is one that cannot be escaped. There are two patterns eternally set before men, the one blessed and divine, the other godless and wretched; and, in their utter folly and infatuation the evil do not see that they are growing like the one, and unlike the other, by reason of their evil deeds; and the penalty is that they lead a life answering to the pattern which they resemble."⁹ Therefore, retribution is not regarded as in the karma doctrine on the principle of *lex talionis*, an eye for an eye, a tooth for a tooth, meted out in an exact proportion on the basis of vegeance and retaliation, justice and desert. But as Plato conceived all souls as having had a divine origin their activities are essentially moral, and transmigration is a natural corollary unless release from the body could be secured to make it possible to embark on a purely spiritual career in the afterlife.

The soul being capable of striving after "wisdom", and by its essential nature surviving the dissolution of the body it has animated, it is imperishable and immortal, distinct from its corporeal integument as a "separable entity" derived from the supreme deity. Its purpose is to correlate absolute reality apprehended by pure knowledge with the phenomenal world, known by sensation, and to bring the body into harmonious relationship with the idea of the Good. But successive lives of the soul are required to secure purification and wisdom by philosophy, thereby setting free the individual from the body altogether, and enabling it to return to the heavenly sphere whence it came. This may be not less than three thousand years even for "the guileless and true philosopher", but for the majority a cycle of ten thousand years will be required to free the soul from its carnal appetites.¹⁰ As emancipation of the soul is essential for the complete mystical apprehension of pure Truth and Being, divine communion is impossible of attainment while physical conditions still survive and deity plays no part in the Platonic process of obtaining eternal life. The divine element in the soul has to render itself indestructible by its own unaided efforts to become immortal.

How far Plato believed in a personal immortality is a matter of debate, but that he would have subscribed to Wordsworth's "Ode to Immortality" is difficult to believe in the light of his conception of the pre-existence of the soul involving its survival after death in terms of the Orphic-Pythagorean notion of transmigration. As in the theory of Ideas the natural world is set over against the ideal spiritual world, so in the human organism the material body is contrasted with the rational or immortal aspect of the soul, which, as Aristotle maintained, alone survives the death of the body, being connected with God through the active reason. For Aristotle the self-consciousness of the individual, which depended upon memory and its physical attributes, perished at the dissolution, whereas the higher part of the soul at the top of the body possessed attributes of divine intelligence (i.e. the active reason) which made it immortal. All other activities, knowing, feeling, memory and moving, were bound to the body and, therefore, destined to be destroyed, the reasoning element alone being independent of the phenomenal world and so eternal. Pre-existence was denied, parentage being regarded as the cause of succession in offspring, and so eliminating reincarnation and transmigration.

The Apocalyptic Afterlife

In post-exilic Judaism and Christianity the hope of immortality developed along different lines in spite of the very close resemblance between the Hebrew Sheol and the Greek Hades, and the influence of the Platonic and Aristotelian conceptions of the nature and destiny of the soul on the Patristic and Scholastic formulation of the Christian doctrine. In Israel this was due in the first instance to the extension of the universal sovereignty over Sheol of Yahweh after the Exile (Is. 26. 19; Wisdom 2. 1–9; 4. 17–19; Dan. 12. 2), though it was not until the emergence of the apocalyptic literature in the second century B.C. (180 B.C.–A.D. 100) with its Iranian eschatological background that a resurrection of the dead with retribution was definitely established. Sheol then became an intermediate state for the faithful Israelites, and the final abode for the rest of mankind (II Macc. 7. 9–11; 12. 43 ff.). By about 170 B.C. it had been located in the far west and divided into departments for particular cross-sections of the community with appropriate rewards and punishments respectively for the righteous and the wicked (I Enoch, 22. 2; II Enoch, 3–21; II(IV) Esdras 6, 81–98; III Baruch, 2–11)

The Christian Conception of Immortality

No attempt, however, was made to systematize either the Jewish or the Christian apocalyptic eschatology and the final state of the righteous or the wicked was variously situated and of different durations. Thus, as Paradise was placed in the celestial regions such as the third heaven, or in some unknowable place outside the earth, so the infernal regions were regarded as being on earth, in Sheol and of unknown provenance. In the synoptic gospels in the New Testament Gehenna was the state allotted to sinners, equated with unquenchable fire, weeping and gnashing of teeth, either interminably or as remedial and variable. [11] Only once, however, is eternal punishment quite definitely asserted, and then as the consequence of everlasting separation from God by persistent impenitence (Matt. 25. 46). Although the imagery of rewards and penalities is indistinguishable from that of apocalyptic Judaism, as is the general eschatological setting, the emphasis is on an immediate parousia of Christ. His second advent would bring the existing era summarily to an end with the elimination of evil and the establishment of a new heaven and a new earth wherein righteousness would prevail. Then evil was destined to be destroyed for ever and God to become all-in-all.[12]

Comparatively little is said about the fate of the damned except in the few Matthaean references to eternal punishment. In the fourth gospel the emphasis is on eternal life which Christ as the Logos bestows upon the faithful here and now, and whom at the Parousia he will gather together to share in the general resurrection.[13] Only once is it asserted in this Gospel that the wicked will have any part in this consummation, though it is said that "he who believeth not in the Son shall not see life but the wrath of God abideth on him" (John 5. 28 ff.; 3. 36). His ultimate destiny is spiritual death as the result of being eternally separated from God, and, therefore, excluded from heaven.

Christ it seems assumed the existence of a future life, apparently in the apocalytic terms current in Palestine at the time, without advancing any arguments in support of the contention, or throwing any new light on the problem by his teaching, so far as it has been recorded in the New Testament. But the conviction that in him the Messianic hope was fulfilled led him to assert that there were standing with him those who should not taste of death till they had seen the Son of Man coming in his kingdom (Matt. 16. 28). Thus, it would appear that at first the reign of God on earth was expected to be achieved within the existing generation, eternal life as a present reality being an inevitable consequence of membership of the kingdom transcending all temporal and spacial limitations. Unlike the Deuteronomic contention that the dead were outside the jurisdiction of the God of Israel, the Christian hope of immortality was grounded in the union of the soul with the living God which cannot be severed by death, its citizenship being in heaven rather than in a chosen nation on earth. "For here we have no continuing city, but seek one to come" (Heb. 13. 14). Consequently, the relationship of man to God begun under existing conditions finds its completion sealed by the resurrection of Christ, because he had established "a new and living way" to the life of the age to come here and now. His followers were conscious of "the power of an endless life" by virtue of their status and spiritual endowment. They realized that "to be carnally minded is death, but to be spiritually minded is life and peace" and "the body is dead because of sin; but the spirit is life because of righteousness" (Rom. 8. 6, 10). In this state of salvation "though our outward man perish, the inward man is renewed day by day" (II Cor. 4. 16). As St. Paul recognized, to walk in the spirit it is necessary to die daily by "crucifying" the flesh with the passions and lusts thereof (Gal. 5. 24 R.V.). Thus, the death and resurrection of Christ introduced a new approach to the Jewish conception of immortality by making eternal life an ever-present experience realized in this world as a mystical dying with him in order to be raised from death to newness of life in the fullness of redeemed humanity, as this was incarnationally in him. Moreover, it made it possible to look forward with hope and confidence to the consummation not only beyond the grave but at the end of time as an accomplished fact begun under temporal conditions.

The Pauline Doctrine

While it was within Judaism that the Christian doctrine of immortality and its eschatology arose in the first instance, nevertheless, in it several streams of thought and practice current in the Hellenistic age met and were diverted in its own main channel. From Judaism, in addition to the current apocalyptic ideas, the Pauline belief in the dualism of the flesh (*sarx*) and the spirit (*pneuma*) was inherited as constituting the personality. The sharp distinction, however, between the carnally minded and the spiritually minded is suggestive of Hellenic influence, notwithstanding the absence of the Orphic-Platonic doctrine of the flesh as inherently evil. Thus, St. Paul by affirming that the body is "the temple of the Holy Spirit" capable of being made "a living sacrifice, holy, acceptable unto God" (I Cor. 6. 19; Rom. 12. 1) clearly did not regard it as fundamentally evil. Distinguishing the *psyche* as the animating principle, and the *pneuma* as the higher spiritual life, equated with the *nous*, or mind, he enunciated a doctrine of the resurrection of the body as distinct from the immortality of the soul. It was not the *nous* as a divine principle of our intelligence that survived the dissolution and became absorbed in the Ultimate Mind, or a pre-existent immortal soul of simple structure akin to the immutable Idea that regained its place in the eternal world when it was divested of its fleshly integument, as the Platonists maintained. Nor was it the resuscitation of the mortal remains as the apocalyptic school supposed. While "flesh and blood cannot inherit the kingdom of God", even in this life the spiritual resurrection of the redeemed, it is contended, is an accomplished fact; the body having been made an "instrument of righteousness" subservient to the interests of the spirit (I Cor. 15. 44; II Cor. 5. 1–10). Therefore, in the hereafter, and when the present mundane order vanishes away at the imminent Parousia, the soul will be clothed with a body "not made with hands, eternal in the heavens". Then death will be swallowed up in victory, the body that is raised will become spiritual though it will be identical with that which was "sown" because the entire personality has been redeemed (I Cor. 15. 42 ff., 54; Rom. 6. 5–8). A disembodied state will not suffice because along this Pauline line of reasoning, which is not without its obscurities and conjectural constructions and interpretations, human personality is represented as neither corporeal nor solely spiritual. So in the afterlife it must continue to function in an incorruptible celestial body.

The Resurrection Body and Everlasting Life

Unlike the animistic survival of the disembodied soul and its phantasmal manifestations, in which the earthly conditions are reproduced in the spirit world, as in so many mortuary cults, the Christian hope of immortality is primarily that of resurrection to eternal life, dependent upon the death and resurrection of Christ. In this tremendous event time and eternity meet, and those who are risen with Christ experience both on earth and in the eternal world this gift of God through him. This is possible because man is endowed with a quality of life, and is capable of a relationship with God transcending temporal conditions and limitations. He is immortal both by divine right, having been created with an immortal soul, and by grace through incorporation in the risen life of Christ which has already triumphed over death. This is an experienced reality here and now under existing conditions for those who are living on a higher spiritual plane by virtue of their baptismal union with God through Christ. By incorporation in him they have already passed from death into his risen life experiencing newness of life destined to endure and reach its climax beyond the grave in the eternal world (Rom. 6. 4; Col. 3. 3 f.; John 11. 25 f.).

In the New Testament, it is true, there is some confusion about a realized and futurist eschatology because the Parousia was at first expected to be an imminent occurrence at any moment. Then the final state would be determined as in the Iranian-Judaic last judgment, and sentence passed by God upon both the body and soul of each individual. This opened the way for the introduction of the idea of a bodily resurrection as an immediate event (I Thess. 4. 13 ff.) in Christian eschatology, which has recurred from time to time ever since, often with not very edifying results, not least in the modern Adventist sects. For the apostles who had been the daily companions of Jesus during his incarnate life, and who were convinced that they had been called to be witnesses of his death, resurrection and ascension, the apocalyptic second advent and judgment in the immediate future were the natural sequel to all they claimed to have beheld and experienced, and the commission they had received (Acts 10. 42). It was, however, recognized that Christ himself had declared that "it was not for them to know the times or the seasons which the Father had set within his own authority." Moreover, "it is not yet made manifest what we shall be. We know that if he shall be manifested we shall be like him for we shall see him even as he is" (Acts 1. 7; I John. 3. 2). When the process of redemption is completed "all will attain unto the unity of the faith, and of the knowledge of the Son of God unto a fullgrown man, unto the measure of the stature of the fullness of Christ" (Ephes. 4. 13). In the eternal world the mortal body will be "clothed upon" to fit it to be the instrument of its own personality in its spiritual environment (II Cor. 5. 1–5).

This conception and interpretation of immortality has at least the merit of fulfilling the more edifying and essential elements in the universal belief that death is not the ultimate end of either human existence and personality, or of the cosmic order. It is now sometimes asserted in theological circles that it is only concerned with eternal life as a particular quality of life and relationship with God in Christ, not with human survival after death. This, however, is to ignore the fact that eternal life of any kind presupposes immortality, and the Christian hope is deeply rooted in the universal belief in the continuation of life in some form or another beyond the grave, whatever may be its location, character and duration. Arising in Judaism and then passing into the Graeco-Roman world, the Christian doctrine maintained the salient features of its Judaeo-Iranian apocalyptic background. It went, however, beyond them in its assertion of a Messianic expectation that had been fulfilled, involving the resurrection and reunion of the body and soul in and through the risen Christ. It also looked for a final consummation in which all things would become subject to the perfect will and purposes of God in infinite time; all creation being centred in him and sharing in his victory over sin and death (Col. 1. 16 f.).

This went far beyond the Greek conception of immortality, though it was under the influence of Platonic and Aristotelian conclusions that the Christian doctrine was formulated by the early Fathers of the Church and the Scholastics in the Middle Ages. As a Platonist St. Augustine maintained that the soul was neither corporeal nor material, being a higher kind of existence *sui generis* than body or matter.[14] At the general resurrection the righteous would be clothed upon with a spiritual body, while Aquinas in the thirteenth century brought together body and soul as a fundamental unity. The soul being, however, independent of the body could lead a separate existence from its physical integument, but a disembodied entity was not a complete human personality. Therefore, at the resurrection the body was an essential requirement in the afterlife. Man representing the connecting link between the temporal and the eternal orders, "form" and "matter" united as a microcosm only could fulfil their proper conditions inherent in human personality. The soul as "form" gave substantiality to the body, unifying and determining it, and being intelligent and rational in man endowed with the power of reflection, intrinsically independent of the body, it neither grew nor decayed with it; hence immortality.[15]

This made possible the Christian interpretation of the soul endowed with eternal life, created independently *ex nihilo* by God as capable of conscious existence separate from the body. In the Middle Ages this conception of the independent creation of each human individual as a special divine creation at birth was generally held in opposition to the view, usually known as "traducianism", that the soul was a product of generation transmitted by the parents to their children. This theory had been advocated by some of the early fathers (e.g. St. Gregory of Nyssa, Tertullian, Apollinaris), and by St. Augustine as a spiritual generation, to account for the transmission of original sin, either by the process of generation, or from the soul of the parents. While in any of its interpretations it was rejected almost unanimously by the Scholastics, it was revived at the Reformation, especially by the Lutherans, and in more recent times by a few Roman Catholic theologians (e.g. Rosmini, Gravina and Hermes). But whatever may be the place and function of the parents in the process of procreation in relation to the soul, and the precise moment when it becomes infused in the unity of human personality as a rational being, for the theist it is a divine creation. The alternative has been pre-existence and reincarnation of a disembodied soul which invariably has ended in a state of nirvana, or passionless peace in which individuality was absorbed in the divine spirit as a river is lost in the ocean.

Against this the Christian doctrine of the hereafter has maintained the idea of the "spiritual body" as the "form" of the human spirit which passes into the life everlasting. "It is sown a natural body; it is raised a spiritual body," as St. Paul affirmed. Only such an affirmation of a body which is continuous with our present body and yet is of a different nature makes sense of the survival of the individual as a spiritual personality. Behind this interpretation of eternal life lies the worth of human beings as persons, possessing everlasting value in the eyes of God, capable of development in the spiritual sphere as they are in the mental and physical orders in the evolutionary process in its mundane manifestations. It is this conception of a conscious afterlife that has found expression in a progressive intermediate state between life on earth and its final achievement in the eternal world. Equipped with a spiritual body quickened anew by the divine spirit, the faithful departed have been conceived as going from strength to strength until at length they attain a state of perfection and the unhindered vision of the majesty of God. In the words of St. Thomas Aquinas, "there may be some impediment on the part of the good in the way of their souls receiving their final reward in the vision of God immediately upon their departure from the body. To that vision transcending as it does all natural created capacity, the creature cannot be raised before it is entirely purified: hence it is said that nothing defiled can enter it, and that the polluted shall not pass through it. Such persons must be cleansed in the next life before entering upon their eternal reward."[16]

In its medieval form too much stress doubtless was laid upon purgation conceived in accordance with the judicial practice of the age, and too little on a spiritual development in the attainment of the beatific vision in its fullness. Nevertheless, it embodied a conception of the nature of man and of the future life which is in harmony both with our evolutionary knowledge and thought today, and the strivings of the human mind throughout the ages to grapple with the problem. From time before memory man has seen in the rhythm of nature the prototype of his own progressive sequence from the cradle to the grave, and that which lies beyond death is a renewed and regenerated immortality. "The path of the just is as a shining light that shineth more and more unto the perfect day."

The Islamic Afterlife

In the parallel Muslim approach to the problem by Averroes which Aquinas incorporated in his Christian philosophy and theology, with the introduction of translations of Aristotelian works from Arabic sources at the end of the twelfth century, Aristotelianism was conceived increasingly in a Neoplatonic sense, excluding altogether personal immortality and the creation of the soul and of the universe *ex nihilo*. Taking as his model the unorthodox *Grand Commentary* of Averroes, Aquinas controverted the theory of the Active Intellect and the Passive Intellect as separate from the individual soul.[17] This view destroyed human personality so far as rational thought is concerned, and renders immortality at most a question only to be settled by revelation, as Averroes maintained. Indeed, Al-Ghazali, the Muslim Sufi mystic theologian, accused Averroes of denying resurrection. This charge its founder denied, affirming that while the body in the hereafter will be the same as that of this life, being "a representation of what is seen in this world, it will not be that very thing *in essentia*. For what has persisted cannot be born again, except in so far as it is individualized; and existence can be bestowed only on the semblance of what has perished, not on the object that has perished in its identity."[18]

In Islam the doctrine of resurrection was borrowed mainly from Judaism and Christianity with Zoroastrian additions. The body would be corporeally resuscitated on the day of judgment "as at the first creation", but in the Qur'an little is said about the abstract aspects of the body-soul relationship. Attention is concentrated chiefly on rewards and punishments in the afterlife, with vivid descriptions of the conditions of heaven and hell based on the Iranian and Judaeo-Christian apocalyptic imagery and eschatology with important differences. Whether or not the soul is inherently immortal is not discussed philosophically as in n.edieval Christianity. In the Qur'an the future life is regarded as a divine gift rather than as survival. After death everyone is thought to be visited in the grave by two angels who interrogate them before their ultimate fate is determined. Those who are able to give satisfactory answers concerning their faith are allowed to sleep undisturbed until the Last Day, but the infidels are assigned to the torments of hell. Unbelief, in fact, is the sin *par excellence* in Islam, and the horrific "wrath to come" awaiting the unbelievers is unsurpassed in any other eschatology, as are the catastrophic convulsions when the trumpets will be sounded by the angel Israfil. The antichrist will be slain by Jesus, God and Magog will be released, all creatures will die and be released at the general resurrection to give an account of their deeds, and their works will be weighed in the balance, as in the Egyptian Osirian Judgment. Those who successfully cross the bridge pass over hell and go to the seven regions of paradise.[19]

These delights of paradise, like the torments of hell, are understood literally in the sense of the terrestrial experiences of the men of the desert. Thus, the joys are of purely mundane character "mid gardens and delights, and rejoicing in what their Lord hath given them, and that from the pains of hell-fire their Lord preserved them." They will "eat and drink with healthy enjoyment, recline on bridal couches served by dark-eyed houris and youths like pearls. Therein shall they pass to one another the cup which shall engender no light discourse, no motive of sin". The trees are of pure gold with branches laden with precious stones and delicious fruits hanging within easy reach of believers, their taste being unknown to mortals.[20] This goal of idealized earthly life of luxurious living and unrestricted carnal indulgence, which surpasses anything conjectured in the Egyptian Elysian fields, implies the resurrection with a body capable of enjoying these sensuous pleasures. To what extent, if at all, they were understood as allegorical expressions of spiritual ideas, comparable to the interpretations given to their counterparts in the Johannine apocalypse, is difficult to know. In some of the later sects they were to some extent so regarded, but this has not been the orthodox view of either the bodily enjoyments of believers, or of the inconceivable tortures of the damned. Both are determined by belief or disbelief rather than by ethical considerations, independent of any spiritual satisfaction in the bliss of the beatific vision, or of remorse at the deprivation of its realization by those doomed to suffer condemnation.

In the Sufi movement, under the influence of Al-Ghazali, the divine spirit in man is regarded as restless until it finds union with the Creator in a mystical relationship which, however, involved bringing the soul and God together in an increasingly pantheistic unity nearer to that of its Indian prototypes than to either Islam or Christianity. Nevertheless, it was conditioned by its rigidly monotheistic Muslim background and by Christian influences.[21] As it became established in the scholastic period, mystical ideas gained popularity and Al-Ghazali was able to combine his Sufistic mysticism freely with orthodox traditionalism, often hardly distinguishable from that of the Christian mystics. Similarly, the Spanish and orientalist Archbishop Raymond Lull, in his attack on the Averroists in the twelfth century, fought the philosophy of Islam with an intimate knowledge of its tenets and the common ground with Augustinianism and the Aristotelianism of the Schoolmen, in which the maintenance of the resurrection of the body and the eschatology of the Qur'an were cardinal dogmas. The Averroistic contention that the soul in all men was one, its parts being separate only in the bodies it animated, was anathema both to Muslims and Christian theologians, though Averroes and St. Thomas Aquinas agreed in their harmony of faith and reason, and their common Aristotelian approach.

Indeed, until the eighteenth century the Scholastic philosophy of immortality remained substantially the basic attitude to the future life and the nature of the soul. Thus, in Europe Descartes (1596–1650) fell back on the Platonic distinction of mind and matter, while for Leibniz (1646–1716) the soul was the primary "monad", or simple spiritual substance, in human nature, self-active, indestructible and pre-existent, and, therefore, immortal. The pantheism of the Dutch Jewish philosopher Spinoza (1632–77), on the other hand, left no room for personal immortality. God was infinite substance with a number of attributes, and mind and matter were two aspects of one underlying divine Reality with extension as one of them. Since the human mind was regarded as part of the divine impersonal intellect, freewill, personality and immortality were ruled out. Kant (1724–1804) maintained that a moral law grounded in an absolute good demanded an "endless progress possible only on the supposition of an endless duration of the existence and personality of the same rational being, which is called the immortality of the soul".[22] But while the moral life is the pursuit of an ideal hardly realizable in its completeness in this world, it has been generally recognized by those most advanced in the spiritual life that it is not confined to the requirements of the moral law and its demands. All that has been accomplished on earth has yet to reach its consummation, and the Christian hope of immortality is based on the conviction that Christ having overcome death and opened the way to eternal life by virtue of his resurrection has made this attainable. Human personality having been endowed with a soul transcending the limitations of time and space is destined to be immortal. This is at once a quality of human life and a divine gift capable of completion when "we all attain unto the unity of the faith, and of the knowledge of the Son of God, unto a fullgrown man, unto the measure of the stature of the fulness of Christ" (Ephes. 4. 13).

FURTHER READING

Baillie, J., *And the Life Everlasting*, 1934
Budge, E. A. W., *Egyptian Heaven and Hell*, 1906; *Osiris and the Egyptian Resurrection*, 1911.
Charles, R. H., *Eschatology: A Critical History of the Doctrine of the Future Life*, 1913
D'Arcy, M. C., *Death and Life*, 1942.
Edwards, I. E. S., *The Pyramids of Egypt*, 1961
Farnell, L. R., *Greek Hero Cults and Ideas of Immortality*, 1921
Frankfort, H., *Ancient Egyptian Religion*, 1948
Hügel, F. von, *Eternal Life*, 1912
Moore, C. H., *Ancient Beliefs in the Immortality of the Soul*, 1931
Nilsson, M. P., *Homer and Mycenae*, 1933
Oesterley, W. O. E., *Immortality and the Unseen World*, 1921

Pringle-Pattison, A. Seth, *The Idea of Immortality*, 1922
Rhode, E., *Psyche*, 1925
Taylor, A. E., *The Christian Hope of Immortality*, 1938
Webster, T. B. L., *From Mycenae to Homer*, 1958
Woolley, L., *Excavations at Ur*, 1954

Chapter Eight

RELIGION, REASON AND REVELATION

THE determination of the place, significance and function of Christianity in the history of religion presupposes that it is a particular discipline in a wider relationship; in other words that it is one among many different religious systems which collectively constitute a universal phenomenon from the beginning of human culture. This, however, raises a question of terminology in the present climate of opinion since recently it has been suggested that Christianity should no longer be regarded as a religion at all. Theism, it is said, in Frazerian fashion, having been replaced by a scientific interpretation of the universe and its processes devoid of transcendental religious beliefs and practices, should be abandoned in favour of a demythologized secular, or "religionless", way of life and service to humanity in love and right relationships, therein finding "God" in the infinite depth and ground of all being.[1] This atheistic conception of "unconditioned transcendent depth", however, is virtually indistinguishable from, though less intelligible or reasonable than, oriental pantheism at the best, which, as we have considered in some detail, is in fact an important and significant religious system rather than a "religionless" phenomena.

Religionless Christianity

The conventional use of the word "God" and of "religion" often has obscured their meaning, but separately or together they include the recognition of an order of reality which transcends the ordinary and commonplace, the temporal and the secular, and in divers forms and manners, is responsive to human needs. Deity, as we have seen, is not confined to a personal supreme being, or even to "a belief in spiritual beings", as Tylor contended, as the term may be employed as the evaluation of the experience of the numinous, or of the eternal world in some capacity. Nevertheless, religion can be differentiated from other cultural institutions by virtue of its reference to supra-mundane beings more powerful than man upon whom man depends, or to a transcendental order of reality. But since, as Durkheim affirms, "religion cannot be defined except by the characteristics which are found wherever religion itself is found",[2] the various religions of the world must be investigated in their concrete reality to discover what they have in common. Every religious system has its own explicit and implicit beliefs concerning the sacred order, and man's relation to it by the prescribed ritual techniques or mystical experiences, all of which claim validity. What these consist of it is the business of the comparative study of the phenomena to determine and assess. Christianity being one of these "concrete realities", it has now become increasingly aware in recent years of its position in a world-wide discipline, and anxious not merely to assert its claims to uniqueness but to ascertain the common ground it shares with other faiths both ancient and modern, recognizing that at sundry times and in divers manners God has not left himself without witness in his self-disclosures to mankind. This has not been vouchsafed so much in dogmatic pronouncements and propositions, as formerly often was supposed, as in divine acts and events in the process of history reaching their climax in the incarnation and resurrection of Christ.

To cut off Christianity from these fundamental religious contexts and substitute for this supreme revelation a human discovery of purpose, love and ultimate reality in the depth of man's being and in the concrete situations of human relationships in the meeting of man and man, as Bonhoeffer demands, is to render it inoperative by destroying the essence of its faith and practice. In becoming "religionless" it ceases to be a theistic discipline in any definable sense of the term without putting anything at all equivalent in its place. For good or ill Christianity stands or falls on its cardinal doctrines of Creation, Incarnation and Redemption as historical occurrences, with Christ as the Son of God at its centre. "We preach Christ crucified, unto Jews a stumbling-block and unto Gentiles foolishness; but unto them that are called, both Jews and Greeks, Christ the power of God and the wisdom of God. Because the foolishness of God is wiser than men; and the weakness of God is stronger than men" (I Cor. 1. 23–5 R.V.) This Pauline injunction goes to the heart of the uniqueness of the Christian revelation, and to abandon it is to reject the faith in its entirety, to all intents and purposes.

A good deal of the confusion that has arisen is the result of Schleiermacher's dichotomy of religion and science-and-morality, resulting in the dualistic separation of God and the world, of the sacred and the secular, issuing in a sharp distinction between natural and revealed religion. As we have seen, in the ancient world and in primitive states of culture no such differentiation was or is contemplated. The natural and the supernatural are so interwoven that divine activity is recognized in each and every occurrence that lies outside the normal sequence of events directly under human control and within the range of human experience, arousing the sense of the numinous. No hard and fast distinction has been made between an order of uniform happenings and an extra-mundane higher order of miraculous supernatural events. When these two spheres become differentiated as a clearly defined duality, an external transcendent deity has assumed an independent role with his own religious dogmas and rites as prescribed propositions and cults in the form of special disclosures; or the divine has become merged in the universe pantheistically identified with its processes in a manner that leaves little room for the exercise of sovereign rule, creative guidance, or revelational communications.

The Mystical Approach

Man may acquire an immediate first-hand mystical experience of the divine within the soul in the contemplative life theistically, as in Christian mysticism which is essentially "this worldly", down to earth. But when the aim and purpose are the attainment of unity with the Absolute, pantheistically or monistically conceived, the phenomenal order tends to be regarded as an illusion (*maya*), and the relationship established is then impersonal, independent of divine grace or redemptive mediation. This has been by no means always the case in Hinduism where latent in the Brahmanic Upanishadic equation, 'That Thou art', there is a personal element in the identification of the individual soul with the world soul, though it leads to absorption into Ultimate Reality as a divine unity, comparable to the merging of rivers into the ocean. In Christianity the apprehension of God as supra-personal is a prerequisite centrally inherent in the Incarnation as the supreme self-disclosure of deity in this world.[3] Therefore, in its mystical approach this must be retained and the distinction between the Creator and the creature maintained, while the erotic element in a sensuous union of the soul with God in terms of a sacred marriage requires sublimation to be either edifying or allegorical. This, indeed, applies no less to its oriental counterparts, but it is all-important in its Christian manifestations because God is there revealed as himself love. It recurs in the Sufi movement in Islam with its Judaeo-Christian background, and has been introduced into Hinduism under Bhakti influences. In monism and in original Buddhism it is as unknown as is the basic personal I-Thou relationship.

It has been, in fact, primarily and essentially in the religions rooted and grounded in a supra-personal conception of the living God in which transcendentalism and immanentalism have been brought into conjunction, that revelation, divine grace and meditation have provided the spiritual dynamic required to meet the deepest needs of the human spirit in the world as it actually exists. A religionless Christianity would not fulfil these functions if the Ultimate Reality was merely an abstraction, just the Ground of Being equated with love within the hidden depth of human nature. God must be himself love, the creator manifest in nature and in history as "the light which lighteth every man that cometh into the world", disclosing himself as the Word made flesh in the incarnate Christ. But for Jesus of Nazareth to be the centre of history, as indeed Tillich affirms,[4] he has to have been a historical person, and the Incarnation and Resurrection to have had more than a symbolic significance. If "God" is only a designation of a purely immanent and impersonal "Ground of Being" it is a metaphysical abstraction so far removed from the "God and Father of our Lord Jesus Christ" that it cannot be the concept of deity on which the Christian revelation ultimately rests; or, in fact, of those divine self-disclosures that have been manifest in the other theistic religions of the world.

Natural and Revealed Religion

The traditional view that divine truth may be either "natural theology" or "revealed knowledge" cannot, however, be sustained in its former presentation and rigidity, as, for example, by Butler in his *Analogy of Religion* (1736). The empirical investigation of the relevant data now generally adopted in the study of religion as a universal phenomenon, has had far-reaching results in the critical interpretation of the biblical evidence, and of the nature and content of religious belief and practice everywhere. The substitution of an inductive scientific method in which the facts are carefully attested and verified, and conclusions drawn objectively from the inquiry, for the former deductive method based on revelational presuppositions, has put a different complexion on the theological situation. Science has now become the determining factor, and revelation, from being a process through which clearly defined theological propositions have been disclosed in the form of articles of faith deducible by reason from explicit decrees of verbally inspired scriptures, or infallible formularies of the Church, taken in an oracular sense, has now given place to verifiable claims. As A. E. J. Rawlinson has said, "the final appeal is to the spiritual, intellectual and historical content of divine revelation, as verifiable at the threefold bar of history, reason and spiritual experience".[5] This, of course, is not to fail to recognize that in the case of religious knowledge its most fundamental elements are rooted and grounded in the eternal world lying beyond the scope of an inductive category confined to the phenomenal order, where a distinction between "natural" and "revealed" religion is relevant. Transcendental truth, however, is capable of spiritual and intellectual verification in the light of reason.

Thus, in the evaluation of the concept of deity the "how" of science, the "that" of history and the "why" of theology, philosophy and spiritual experience are all required; cause being subordinated to purpose, origin to validity, and historico-empiricism to teleology and cosmology. In the understanding of theistic religious phenomena the ultimate purpose and significance of the concept, together with the empirical data and inductive knowledge of God, are vital considerations. This raises the question of the duality of the temporal and eternal, of natural and revealed religion and of general and special revelation, since the phenomena of religion fall within both these spheres of being. The function of reason in relation to revelation is that of subjecting the alleged divine disclosures to a strictly rational inquiry as against the claims of all direct and oracular guarantees of inspirational and revelational truth and reality. Reality must be capable of verification within the limits of its own subject matter. Because the finite human mind is incapable of knowing in all its fullness the essential being of the Infinite, it is no excuse for assuming with Schleiermacher and his followers that religion has nothing to do with knowledge,[6] or with Barth and the neo-Calvinists that "truth comes in the faith in which we begin and in the faith in which we cease to know", and depends solely upon God's self-unveiling.[7] Such an antithesis of revelation and reason is as indefensible as the traditional dichotomy of natural and revealed religion.

The historical and comparative study of religion as an empirical discipline is a corrective of ill-founded a priori assumptions and dogmas based on supposed doctrinal disclosures in conflict with ascertainable and verifiable knowledge. But as Professor Laird has said, "natural theology could never be the whole of Christian theology, even if it uniformly supported that theology. It must always be less than Christian, and would seem to be narrower in principle than the theologies of many other religions. That in itself is not an objection to natural theology; but there would be serious reason for complaint if the limitations of the sphere of natural theology were sedulously and not quite candidly concealed."[8] Thus, it cannot pass judgment on the doctrine of the Holy Trinity because, as Aquinas and the Scholastics reasonably affirmed, it is knowable "only by faith as a revealed truth". This applies to the incarnation and resurrection of Christ as the eternal Son of God, except in so far as the historical occurrence of the alleged events is capable of verification in relation to the observable facts and the reliability of the literary records bearing upon them. And because these cardinal doctrines are of such crucial importance in a revelation which claims to be unique and final, every effort should be made to establish their validity within the limits of the available data.

To exempt such divine disclosures from critical investigation on the ground of their being God-given infallible propositional communications and miraculous interventions, beyond all human powers of investigation and evaluation, is to remove them from the life, thought and knowledge of the phenomenal world altogether. This leaves them at the mercy of unrestrained speculation and naïve fantasy, which in fact have gathered round them, notably in the apocryphal literature. Moreover, to make a fundamental distinction between what can be known about God by the "unaided reason", and the "saving knowledge" bestowed by him on his elect recipients, opens the way for a disastrous dualism in the quest of truth. Thus, the conception of incarnation in Bhakti Hinduism, Mahayana Buddhism and in Christianity, though very different in origin, character and purpose, as has been considered, is sufficiently parallel to rule out entirely a clear-cut division devoid of a common element disclosed exclusively to any one faith. It is not, in fact, ready-made theologies that have been or are revealed at any time, or in any place or religion; common features recurring in them often emerging from a common background deeply laid in history. In Christianity, Hebrew prophecy and Judaeo-Iranian apocalyptic, together with Hellenic philosophy and Graeco-oriental Mystery cults, met in the second century of the new era, interpreted in terms of a *praeparatio evangelica* of a common faith centred in the Incarnate Christ. The Old and New Testaments, however unique as vehicles of revelation, cannot be set apart exclusively from all other records of religious belief and spiritual experience, as has now become widely recognized. Thus, modern biblical scholarship freely employs the available archaeological, historical and literary material collected from other relevant sources and contemporary cultures to elucidate its own specialized data. To this is being added, largely under the inspiration of the ecumenical movement, the sacred literature, beliefs and practices of the Asian peoples among whom, it has become apparent, God "left not himself without witness".

This is hardly surprising since the Christian Church claims to be catholic with a universal faith for all mankind. This has led some apologists to differentiate a "general revelation" common to the religious consciousness of the entire human race, from a "special revelation" mediated through particular historical episodes, persons, nations and situations as the means whereby the truths of "general revelation" are apprehended.[9] This avoids the former dualism based on revealed propositional truths contrasted with unaided natural knowledge, and leaves room for the interpretation of the unique contribution of Christianity, without excluding a divine self-disclosure at sundry times and in divers manners among the non-Christian religions everywhere. If, as St. Augustine contended, all knowledge becomes superfluous,[10] even so this does not preclude degrees of disclosure, inspiration and illumination in the giving, perceiving and evaluation of higher truth. "General" revelation bestowed through the medium of nature or history becomes a "special" revelation when it is experienced and appropriated by a particular religion and given a specific interpretation and significance.

Throughout the history of religion the divine powers, believed to have created the universe and controlled natural events and human destinies, have been thought to communicate their will and purposes to mankind in a variety of ways, as we have seen, such as through divination, ecstatic experiences, omens, auspices, oracles and astrological lore, until at length the living God has been regarded primarily as unveiling himself as a Person to persons through events rather than in oracular signs, wonders, portents and mantic utterances and knowledge. Alternatively when the divine order has been merged in the universe and identified with its processes, little room has been left for the independent exercise of sovereign rule, creative initiative and guidance, and revelational self-disclosure or communication. Man may seek immediate knowledge of the Absolute with the soul, but an impersonal monistic or pantheistic Ultimate Reality cannot reveal itself like the transcendent Creator in a personal relationship with his creation.

Divination

In primitive society this has been achieved by divine activities ordering and controlling the course of nature and history through interventions, prescriptions and manifestations in theophanies, handed down from age to age in the sacred tradition as myths, ritual and cultus. The medium of the revelations has ranged from visionary experiences and shamanistic occult methods to oracular inspiration and ecstatic insights, as disclosed respectively by the Pythia at Delphi or the Bacchoi in Thrace, and the "prophets" called *nebi'im* in Israel. In Greece, however, the wilder shamanistic orgiastic practices were never established as Hellenic tradition, the Dionysian frenzies, as we have seen, having been brought under the sobering influence of Apolline divination and the Orphic mysteries. Similarly, the esoteric revelations at Eleusis were confined to sacred objects, sounds, sights and illumination, to effect a change sacramentally in the spiritual condition of the neophytes rather than the liberation of a divine element from a hampering body. Furthermore, when the Dionysian-Orphic tradition was incorporated in the Platonic soma-sema relation and in the doctrine of reincarnation, it became a vision of eternal truth, beauty and goodness in the world of Ideas, where the liberated soul was like God, "holy and just and wise".[11] Divination, it is true, played its part inherently in the process, Socrates having attributed his pursuit of truth to a supernatural gift bestowed by a "Daimonian", or "inward voice", and turned for guidance to the Delphic oracle declaring its Pythia to be "the wisest of men", and placing himself in the service of Apollo.[12] So deeply laid, in fact, was divination in the Graeco-Roman world that Plotinus developed a doctrine of ecstatic communion with the Absolute, unknowable directly by reason. In the fourth and fifth centuries A.D. Neoplatonic mysticism readily degenerated into a means of communication with the Olympian gods by oracles, and from them receiving revelations.[13] The popular appeal of the Sibylline oracles in and after the fifth century B.C. with their ecstatic prophecy written in Greek hexameter verses with acrostics guaranteeing their genuineness, increased the belief in the direct communication of the divine will through inspired seers. This continued until their final suppression in A.D. 363; in the meantime they had acquired Jewish and Christian interpolations.

So important, significant and complex became the mantic tradition in Greece and the Ancient Near East, especially in Mesopotamia, that highly trained experts were set apart to proclaim and interpret oracles, omens and astrological phenomena and other divinatory communications. Thus, it became a pseudo-science under the direction of diviners, seers and astrologers engaged primarily in disclosing hidden wisdom, determining the course of events by visionary experience and prognostications, and establishing verbal communion with a god by an exchange of words. The revelation thus received was made known as a divine oracular pronouncement having an absolute validity as the expression of the will and purpose of the deity with whom the seer had been *en rapport*. The divine voice spoke through him conveying a message, a warning or a declaration, or, if it was unintelligible, it gave expression to a deep-seated state of emotion. In this condition of divine inspiration the seer, like the Syrian mantis Balaam only could speak the words put in his mouth as an inspired utterance by his divine control (Num. 22. 38); or in India the Vedic *hotr*, or reciting priests who reiterated the syllable OM, or sang the Rig-Veda as Words of Power, when they were

filled with Brahman as the constraining energy.[14] The words uttered
and the sacred actions performed established a condition of *rapport* with
the divinity, the human situation, environment, portents and hidden
potencies, independent of the meaning of the words spoken. Their
utterance had a numinous effect very much as has the recitation of the
Qur'an in mosques in non-Arabic speaking Muslim countries, or the
saying of Mass in Latin, or the reading of some of the epistles of St.
Paul, among an uneducated congregation unfamiliar with the language
and terminology employed.

When the purpose of mantic devices was to establish union with the
sacred order, to convey supernatural power and to influence the course
of events, gaining superhuman knowledge was a secondary consideration. Glossolalia, or speaking in an unintelligible manner ecstatically,
did not fulfil the practical purposes of mantic prediction, prognostica-
tion, astrology and necromancy, although it has been a recurrent
phenomenon, prominent in apostolic Christianity as "speaking with
tongues", or "prophesying" in this manner (Acts 2. 14 ff.; 10. 46), and
recurrent in subsequent revivalist movements (e.g. among the Quakers,
Ranters, Irvingites and other Adventist sects).[15] But the main purpose of
the diviner always has been to determine, disclose and interpret occurrences of critical importance, and it was in the Hellenic-Roman and the
Babylonian-Assyrian world that the practice was most firmly established both in the official cult and unofficially in an array of private
augurs and soothsayers.

In Mesopotamia many of the mantic offices went back to Sumerian
times when some of the omen-texts and inscriptions, such as the *Enuma
Anu-Enlil* series, were already in existence. The special class of seers
known as the *baru*, however, also resorted to more direct methods to
obtain portents, as, for instance, night visions. It was, in fact, from
Babylonia and Assyria that this type of divination reached the Graeco-
Roman world through the Etruscans who had adopted it. But it would
seem from the Jewish apocryphal book of Tobit, where the liver of a
fish is represented as being employed for exorcism, and other similar
references to the practice (Tobit 6. 4–16; Ezek. 21. 21), that Judaism also
came under these influences, as did Anatolia.

Cultic and Canonical Prophecy

In Israel, however, revelation developed along very different lines
notwithstanding the prominence of cultic prophecy among the Hebrew
nebi'im, or "prophets", while the *kohen* was the equivalent of the Arabic
kahin, or diviner, who was mainly concerned with obtaining oracles,

often with the aid of the Urim and Thummin, answering "yes" or "no" to specific questions. But in Israel the nebi'im were primarily ecstatics attached to sanctuaries like Bethel, Gibeah, Rama and Carmel, rather than soothsayers, sorcerers and diviners. Thus, when Saul had been anointed king by Samuel he is said to have encountered a band of ecstatics (nebi'im) in Mount Gibeah, and under their inspiration he was "turned into another man", the spirit (*ruach*) of Yahweh coming mightily upon him. Henceforth he frequently displayed ecstatic symptoms even after the divine afflatus had left him and descended upon David (I Sam. 16. 13 ff). Samuel himself was a seer who had night-visions, mystical auditions and superhuman knowledge of events, and Elisha was a typical nabi; his predecessor Elijah also occasionally behaving ecstatically, as, for instance, after his triumph on Mount Carmel when he ran before Ahab to Jezreel (I Kings 18. 46).

In the Northern Kingdom from the eleventh to the ninth centuries nabi'ism seems to have been more ecstatic than in Judah where Nathan and Zadok occupied a prominent position in the Davidic hierarchy and in the Temple ritual as the court priest-prophets. In the north Elijah, Elisha and Micaiah were powerful influences, and it was at Bethel that the earliest of the canonical prophets, Amos, though himself a southerner, first proclaimed "the Word of Yahweh" as he had received it in the disclosures vouchsafed to him in visionary experiences in Tekoa in the middle of the eighth century B.C. (Amos 1, 7. 12–15). It now appears that both types of prophets, with the priests, were engaged in the communication of a divine knowledge and information in their respective spheres, and by their duly appointed methods, under the direction of Yahweh. Behind it, in fact, lay the Canaanite ecstatic tradition which in Israel may go back even to the time of Moses (Deut. 34. 10), though the early developments of the prophetic cultus are very obscure and conjectural.[16] But as the special spokesmen of Yahweh revealing the divine word, they were widely consulted for oracular guidance by the laity, the divine decrees being transmitted to them as a cultic revelation.[17] Indeed, it is now clear that the Hebrew prophets were not in violent opposition to the cultus and its priesthood, as was formerly supposed, all the functionaries, sometimes perhaps living together in cult associations, being engaged in the common task of making known the message and directions of Yahweh to his people.

The methods and techniques adopted in the exercise of their vocation were of various kinds, and if these not infrequently included cultic ecstatic activities, they were not confined to this mode of obtaining and imparting divine oracles. That they were convinced that they were moved by the God of Israel to proclaim what had been revealed to them is evident from their use of the refrain "Thus saith Yahweh" and concluding with the words "Oracle of Yahweh". As his "messengers" they held converse with God and received their orders from him becoming, in fact, a projection of his "corporate personality", and so virtually a divine *malach*, or "messenger".[18] This gave them insight into his will and purposes, and led them to declare "the Word of Yahweh" they had received, determining events and the history of the nation, whether the people would hear or whether they would forbear.

The classical prophets, beginning with Amos in the eighth century, were much more apprehensive about the course of events. The Exodus and occupation of the promised land had not achieved their hopes and expectations through the backsliding of Israel, and now another exile and captivity were looming conspicuously on the horizon. This occurred first in the Northern Kingdom with the ascendance of Assyria, and then in the south when the military and political centre moved from Nineveh to Babylon with the rise of Nebuchadnezzar to predominance in the sixth century. What lay beyond this course of approaching tragic events was only dimly perceived, attention being concentrated on prophetic utterance and symbolic signs of the imminent catastrophe (Amos 3. 8; Hos. 1. Jer. 20. 8 f.), though redemption and restoration were latent in their proclamations of the Word of Yahweh. But it was always recognized that behind and in all the vicissitudes of the history of the nation was the one omnipotent will of the Holy One of Israel, the righteous ruler of creation and the doer of justice, whose law was holy and whose power was infinite. Unlike the gods of the surrounding countries whose existence was not denied, Yahweh was not sporadically beneficent when he was propitiated and in a favourable mood, nor was he dependent upon the fate of cities and their priesthoods. His tender mercies were over all his works, but he demanded obedience to his commands and conformity to his standards and requirements by every member of the holy nation. Being divine self-disclosures and precepts the word of Yahweh, and subsequently the Torah, constituted this absolute standard of belief and conduct binding on Israel and all its personnel by virtue of the covenant relationship between them. Indeed, it was this intimacy that led Amos to cry in the name of Yahweh, "You only have I known of all the families of the earth: therefore I will punish you for all your iniquities" (Amos 3. 2). It was this unique relationship that rendered its rebellion and infidelity so heinous, bringing judgment upon itself. But it carried with it the hope of restoration. As Hosea was led to declare, in terms of his own nuptial symbolism, the day would come when Yahweh would betroth them to him for ever in righteousness, in justice, in steadfast love, and in compassion, mercy and faithfulness (Hos. 2. 16–20).

Post-Exilic Revelation in Judaism

The corporate personality of the nation, however, could fulfil its vocation and covenant relationship only by every member realizing his responsibilities and the demands made upon him by Yahweh as the righteous God of Israel. Moreover, it required the humiliating experience of the Exile to effect the restoration and re-establishment of Judaism on a new and firm theocratic basis after the prophetic movement had done its work. It was only a remnant that was destined to return, rebuild Jerusalem and its Temple, and restore its worship with a reorganized Levitical priesthood and sacrificial system, and with the Torah as the verbally-inspired Law taking the place of the prophetic Word of Yahweh. The classical prophets declared the truth in the same measure as they were convinced that they had received it from him. They believed they knew his divine will and mind because they had been called by him to their office, stood in his council and heard his word, which they transmitted to the people (Jer. 23. 18–22). Isaiah in a visionary experience saw Yahweh sitting on his throne, high and lifted up and surrounded with angelic beings. In this ecstatic condition he heard the divine voice saying to him, "Whom shall I send and who will go for us?" And in abasement, filled with numinous awe and wonder, he replied, "Here am I, send me" (Is. 6. 1–8). So with the rest of these unique personalities. But in the post-exilic community their place was taken by the sacerdotal schools primarily concerned with the collection and canonization of the Pentateuchal sacred literature, attributed to Moses and so assigned supreme authority as a divine oracle. This made prophecy of secondary importance and with the rise of synagogues those who sought to know the will of Yahweh betook themselves to the scribes as the official teachers of the Law. As they claimed to sit in Moses' seat all that they taught and commanded had to be obeyed (Matt. 23. 2 f.).

God was praised daily for having sanctified his people by his commandments whose words were their life and "the strength of their days", if no distinction was made between ritual observances, the pious duty respecting the burial of the dead, and "doing justly, loving mercy and walking humbly with God", which the prophets had insisted was the primary concern. For them the redemption of Israel had a much wider application and significance than that conceived in post-exilic Judaism, finding its consummation in Yahweh becoming "king over all the earth", his righteous rule being extended to the ends of the world. If, however, prophecy in its former sense ceased to function and the prophetic office fell into disrepute, its more optimistic predictions having failed to be realized, nevertheless, the words of its great exponents were held in the highest regard as divine utterances, side by side with the Law in its all-embracing entirety, and its cultus which was claimed to have been directly revealed by God on the Holy Mount.

Thus, it was through the nebi'im, the canonical prophets and the priests that Yahweh was believed to have spoken most clearly and directly to his people, though subsequently also by the wise men whose divine observations are recorded and semi-personified in the Wisdom Literature, and eventually embodied in Christ. Behind this Hebrew Wisdom movement lay the "Teaching of Amen-em-ope" as its prototype in ancient Egypt, being identical in form with Proverbs 22. 17–23. 11, and earlier in date. In Israel it included magicians, sorcerers, and "Chaldaeans", all of whom were regarded as endowed with supernatural knowledge as a divine attribute through which Yahweh disclosed his will and intentions. Therefore, their words were thought to be the words of God and so acquired a revelational significance in the divine direction of human life, and became part of the Torah. Throughout the Hebrew conception of revelation it was, however, Yahweh who made himself known to the nation with which he stood in such a unique relationship. It was he who was alleged to have spoken to Moses and ratified the covenant. He gave the Law and used the prophets as his mouthpiece, demonstrating his power and purposes in history by mighty acts and signs, and the control of natural events and processes in the establishment of his kingdom. The compilers of the record of this revelation, therefore, were not displaying their own inspirational insight, though their minds may have been divinely illuminated to discuss the activity of God in that which they interpreted. In any case, they themselves believed they were the instruments of Yahweh impelled to declare what had been revealed to them, if, indeed, they always understood the message they felt they had received.

The Christian Revelation

This transcendental conception of revelation recurs with equal insistence in the New Testament. As Yahweh was alleged to have manifested himself to Moses, so in the Christian dispensation the fundamental assumption was the Incarnation. Thus, the mystery of faith was rooted and grounded in the belief that God had broken into the world of time and space in a stupendous intervention. This was more than just another stage in a progressive divine disclosure in a Judaeo-Christian sequence of events. It was rather, as C. H. Dodd has said, "a cutting across of purpose by events; the entry into history of a reality beyond history".[19] Upon the unique understanding and interpretation of the vicissitudes of historical events in Israel, and their predictions, which characterized the Judaic revelation, a Christian theology was built up around the incarnation, death and resurrection of Christ as the climax and fulfilment of all that had gone before, but different in kind rather than in degree. It went beyond the mighty acts that had been manifest already, Jesus affirming that the Messiah had come and the ancient prophecies and promises had been fulfilled, "the reign of God had begun" (Mark 1. 14 f.).

This was the assertion and the challenge that introduced a new era as well as a new epoch in revealed religion. That they were made and in due course widely accepted, becoming the spiritual dynamic in the Graeco-Roman world, is beyond dispute, however the outstanding events are explained and evaluated. Moreover, it was in accord with what had been predicted inasmuch as it renewed the Hebraic covenant and established the mystery "kept silent through times eternal and now manifested" (Rom. 16. 25–6). It was proclaimed in its *kerygma*, or message preached, to be the final and complete revelational event in the history of the world, constituting at once the fulfilment of all that had gone before in the world-wide *praeparatio evangelica*, and at the same time marking a break with the past. Eternity had entered into the conditions of time incarnationally, giving an eternal significance to the temporal order it did not formerly possess. The kingdom had come with power, and although its consummation had yet to be achieved "the life of the age to come" was here and now an experienced reality. The omnipotent deity who had made himself known by his mighty acts in Israel had created a new humanity manifesting therein his divine power and love. The Kingdom of God having come already in a "realized eschatology"[20] those initiated into it were recipients of the new revelation and partakers of its power and grace.

The esoteric disclosures of the pagan mystery cults became in Christianity a revelation foreshadowed in the old dispensation and made known in all its fullness in the New Israel as the Kingdom of God, wherein the Gospel is proclaimed and its hidden meaning, wisdom and knowledge perceived. The "mystery of the Kingdom" was centred in the humiliation and exaltation of Christ as the suffering Messiah, set forth in what in all probability is a pre-Pauline hymn incorporated in the epistle to the Philippians (2. 5–11), and expressed in terms of a *kenosis*, or "emptying", in which he laid aside his divinity when he was born in the likeness of man, taking the form of a "servant". Thus, he "became obedient unto death, even the death of the cross, God having exalted him and given him a name which is above every name" (i.e. *kyrios* "lord"); the whole of creation acknowledging him at the Parousia as sovereign Lord. This equation of the historical Jesus with the Messiah and the Isaianic Servant exalted as the Lord in glory, differentiated the new dispensation from the whole of previous history.[21] Henceforth, the perfectly surrendered will and life laid down by the Redeemer was the crucial factor in the Christian mystery on which all divine revelation and intervention in the temporal order converged.

As Edwyn Bevan has maintained, "the great dividing line is that which marks off all those who hold that the relation of Jesus to God — however they describe or formulate it — is of such a kind that it could not be repeated in any other individual — that to speak, in fact, of its being repeated in one *other* individual is a contradiction in terms, since any individual standing in that relation to God would *be* Jesus, and that Jesus, in virtue of this relation, has the same absolute claim upon all men's worship and loyalty as belongs to God. A persuasion of this sort of uniqueness attaching to Jesus seems to me the essential characteristic of what has actually in the field of human history been Christianity."[22] It is this which gives the faith its unique position in the history of religion. Arising among the Jews it inherited and adopted their relevant revelational predictions, though it was not content merely to maintain the Judaic Messianic tradition. Since the Incarnation was a new creative act which set the seal on the divine intervention by which God had made known and worked out his purpose in Israel and in human history everywhere, all that proceeded from it gained a new spiritual and redemptive significance. Christ was declared to be the Son of God because of what he *was* rather than what he did and said. This was confirmed by his resurrection from the dead as an historical event of unparalleled uniqueness. The conviction that a reconciliation had been achieved through his moral perfection sealed in this great redemptive act in history, and that in its accomplishment "he who was dead is alive for evermore", constituted the core of the Christian faith (I Cor. 15. 3). To it the sacred literature of the New Testament bears witness, acquiring in due course the authority of an inspired record comparable to that which formed the basis of Judaism, though it was the events and the message rather than the actual books that disclosed the revelation.

The delay in the Parousia gave increasing significance to the Kingdom of God on earth, the Church, as the divinely appointed sphere in and through which this absolute revelation was made known to mankind as a *living* tradition. It had been instituted by Christ himself to bear witness to his resurrection and to perpetuate for all time his atoning sacrifice once offered as an historic oblation. This conception of its office, work and function as an apostolic fellowship and spiritual society united by a common faith and worship, and committed to a particular way of life grounded in its basic doctrines, arose quite naturally from the Judaic theocracy; but invested with its own distinctive claims of faith and practice. Thus, it reserved to itself the right to interpret Scripture in accordance with its own official formularies, but in maintaining its standard of orthodoxy in terms of a revelation, it readily tended to make inspiration oracular, reducing the Church and the Bible to the level of the Delphic oracle. This was apparent in the fourth century when these ideas of divine disclosures were current in the Graeco-Roman world. It recurred in the Middle Ages and in the sixteenth century, and in recent years in the obscurantist reaction to critical scholarship. But neither the Scriptures nor the Church have independent authority apart from Christ, though both bear witness to and declare the truths he revealed.

The words written down in the documentary records, biblical and credal, are those of human beings living at a particular time and in a specific country under the prevailing historical conditions, with their limitations. The apprehension of the revelation, therefore, is dependent upon the human mind perceiving and interpreting the meaning of what has been disclosed, and this involves a subjective element. An act of faith is required to evaluate correctly the event or doctrine and its record, but room is left for finite and even erroneous judgments in matters of interpretation and presentation, and of historical detail. Consequently, no hard and fast distinction can be drawn between the objective and the subjective aspects of revelation, or between natural and revealed religion. Revelation must always be a revealed reality on the part of its recipient, neither wholly objective nor entirely subjective.

In the Judaeo-Christian scriptures human and historical events are perceived as the saving acts of God in the working out of the divine purpose, first in and for Israel and then for all mankind and the world at large through the Holy Spirit illuminating the minds of the prophets and apostles and their successors. To dismiss all this as Jewish and Hellenistic mythology, and with Bultmann reduce the Gospel to God confronting man demanding an absolute decision in an existential situation in which the whole of the narrative from the Virgin Birth to the Ascension is "demythologized", is to destroy the entire revelation and the historicity of Christ and Christianity. If Jesus was not historically "the image of the invisible God" that is disclosed and maintained in the scriptures (Col. 1. 15) and defined in the creeds, the traditional faith of

Christendom is devoid of ultimate reality and revelational significance. In the interests of truth, and in fairness both to believers and unbelievers, Christians and humanists, this must be definitely and unambiguously asserted, for Christianity is primarily and essentially a historical religion. As such it stands or falls. It was at a critical moment in history when the Roman Empire seemed to be at the height of its power and glory, before the clouds had gathered and shadows crept across the fair landscape, that a figure appeared among the hills of Galilee who was destined to shake its foundations and lay the fabric of the current civilization in the dust. Only in an obscure fellowship of spiritually alert minds and perceptions was it realized that they were standing at the very focal point of history. Although for the most part they were ignorant and unlearned men, they felt themselves compelled to make known far and wide the Gospel that they had received and the events they had themselves witnessed as a divine encounter, under the inspiration of the Holy Spirit, through historical situations and occurrences.

As Dr. Leonard Hodgson has pointed out, theology is the study of Christian history with a view to determining the exact nature and meaning of its contents.[23] Therefore, it has to take account of the historical situation out of which the faith arose, and of the beliefs of those who had first-hand knowledge of what had been disclosed, made known and experienced. If the revelation was of God himself and his purposes in Christ, this could only be understood and made intelligible to others through the thought-forms and expositions of those who were convinced that they had "seen God in the face of Jesus Christ". It was the function of the Church to interpret the mysteries of the faith which it claimed to have been commissioned to expound and preserve as its custodian. But in the absence of revealed systematized doctrines, credal formulation proved to be a protracted and highly controversial process, and when at length at the Council of Chalcedon in 451 a settlement was reached, it was in the nature of a compromise, the Christological inconsistency in the *Tome of Leo* having been unresolved. Nevertheless, the definitions of the faith concerning the Person of Christ made by the ecumenical Councils of Nicaea and Constantinople were reaffirmed, and by maintaining the two natures, divine and human, in the one Christ, united indivisibly and inseparably, at least his unique personality was established, notwithstanding their rejection by the monophysite heresy for the next two centuries. By the end of the seventh century the Nicene faith was generally received, however, both in Eastern and Western Christendom, and it has remained the cardinal doctrine of Christianity.

The theological implications of the nature of the Godhead originated in Christian experience of the ethical monotheism revealed in Judaism, combined with the Person of Christ, interpreted in the light of the risen and ascended incarnate Lord; and the work of the Holy Spirit realized in the lives and witness of his followers as a divine afflatus, often sealed by their blood. Each of these modes of experience was distinct yet they were experience of the one living God, Creator, Redeemer and Sanctifier. It was this apprehension which was given credal formulation in the language and thought of the fourth century, and the affirmations have stood the test of time as the generally accepted theistic definition of the faith because they expressed the fundamental conception of deity which Christianity had made its own particular revelational interpretation of the divine being, confirmed by the spiritual experience of those who embraced it.

Apart from the academic question of credal definition, however, the Godhead attributed to the founder of Christianity, alike in the New Testament and by the Church, renders it unique in the history of religion. Nowhere else had it ever been claimed that a historical founder of any religion was the one and only supreme deity. Divinities in a pantheon frequently have been venerated, especially in the mystery cults, as we have seen, but Christ was not regarded as one of many gods. He was God in the monotheistic meaning of the definition set forth in the Nicene Creed. This is a very different conception from that of Krishna and Rama in theistic Bhakti Hinduism, where the reincarnations of Vishnu as mythical heroes were far removed from Christ, or, indeed, from a Hebrew prophet, there being sages but no prophets in Hinduism. Vishnu constantly appeared in an indefinite number of avatars in varying forms in contrast to the one and only Mediator, who alone effected deliverance from sin as moral evil, rather than from ceaseless reincarnation leading to release (*moksa*) from temporal existence for the purpose of the attainment of nirvana.

In Buddhism, again, while Gautama had a great compassion for suffering humanity, relinquishing his own entrance to this state of bliss for the sake of revealing his middle way of "salvation" to mankind at his enlightenment, he repudiated any conception of deity or redemption. Similarly in the Mahayana Great Vehicle the Bodhisattvas, Christlike as they were in their self-sacrificing efforts on behalf of humanity, were animated by the same desire to secure escape from the misery and pain of phenomenal existence; the Buddhist denial of the substantiality of the "self" rendering personal immortality impossible. Thus, notwithstanding the introduction of Pure Lands en route for the ultimate goal of nirvana in some of the Mahayana sects in China and Japan, the

Christian hope of an afterlife was excluded, and with it any comparable conception of salvation. Therefore, while undoubtedly there has been a *praeparatio evangelica* among the Asian peoples, it is most apparent in the great prophetic religions having historical founders, such as Judaism, Zoroastrianism and Islam.

Like the Hebrew prophets Zarathustra and Muhammad claimed to have been the recipients of a special revelation from God, vouchsafed either gradually, or, as in the case of Muhammad, as an overwhelming sudden experience compelling him to "recite in the name of the Lord who created man from a clot of blood", and record the message he had received in the Holy Qur'an. To Zarathustra, Ahura Mazdah manifested himself as the one and only wise Lord, Creator and Judge, attended by a number of spirits representing abstract ideas (e.g. Good Mind, Righteousness, Immortality). In due course this developed into a dualistic struggle between two opposed forces of good and evil, personified as twin spirits who eventually became rival Mazdaean gods. How this original ethical monotheism, prior to the later dualism, emerged out of Vedic polytheism is not easily explained, as the earliest hymns in the Avesta throw no light on the problem. In them Ahura Mazdah is the sole deity, but to what extent Zarathustra succeeded in converting his fellow settled husbandmen from their earlier polytheism is by no means clear. It was not until the Achaemenian period (c. 540 B.C.) that the dualistic eschatology, characteristic of the later literature, appeared, centred in the coming of the Saoshyant, or saviour, and in the last judgment. In the Sassanian Empire (A.D. 226–652) this remained the orthodox faith with Ormuzd and Ahriman as the two rival gods, modifying the original revelation of Zarathustra.

In Islam the utterly transcendent disclosure of Allah to Muhammad made him the passive recipient of a verbally-inspired revelation beyond critical examination, given once and for all as a divine message to be accepted by believers with unquestioning faith. From the beginning Islam has been "the religion of the Book" (i.e. the Qur'an) universally followed by all Muslims as the completion of the revelations earlier given to the Jews and then by Christ, whom Muhammad regarded as the Messiah within the limits of his understanding of the office and its functions and significance. Except by the Mu'tazilites, the eternity of the Qur'an is maintained, containing the speech of Allah as an infallible self-existing oracle, be it "from Moses or other prophets, from Pharaoh or from Satan", sent down from heaven complete to the founder, who was the "seal of the Prophets" since he was the bringer of the Qur'an as the Word of God. This makes him the last and the chief of the instruments of divine self-disclosure, "the Messenger of God" *par excellence*, and Islam the final revelation superseding all the previous inspired records.

These claims, of course, have given the faith an enormous appeal, coupled with the relative simplicity of the basic creed and its duties, summed up in the "Five Pillars" to be performed with sincere intention (*niya*). Here lies the challenge to and the real problem for Christianity. Accepting substantially, as it docs, the Judaeo-Christian revelation as its precursor, Islam historically and theologically is essentially an integral part of one and the same religious tradition. Indeed, as has been pointed out, Muhammad at first sought the co-operation of Jews and Christians in Arabia when he launched his movement in Mecca. It was not until their refusal to accept his advances to them and their repudiation of his revelations that he organized his Muslim community at Medina as a theocracy distinct from Judaism and Christendom. As such it was destined to become a world-wide religious civilization comprising some three hundred and fifty million adherents, representing the dominant faith in North Africa, Zanzibar, and Tanganyika, in Pakistan, the Malay Peninsula and the East Indies, with scattered groups still surviving in the Balkans and elsewhere.

Nevertheless, the fact remains that the claims are based to a considerable extent on a very imperfect knowledge and understanding of the Judaeo-Christian revelation and especially of the founder of Christianity as the incarnate Son of God, as this claim is demonstrated by his life, teaching, death and resurrection, subjected to a critical examination in the penetrating light of modern investigation which has been and still is resisted in orthodox circles in the study of the Qur'an. It is, of course, true that in Christianity, and other parallel religions, there has been always a rigidly conservative obscurantist element upholding the literal inerrancy of scripture, and of what are assumed to be unalterable revealed doctrines, regardless of literary criticism and of historical and scientific evidence, no less fundamentalist than that adopted in Islam. But with the advance of modern knowledge, outside these restricted circles, the study of the New Testament, the interpretation of the Person of Christ and the cardinal doctrines of the faith, have been predominantly objective, with a view to the determination of the truth and validity of the inherent beliefs, often with very different results from the foregone traditional conclusions.

It has become increasingly recognized, in fact, that progress in empirical knowledge is an aspect of divine revelation, keeping in mind that transcendental reality belongs to a different domain of thought and inquiry from that confined to the factual phenomena amenable to the scientific method of investigation. But revelation and spiritual insight disclosing fundamental truth have to be expressed in such a way as to be intelligible in the particular cultural, social and intellectual conditions in which they occur to afford a deeper understanding of divine truth at varying human levels of perception and understanding. Nevertheless, as Professor H. D. Lewis so truly says, "the unique events narrated in the Gospels are the core of the Christian faith. These are not to be taken as mere symbols of something beyond them, whether in depths of our own experience, or in the absolute being of God. They are not just pictures, but supreme reality. The Christian faith as a distinctive faith, cannot survive the surrender of particularity."[24] In it the highest insights of Judaism, Islam, Zoroastrianism, Hinduism and Buddhism have been realized, fulfilling alike the prophetic revelations and mystical knowledge of God, and of sacramental union with him in its transcendental and immanental aspects. Therefore, these basic elements being foundation truths must be held fast if Christianity is to retain its unique place and function in the history of religion. But, as was affirmed at the recent Vatican Council, "although the Church sees the fullness of truth in Christ and his message, she does not on that account reject anything true and holy in the other religions, looking with great respect on Hinduism and Buddhism, and especially on Islam which also worships the one God and honours Jesus as a prophet." Indeed, it is recognized that "all the peoples of the earth with their various religions form one community; each and all of them attempting to answer the same vital questions in different ways." To discover the reality of Christ in all the religions of the world is the essence of the ecumenical approach.

FURTHER READING

Baillie, D. M., *God was in Christ*, 1955
Bevan, E., *Hellenism and Christianity*, 1921
Bouche-Leclereq, A., *Histoire de la Divination dans L'Antiquite*, 4 vols., 1879–82
Cumont, F., *Astrology and Religion among the Greeks and Romans*, 1912
Guillaume, A., *Divination and Prophecy*, 1938
Haldar, P., *Cultic Prophets among the Ancient Semites*, 1945
Halliday, W. R., *Greek Divination*, 1913
Hodgson, L., *The Doctrine of the Trinity*, 1944
Hooke, S. H., *Prophets and Priests*, 1938
James, E. O., *The Concept of Deity*, 1950
Jenkins, D. E., *Guide to the Debate about God*, 1966
Johnson, A. R., *The Cultic Prophets in Ancient Israel*, 1944

Knox, R. A., *Enthusiasm*, 1950
Parke, P. M. and Wormell, D. F. W., *The Delphic Oracle*, 2 vols., 1956
Richardson, A. (ed.), *Four Anchors from the Stern*, 1963
Tavard, J. H. T., *Paul Tillich and the Christian Message*, 1962
Terry, M. S., *The Sibylline Oracles*, 1890
Warde Fowler, W., *The Religious Experience of the Roman People*, 1912
Welch, A., *Prophet and Priest in Old Israel*, 1953

ABBREVIATIONS

A.B.	*Anat-Baal texts*
ANET.	*Ancient Near Eastern Texts relating to the Old Testament* Ed. J. B. Pritchard, 1955
BSA.	*Annual of the British School at Athens*
CGS.	*Cults of the Greek States,* L. R. Farnell, Oxford
ERE.	*Encyclopaedia of Religion and Ethics,* Ed. J. Hastings
GB.	*The Golden Bough,* J. G. Frazer, 3rd. Ed.
JAOS.	*Journal of the American Oriental Society,* New Haven
JHS.	*Journal of Hellenic Studies*
JNES.	*Journal of Near Eastern Studies.* Chicago
JRAS.	*Journal of the Royal Anthropological Institute.* London
PPS.	*Proceedings of the Prehistoric Society*
PT.	*Pyramid Texts*
RV.	*Rig Veda*
SBE.	*Sacred Books of the East*

NOTES

Introduction

1 C. Darwin, *The Origin of Species*, 1st ed., 1859, p. 310; A. R. Wallace, *Darwinism*, 1889, p. 8.
2 E. B. Tylor, *Primitive Culture*, Vol. 1, 1871, pp. 34 ff.
3 A. Lang, *Custom and Myth*, 1904, pp. 25 ff.
4 J. G. Frazer, *The Golden Bough*, Part X, Vol. I, 3rd ed., 1914, pp. vi ff.
5 J. G. Frazer, *The Worship of Nature*, 1926, pp. 9 ff.
6 J. G. Frazer, *Early History of Kingship*, 1905, pp. 12 ff.
7 J. G. Frazer, *The Golden Bough*, Part IX, p. 306.
8 R. R. Marett, *The Threshold of Religion*, 1914, pp. xxxi, 1-28.
9 R. Otto, *The Idea of the Holy*, E. T. rev. 1929, pp. 7, 15 n.1.
10 C. Dawson, *Religion and Culture*, 1948, p. 57.
11 E. Durkheim, *Elementary Forms of the Religious Life*, E. T. 1915, p. 206.
12 A. M. Ramsey, *Sacred and Secular*, 1965, pp. 17 ff.
13 E. E. Evans-Pritchard in *Blackfriars*, 1960, pp. 109 f.
14 R. C. Zaehner, *Mysticism Sacred and Profane*, 1957, pp. 168, 184, 198.

Chapter Two

1 J. G. Frazer, *The Golden Bough*, Part IV, Vol. 1. 3rd ed., 1914, p. 5.
2 F. E. Zeuner, *Dating the Past*, 1953, pp. 264 ff.
3 H. Breuil, *Four Hundred Centuries of Cave Art*, 1952, pp. 167, 176.
4 A. Loisy, *Essai historique sur le sacrifice*, 1920, p. 22.
5 G. Elliot Smith, *The Evolution of the Dragon*, 1919, p. 151.
6 A. Lang, *The Making of Religion*, 1898, pp. 160 ff.; A. W. Howitt, *The Native Tribes of South East Australia*, 1904, pp. 488 ff.; K. Langloh Parker, *The Euahlayi Tribe*, 1905, pp. 5 ff.
7 B. Spencer and F. J. Gillen, *The Northern Tribes of Central Australia*, 1904, pp. 488 ff.
8 K. Langloh Parker, op. cit. pp. 2, 5.
9 W. Schmidt, *The Origin and Growth of Religion*, E. T. 1931, pp. 220 ff.
10 E. E. Evans-Pritchard, *Nuer Religion*, 1956, pp., 2 ff., 118, 124, 200 ff.
11 W. Schmidt, op. cit. pp. 150, 269, 273
12 L. Lévy-Bruhl, *La Mentalité primitive*, 1922, p. 19; *How Natives Think*, E. T. 1926, pp. 35 ff.
13 R. R. Marett, *The Threshold of Religion*, 1914, p. 109.
14 B. Malinowski, *The Foundations of Faith and Morals*, 1936, pp. viii ff., 62.

Chapter Three

1 *Pyramid Texts* 1048 b. Utterance 488; S. A. B. Mercer, *The Pyramid Texts*, Vol. III, 1952 p. 527 f.

2 A. Erman, *The Literature of the Ancient Egyptians*, E. T. 1927, p. 286.

3 J. A. Wilson and A. Scharf, *Hieroglyphic Texts from the Egyptian Stelae*, Part VIII, Brit. Mus., p. 24.

4 E. A. Wallis Budge, *Tutankhamen, Amenism and Egyptian Monotheism*, 1913, pp. 21, 113.

5 A. Erman, *op. cit.*, p. 289; C. Davies, *Rock-Tombs of El-Amarna*, Vol. VI, 1903-5, Parts xxvii, xxix.

6 J. H. Breasted, *The Development of Religion and Thought in Ancient Egypt*, 1914, p. 9.

7 S. N. Kramer, *Sumerian Mythology*, 1944, pp. 39 ff.

8 T. Jacobsen, *The Intellectual Adventure of Ancient Man*, 1946, pp. 140 ff.

9 S. Langdon, *The Babylonian Epic of the Creation*, 1923, Tablet vii, p. 207.

10 Aleyan-Baal Texts, II. 15-20; IV. 49. 27-29. Cf. C. F. A. Schaeffer, *Cuneiform Texts of Ras Shamra-Ugarit*, 1909, p. 68.

11 J. T. Meek, *Hebrew Origins*, 1950, pp. 97 ff.

12 S. Mowinckel, *The Two Sources of the Pre-deuteronomic Primeval History (JE) in Genesis I-XI*, 1937, p. 55.

13 H. H. Rowley, *From Joseph to Joshua*, 1950, pp. 2 ff.

14 A. R. Johnson, *The One and the Many in the Israelite Conception of God*, 1941, pp. 37 f.

15 R. C. Zaehner, *Zurvan: a Zoroastrian Dilemma*, 1955, pp. 35 ff.

16 *Qur'an* V. 14-18; 77. 79. 116; IV. 155 ff.; III. 41-59.

17 *Qur'an* V. 64; XVIII. 28; LXXVI. 28-31.

18 B. Malinowski, *The Foundations of Faith and Morals*, 1936, pp. 2 ff.

19 C. G. Montefiore, *Some Elements in the Religious Teaching of Jesus*, 1919, p. 93; *The Synoptic Gospels*, Vol. I, 1927, p. cxviii.

20 F. von Hügel, *Essays and Addresses in the Philosophy of Religion*, 1st series, 1921, p. 134.

Chapter Four

1 J. Marshall, *Mohenjo-daro and the Indus Civilization*, Vol. I, 1913, p. vii.

2 *Satapatha Brahmana* V. 4. 4. 10.

3 *Sat. Brah.* I. 9. 29; VI. 7, 2-12.

4 *Sat. Brah.* V I. 1. 2; III. 2.2.4.

5 *Chandogya Upanishad* VI. 3; *Brihadaranyaka Upanishad* I. 4. 22.

6 *Chand. Upan.* II. 2, 3.

7 *Maitri Upanishad* 6. 3.

8 *Isa Upanishad* 8.

9 *Taittiviya Upanishad* II. 4.

10 *Svetasvatara Upanishad* I. 10; III. 2; V. I; VI. 5-3.

11 *Bhagavadgita* X. 1–7; 19–42.
12 *Gita* IV. 7. 8.
13 A. A. Macdonell, *A History of Sanskrit Literature*, 1900, pp. 309 ff.
14 *Digha-Nikaya* II. 100; *Dhammapada* 105, 378. 80.
15 C. F. Rhys Davids, *Manual of Buddhism*, 1932, p. 139.
16 P. Dahlke, *Buddhism and Science*, 1923, pp. 65 ff.
17 *Digha-Nikaya*, 131; *Tevijja*, 4 ff.
18 I. B. Horner, *The Early Buddhist Theory of Man Perfected*, 1936, p. 190.
19 E. Conze, *Buddhism: its Essence and Development*, 1957, pp. 147 ff.; D. Snellgrove, *Buddhist Himalaya*, 1957, pp. 147 ff.
20 D. T. Suzuki, *Essays in Zen Buddhism*, 1927, p. 84.
21 A. Graham, *Zen Catholicism*, 1964.
22 A. Huxley, *The Doors of Perception*, 1954; R. C. Zaehner, *Mysticism Sacred and Profane*, 1957, pp. xv, 55 ff.
23 R. Panikkar, *The Unknown Christ of Hinduism*, 1964.

Chapter Five.

1 S. A. B. Mercer, *The Pyramid Texts*, Vol. II, 1952, p. 4.
2 E. A. Wallis Budge, *The Book of the Opening of the Mouth*, Vol. I, 1909, p. vii.
3 K. Sethe, *Urgeschichte und aelteste Religion der Aegypter*, 1930, p. 85; M. A. Murray, JRAI, vol. XLV, 1915, pp. 305 ff.
4 W. M. F. Petrie, *Royal Tombs of the First Dynasty*, Part II, 1901, Plate II, nos. 13, 14; Pyramid Texts, 370 a–b. Utterance 268. Mercer, *Pyramid Texts*, Vol. II. pp. 172 f.
5 Plutarch, *De Iside et Osiride*, chaps. xv, xvi.
6 Dio Cassius xlvii. 15, 4; liii, 2.4; Tertullian, *Apologeticum* 5; *Ad Nationes* 1. 10 (Varro); Tibullus i. 27–30; Ovid, *Ars Amatoria* 1. 77.
7 *Metamorphoses* xi. 5. 6. 16. 21.
8 *Metamorphoses*. xi. 21, 23–30.
9 Pausanias ii, 17; ix. 3. 1.
10 *De Iside et Osiride* 8.
11 Kramer, *Bulletin Army Schools of Oriental Research*, 183, 1966 pp. 31 f.
12 H. Frankfort, *Kingship and the Gods*, 1948, p. 297.
13 S. Mowinckel, *Psalmenstudien* II, 1922, pp. 201 ff.; A. R. Johnson, *Sacral Kingship in Ancient Israel*, 1956, pp. 54 ff., 61 n.2.; N. Snaith, *The New Year Festival*, 1947, pp. 195 ff. cf. p. 102.
14 H. H. Rowley, *The Servant of the Lord*, 1952, pp. 61 ff.; J. Jeremias, *Deutsche Theologie*, Vol. II, 1929, pp. 106 f.; W. Manson, *Jesus the Messiah*, 1945, pp. 110, 171 ff.; C. R. North, *The Suffering Servant in Deutero-Isaiah*, 1956.
15 T. W. Manson, *The Teaching of Jesus*, 1935, p. 227; *Studies in the Gospels and Epistles*, 1962, pp. 132 ff.
16 C. H. Dodd, *The Apostolic Preaching and its Development*, 1936, pp. 86 ff.
17 M. P. Nilsson, *Greek Popular Religion*, 1940, pp. 51 ff.

18 J. Harrison, *Prolegomena to the Study of Greek Religion*, 1903, p. 377.
19 M. P. Nilsson, *History of Greek Religion*, 1925, p. 205.
20 L. R. Farnell, *Greek Hero Cults and Ideas of Immortality*, 1921, p. 402.
21 F. Cumont, *Textes et monuments figurés anx mystères de Mithra*, 1896.
22 Theodoret iii. 29.
23 N. Smart in *The Saviour God*, 1965, p. 164; T. O. Ling, *Buddhism and the Mythology of Evil*, 1962, pp. 56 ff., 63.

Chapter Six

1 Aquinas, *Summa Theologica* I. q.v. lx.i.iv. Sent i.i.5.
2 W. Robertson Smith, *Religion of the Semites*, 3rd ed., 1927, pp. 245 ff., 345 ff.
3 H. Hubert and M. Mauss, *L'Année sociologique*, Vol. II, 1898, pp. 29 ff.
4 Joshua vi. 26; I Kings xvi. 34; II Kings xxiii. 10; R. A. S. Macalister, *The Excavations of Gezer*, vol. II, 1912, pp. 426 ff.
5 Isaiah lv. 6 f.; xliv. 22; Psalm li. 16 ff.; lxix. 30;
6 Acts 14. 23; 10. 17 ff.; Philippians I. I ff.; Titus 1. 5; Clement 44; Hippolytus *Apostolic Tradition* iii. 4; Ignatius, *To the Smyrnaeans* 8.
7 E. O. James, *Sacrifice and Sacrament*, 1962, pp. 60 ff.; F. C. N. Hicks, *The Fullness of Sacrifice*, 1938; A. Loisy, *Essai historique sur le sacrifice*, 1920.
8 *Lambeth Conference Report* 1930, Resolution 33 c. pp. 49, 136.
9 E. R. Bevan, *Symbolism and Belief*, 1938, pp. ll ff.
10 R. J. de Acosta, *Natural History of the Indies*, Vol. II, Bk. 5, 1880, pp. 356; H. H. Bancroft, *Native Races of the Pacific States*, Vol. III, 1876, pp. 297 ff., 316.
11 E. J. Martin, *History of the Iconoclastic Controversy*, (Church Historical Society) 1930; A. Fliche-Martin. *Histoire de l église*, Vols. V, VI, 1937–1938.
12 *Summa Theol.* iii. 9. 9.v. xxv art. 3.
13 *Law of Manu* IX. I, 3. 85.
14 *Satapatha Brahmana* I. 6. 3. 20; 24; III. 2.2.4.
15 *Sat. Brah.* I. 1–4 ff.; II. 5–7; *Rigveda* X. 119.
16 *Brihadaranyaka Upanishad* I. i. ii; *Chandogya Upanishad* VI. viii. 7.
17 *Rigveda* X, 119.
18 *Yasna* XLVIII. 10; IX; X. 50; XL. 4; XXX. 3; *Yasht* X, 89 f.
19 *Bundahishn* I. i. 5; XXV. 11–5.
20 Justin Martyr, *Apology* i. 66.
21 F. B. Jevons, *Introduction to the History of Religions*, 1902, pp. 365 ff.
22 L. R. Farnell in *Hibbert Journal*, 1904. Vol. II, pp. 316 f.
23 Clement of Alexandria, *Protrepticos* ii. 13; Firmicus Maternus, *De errore profanarum religionum* xviii.
24 L. R. Farnell, *op. cit.*, p. 317.
25 H. Hepding, *Attis; Seine Mythen und Sein Kult*, 1903, pp. 196 ff.
26 *Corpus Inscriptionum Latinarum* VI. 510; VIII. 8203.
27 Sallustius, *De Diis et Mundo* iv. cf. iii. 33. (E. T. by A. D. Nock, 1926)

28 Euripides (ed. E. R. Dodds), *Bacchae*, 1960, pp. xvi f.; L. R. Farnell, CGS, Vol. IV, p. 120

29 J. Harrison, *Prolegomena to the Study of Greek Religion*, 1912, p. 476.

Chapter Seven

1 L. Woolley, *Excavations at Ur*. 1954, pp. 56 ff.
2 I. E. S. Edwards, *The Pyramids of Egypt*, 1961.
3 A. Heidel, *The Babylonian Genesis*, 1952, pp. 148 ff.; *Epic of Gilgamesh*, 1946, pp. 34 f.; E. A. Speiser in ANET, pp. 87, 96. 101 ff.
4 *Iliad* XXIII. 10; *Odyssey* XI. 51. 140 ff.
5 R. Rhode, *Psyche*, 1925, p. 13.
6 M. P. Nilsson, *Homer and Mycenae*, 1933, pp. 155 ff.; A. W. Persson, *New Tombs at Dendra near Midea*, 1942, pp. 12, 69 ff.
7 Cicero, *De Legibus* Z. 36.
8 *De Anima*, Frag. viii. 23; (Strobaeus), ed. Meincke, iv, 107. vol. iv. p. 107.
9 *Republic* 613; *Theaetetus* 176.
10 *Timaeus* 42; Phaedrus 245 f.; Phaedo 63 ff., 81 ff.
11 Matt. 13.42; 18.8; 25.41; Mark 9.43; Luke 16.23.
12 I Cor. 15.24–8; Rom. 6.59; Ephes. 1.20 ff.; Col. I. 16, 20; I, Thess. 5.3; II Thess. I. 6 f.
13 John 3.15 ff.; 5.24, 26; 6.40, 54 ff.; 10.28.
14 Augustine, *De Immortalitate Animae* 387;
15 Aquinas, *Summa Theologica* l. q.v. lxxvi, xc; *Contra Gentiles* II, lxxix, lxxxi.
16 *Contra Gentiles* iv. c. 91.
17 *De Unitate Intellectus contra Averroistos*, 1270.
18 *Tahafut* (Cairo, A. H. 1303), p. 140.
19 *Qur'an*, XL–XLIII.
20 *Qur'an* LV. 45 ff.; LVI. 12–39.
21 D. B. Macdonald, *Development of Muslim Theology etc.*, 1903, pp. 243 ff.
22 I. Kant, *Kritik d. pr. U. Dialektik*, chaps. ii, iv.

Chapter Eight

1 P. Tillich, *The Shaking of the Foundations*, 1948, p. 63.
2 E. Durkheim, *Elementary Forms of the Religious Life*, E. T. 1915, p. 24.
3 Aquinas, *Summa Theologica* I. qu. XXIX. I. I; H. H. Farmer, *Revelation and Religion*, 1954, pp. 27, 57, 79, 325.
4 P. Tillich, *Systematic Theology*, 1957, pp. 138 f.
5 A. E. J. Rawlinson, *Essays Catholic and Critical*, 1929, p. 95.
6 F. Schleiermacher, *On Religion; Speeches addressed to its Cultured Despisers*, tr. Oman, 1893, p. 101.
7 K. Barth, *Doctrine of the Word of God*, E. T. 1936, pp. 14, 368 ff.
8 J. Laird, *Theism and Cosmology*, 1940, p. 38.

9 A. Richardson, *Christian Apologetics*, 1947, pp. 116 ff.
10 Augustine, *De Civitate Dei* Bk. X, chaps. ii–iv.
11 *Phaedrus* 247 ff.; *Phaedo* 64, 66 ff.; *Theaetetus* 176.
12 *Apology* 19A, 40A, 41D; *Symposium* 210; *Phaedo* 66.
13 Plotinus, *Enneads* VI. ix. 3; Cicero, *De Diviniatitone* 2, 112; Dionysius Halicarnassus 4, 62, 1–6.
14 *Rig-Veda* xiv, 163, 179; II. 2, 10; VI. 5, 7. 19; *Aitareya Brahmana* vii. 13.
15 R. A. Knox, *Enthusiasm*, 1950.
16 A. R. Johnson, *The Cultic Prophet in Ancient Israel*, 2nd ed. 1962; A. Jepsen, *Nabi*, 1934, pp. III ff.
17 A. Haldar, *Associations of Cult Prophets among the Ancient Semites*, 1945; N. Porteous in *Studies in Old Testament Prophecy*, ed. H. H. Rowley, 1950, pp. 143 ff.
18 A. R. Johnson, *The One and the Many in the Israelite Conception of God*, 1941, p. 37
19 C. H. Dodd, *History and the Gospel*, 1938, p. 181.
20 C. H. Dodd, *The Apostolic Preaching and its Development*, 1936, pp. 77 ff.; *The Parables of the Kingdom*, 1935, pp. 50, 79.
21 J. B. Lightfoot, *Epistle to the Philippians*, 1868; W. Bousset, *Kyrios Christos*, 1913; H. Lohmeyer, *Philipper, Kolosser und Philemon*, 1913, pp. 90, 97.
22 E. Bevan, *Hellenism and Christianity*, 1921, p. 271.
23 L. Hodgson, *The Doctrine of the Trinity*, 1944, p. 24.
24 H. D. Lewis, *World Religions*, 1966, p. 195.

INDEX

INDEX

AARON, 56, 96
Abraham, 56, 64, 111, 136
Absolute, the, 26, 72 ff., 76, 85, 155, 159
Adapa, the myth of, 136
Advaita, 11, 72, 86, 110
Agni, 70 f., 126
Ahriman, 61, 171
Ahura Mazdah, 60 f., 171
Al-Ghazali, 65, 149 f.
Allah, 64 f., 171
Amidism, 11, 83 f., 111
Amitabha-Buddha, 11, 83 f.
Amon-Re, 48 f., 51
Amos, 162 f.
Analects, the 25 f.
Anat, 54, 93
Anatta (non-ego), doctrine, 79 f.
Angus, S., 132
Animatism, 22
Animism, 21, 40 f., 70, 140
Anu, 52
Apocalyptic imagery, 99 f., 102, 143, 149, 158
Apollo, 102 f., 159 ff.
Apuleius, 90 f.
Aquinas, St. Thomas, 113 f., 125, 147, 148, 150, 157, 180 f.
Aristotle, 65, 141, 146, 148, 150
Aryan gods, the, 69
Aryan invasion, the, 60, 70
Asha, 61
Asherah, 55, 93
Ashur, 53 f.
Asoka, 81
Astarte, 93
Atman, the, 11, 72, 79
Aton, cult of the, 48 ff.
Atonement, the doctrine of the, 12, 82, 110, 116, 132; day of the, 117 f., 110

Attis, 129 f.
Augustine, St., 146 f., 181, 182
Avatar, 11, 72, 81, 109 f.
Averroes, 65, 148 f., 150, 181
Avesta, the, 60 f., 127, 171
Avicenna, 65
Avidya, 11

BAAL, 53 ff., 93 f.
Baillie, D. M., 173
Baillie, J., 151
Bevan, E., 121, 132, 167, 173, 182
Bhagavad-Gita, the, 11, 75 ff., 85, 108 f., 179
Bhakti, 11, 27, 76, 83, 86, 109, 155
Bodhisattva, the, 11, 81 f., 83, 109 f., 170
Bouquet, A. C., 29, 88
Brahman, 11, 26, 72, 161
Brahmana texts, the, 11, 71 f., 126
Brahmins, the, 71 f., 126
Brandon, S. G. F., 112
Breasted, J. H., 51, 68, 178
Breuil, H., 37, 46, 177
Buddha, the, 78 f., 81 f., 86, 110, 170
Buddhism, origin of, 27; creed of, 78 ff.
Budge, E. A. W., 49 f., 68, 151, 178 f.
Bultmann, R., 168
Butler, J., 156

CALVINISM, 65, 157
Carmel, contest on the Mount, 55, 94, 162
Catacombs, wall paintings in, 124
Cave art and ritual, Palaeolithic, 36 ff.
Chalcedon, Council of, 169
Charles, R. H., 151
Christ, the person and work of, 67, 87, 97 ff., 154, 167 f; the Saviour, 96, 112, 132; and Krishna, 76, 85,

Nun, 48
Nut, 48

ODYSSEUS, 138
Oesterley, W. O. E., 133, 151
Omophagia, in the Dionysiac, 12, 130
Omphalos, the, 12
Oracles, 102, 137, 156, 160, 162 f., 168, 171
Ormuzd, 61, 171
Orphism, 103 f., 131, 139 f.
Osiris, 48, 89 ff., 95
Otto, R., 22, 177
Owen, R., 18 f.

PALEY, S. A., 17
Pallis, S. A., 112
Panikkar, R., 88, 179
Pantheism, 65, 69 ff., 72, 81, 85 f., 87, 89, 126, 140, 153
Parke, P. M., 174
Parousia, the, of Christ, 12, 143, 145, 167
Parrinder, E. G., 30
Parsees, the, 63
Patroclus, obsequies, of, 138
Pedersen, J., 68
Persephone, 101
Petrie, W. M. F., 179
Piaculum, 12, 115 f.
Piggott, S., 88
Plato, 103, 140 f., 144, 146, 150, 160, 181 f.
Plutarch, 102, 139, 179
Pluto, 101
Polytheism, 21, 39, 47, 70 f., 131, 171
Praeparatio evangelica, the, 82, 87 f., 91, 158, 166
Prajapati, 71, 126
Pratt, J. B., 88
Prayer, 22
Predestination, 65
Pre-existence, 140 f., 144, 147
Pringle-Pattison, A. S., 152
Prithivi, 70
Prometheus, 32

Prophets, the Hebrew, 58 f., 158 f., 161 f.; Islam, 66, 171
Providence, belief in, 36 f., 41, 43 f.
Psyche, the, 138, 144
Ptah, 48
Pure Land sects, the, 83 f., 111, 170
Purusha, 74, 127
Pyramids, the, 135, Texts, 135 f.

QUICK, O. C., 133
Qur'an, the, 64 ff., 149, 161, 171, 181

RAMA, 76 f.
Ramanuja, 86
Ramayana epic, the, 77
Ramsey, A. M., 27, 177
Ras Shamra (*see* Ugarit)
Rashdall, H., 112
Rawlinson, A. E. J., 156
Re, the sun-god, 48, 50
Redemption, 67, 76, 82, 95 f., 97 f., 111 f., 154, 167
Reformation, the, 15
Reincarnation, 74, 77 f., 79 f., 86, 102 f., 105, 108, 131, 140, 147
Religion, Comparative study of, 7, 15 ff., 20, 153, 157; of early man, 34 ff.; origin of, 20 ff., 33 f.; sociological function of, 23 f.
Rephaim, 137 f.
Resurrection, in Christianity, 134, 142 f., 145 ff., 154, 167 (*see* Christ); Islam, 149; mystery cults, 90, 100, 129 f., 131
Revelation, the Christian, 46, 66, 87, 165 ff., 172 f.; Hebrew and prophetic, 59 f., 161 ff.; Islamic, 64 f., 66, 148 f., 171; natural and revealed religion, 154, 156 ff.; Oracular, 157, 160, 162 f., 168, 171; Primeval, 41; special and general, 158 f.; Zoroastrian, 61, 171
Rhode, E., 138, 152, 181
Rhys Davids, C. F., 179
Rhys Davids, Mrs., 79
Richardson, A., 174, 182

189

Rig-Veda, the, 12, 69, 70, 160
Romantic movement, the, 16
Rowley, H. H., 68, 112, 178 f., 182
Rta, 70 f., 126
Rudra, 70

SACRAMENT, definition of, 113 f.;
   function and significance of, 60 f.,
   85, 87, 105, 160; meals, 60 f., 120,
   127 ff., 129 (see sacrifice, *communio*)
Sacramental principle, the, 113 ff.
Sacred and the Secular, 43 ff.,
   154
Sacredness, 20, 71
Sacrifice, definition of, 115 f.; Chris-
   tian, 119 f., Eucharistic 120 f., 132;
   Hebrew, 118 f.; human, 117; Soma,
   60 f., 127
Salvation, conception of, 12, 89 f.,
   94, 96, 102 f., 105 f., 107, 110, 132,
   144
Samsara, 11 f., 73 f.
Samuel, 157
Sankara, 73
Sankhya dualism, 12, 74 f., 77
Satori, experience of, 84
Saul, 137, 162
Saviour god, belief in, 89 ff., 93,
   95 f., 101, 105 f., 111, 131, 171
   (*see* avatar, incarnation, Christ,
   Krishna, Buddha)
Schaeffer, C. F. A., 178
Schleiermacher, F., 154, 157, 181, 184
Schmidt, W., 40 f., 46, 177
Sedgwick, A., 18
Selden, J., 16
Seth, 48
Shades, 138
Sheol, 137, 142
Sh'ia sects, the, 65, 69
Skandhas, the, 79
Smart, N., 110, 180
Smith, F. H., 88
Smith, G. E., 177
Smith, W. R., 16, 114
Snellgrove, D., 179

Söderblom, N., 68
Soma, 60, 70, 126 f.
Son of Man, the, 97, 143
Sophocles, 100
Soteriology (*see* salvation)
Soul and body, 144 f. (*see* animism,
   nephesh, reincarnation, psyche,
   resurrection)
Spencer, J., 16
Spinoza, 151
Stone, D., 133
Suffering Servant, the, 96
Sufism, 65, 149 f., 155
Sumerian pantheon, the, 52 f.
Sun-god, the, 47 ff. (*see* Re, Atum,
   Aton)
Supreme Beings, belief in, 39 ff., 57,
   60, 73, 86 (*see* Creator), monothe-
   ism)
Suzuki, D. T., 88, 179
Sweetman, J. H., 68

TABERNACLES, Feast of, 94 f.
Talmud, the, 64
Tammuz, 92 f., 95, 97
Taoism, 7, 26
Taurobolium, the, 130
Tavard, J. H. T., 174
Taylor, A. E., 152
Temple in Jerusalem, 58, 60, 164
Tennant, F. R., 46
Terry, M. S., 174
Tetragrammaton, the, 12, 56
Theravada, Buddhism, 12, 79, 81 f.
Thoth, 51
Tiamat, 31, 53, 94
Tillich, P., 153, 156, 181
Titanic nature, the, 103 f., 139 f.
Torah, the Mosaic Law, 13, 59 f., 65,
   163 f.
Totemism, 115, 129
Traducianism, 147
Transcendence, divine, 16, 19, 46, 87,
   89, 131, 155 f., 171 (*see* immanence)
Tress, magical, 32, 99
Tylor, E. B., 20 f., 153, 177